# EXPERIENCE PORTUGAL

YOUR COMPLETE TRAVEL GUIDE TO THE HIDDEN GEMS, SIGHTS, FOODS, BEACHES, & BREATHTAKING VIEWS OF EVERY MAJOR CITY IN PORTUGAL

EXTRAORDINARY TRAVEL

# TABLE OF CONTENTS

PART TWO

## CITIES AND PLACES TO SEE IN PORTUGAL

# INTRODUCTION

> "The world is a book, and those who do not travel read only one page."
>
> SAINT AUGUSTINE

Bem-vindo a Portugal!

Where music from the fado cafés spills out onto the streets, and the culture is vibrant and alive, Portugal is a place unlike any other. Interestingly, "fado" has numerous meanings, including destiny or fate. As luck would have it, fado must have brought you here. It must be a sign that you're destined to go to Portugal.

We understand the intrigue of this beautiful European nation. You've been getting tired of the rat race, and want to take a break and step away from the harsh realities of life. So, you want to go somewhere that offers you everything you need to have a great time. The answer? Portugal. Don't believe us? Well, over 22 million people visited last year, and that's below 2019 levels. Portugal has become one of the most popular tourist destinations in recent years. Once you're there, it's easy to understand why'.

Traveling to foreign countries 'can be a daunting undertaking. Planning a trip and making the effort to understand the country, its culture, and ways of life can be exhausting. It leads to many late-night Google rabbit holes that leave you with more questions than answers. As a result, you've come here, to a single source of information for all things Portugal. Sure, you could just wing it, but spontaneous travel has its downsides.

The downsides include:

- Unpreparedness for just about everything, from accommodation to what to do when in the area, leading to wasted time.
- Lack of awareness of the costs of certain things and how to get the best deals.
- Inconvenience in the form of waiting around for things you could have sorted out ahead of time.
- Missing out on experiences you either weren't aware of or couldn't get to due to delays.

In this book, we're going to cover just about everything. Here's what you gain from progressing through this thoroughly researched guide:

1. You won't miss out on any great experiences across Portugal.
2. You can confidently purchase tickets and book accommodation ahead of time.
3. You'll know what you need to pack and why.
4. You will save time on research while you're in the country, as it eliminates unnecessary decision-making.
5. You can prioritize the things that you want to do while you're visiting Portugal.

It took us years to garner this knowledge, and the best part was all our trips to Portugal. We got to see these things first-hand, making writing this guide so much easier. We explored countless regions of Portugal and saw the magic for ourselves. The historic buildings, the picturesque sunsets, the incredible food, the atmosphere of the people, the beauty around every bend. It was a collection of experiences that made us fall in love with Portugal. As a result of it all, we present to you a book that's current, filled with meticulous detail, and thorough in its research.

Let's get you to Portugal!

# PART ONE
# PLANNING A TRIP TO PORTUGAL

# CHAPTER 1
# WHY PORTUGAL?

So, you've decided it's time to take a vacation. Of all the places on earth, you've narrowed down your list, and somewhere on that list is Portugal. Well, there couldn't be a better place to go on vacation. Across seven regions, Portugal is home to a wide variety of places to visit and explore. It's home to a rich culture and history that you'll be able to experience in this stunning country.

> *"If there is one portion of Europe which was made by the sea more than another, Portugal is that slice, that portion, that belt. Portugal was made by the Atlantic."*
>
> *HILAIRE BELLOC (WRITER/HISTORIAN)*

In this chapter, we will explore the rich history of Portugal, and express some of the many reasons to visit and some interesting facts. By the end of this chapter, you'll be wishing you were there right now!

## PORTUGAL: THE BASICS

Located in Southwestern Europe along the Atlantic coast of the Iberian Peninsula and neighboring Spain, Portugal is home to a diverse landscape. The northern coast is cold and rocky, while the interior is mountainous, sparsely settled, wild, and above all, scenic. Throughout the country, numerous locations offer warm and fertile conditions, like the popular province Algarve.

Portugal is home to over 10.2 million people as of 2023. The country is populated mainly by Portuguese people, who make up more than 90 percent of the population. Still, there's a smattering of other ethnicities such as Brazilian, Marrano, Han Chinese, and various other internationals and Europeans. The vast majority of the nation is Catholic, making up roughly 81 percent of the religious affiliation. Regarding the urban-rural breakdown, more than 50 percent of the population lives in rural areas. Most of the population resides in the country's coastal regions. Finally, the age breakdown of the country shows that it's well divided among the various age groups, with most of the population being under sixty, with the bulk being between thirty and fifty-nine.

At one point, at its peak, Portugal was the wealthiest nation in the world. That's right, the world. Of course, this was through colonization. This changed during the nineteenth and twentieth centuries, with it slowly becoming one of Western Europe's poorest countries. During the mid-1970s, post-revolution, Portugal's economy became disconnected from its possessions in Africa, and they were reoriented towards Europe. Finally, in 1986, they joined what would become the EU, and this is when their economy began experiencing strong and steady economic growth. The country is now dominated by service, manufacturing, and agriculture. Now, in the twenty-first century, Portugal has vastly improved living standards, increased incomes, and low unemployment.

Since 1910, Portugal has been a republic. This followed the overthrow of King Manuel II. This brought about the era of its First Republic when a parliamentary democracy was established. It wasn't smooth sailing throughout the century that followed. They experienced a military coup in 1926, and in 1932, a corporatist dictatorship took hold until 1974, when the Revolution of the Carnations changed things for the final time, at least so far. Since the revolution, Portugal has been a democratic republic. The constitution, first adopted in 1976, brought democracy back to Portugal.

The cultural life in Portugal is vibrant thanks to a long history dating back to Prehistoric times. Traces of centuries of history can be found across the country. Portugal was invaded numerous times throughout its history, including the Roman and Moorish invasions, and you can still find traces of their presence in modern Portugal.

## REASONS TO VISIT PORTUGAL

There are a lot of reasons why you should visit Portugal. While we could tell you them all, we want to focus on the main selling points. Even then, there are a lot of selling points!

**Pastéis de Nata**

The first thing we want to talk about is the food, especially *pastéis de nata*. These pastries are easily the most delicious thing you'll have on your trip and maybe—just maybe—in your life. So, what makes these so unique? The legend goes that only five people know the recipe for these delectable egg cream tarts. You'll definitely want to go and try one for yourself.

Beyond this legendary pastry, the food in Portugal is heavenly. You'll find that most places serve food packed with flavor that

is to die for. You can't go wrong with the food, which is something we're going to talk about in depth later on!

### The Town of Sintra

Sintra is one of the most beautiful towns in all of Portugal. Filled with picturesque façades, quaint narrow alleyways, gorgeous gardens, and glamorous places, it's like something' straight out of a fairytale. If you visit Portugal, this must be on the list of things to do. You won't regret taking a trip to Sintra to explore a place as incredible as this.

### Ancient Castles

Everyone loves visiting old castles, and they have castles in abundance here. Portugal has had the same borders since the eleventh century, which is rare, making it one of Europe's oldest countries. Thanks to these unchanged borders, the history of Portugal has managed to stay mainly intact. This means that the castles and various historical sights are still standing proudly. You won't want to miss some sights, like Guimarães, where the first king was born, Caimbra, where the oldest university resides, or Lisbon, where you'll find the Castelo de São Jorge with its sweeping views.

### It's a Party till the Break of Dawn

New York City has a reputation for being the city that never sleeps, but Portugal can take the title as the nation that never sleeps! There's something for everyone, with a vibrant party scene. From the street bars in Lisbon to the nightclubs in Vilamoura, you'll be partying early and leaving early… the next day, that is.

### The Santos Festivities

If you're considering traveling to Portugal in June, you'll be just in time for the Santos Festivities. This festival celebrates three Catholic saints. The streets come to life with parades, traditional street dances, and even weddings! You'll find fresh sardines are a big deal during the Santos Festivities. The festival starts early in the evening, and in true Portuguese fashion, it lasts well into the night.

### So. Many. Festivals

One thing you should know about the Portuguese is that they love a good festival. They love them so much, in fact, that there are usually many happening year-round. Due to Portugal being predominantly Catholic, they celebrate many saints year-round with parades, music, and delicious food. One of the most famous festivals is the Festa de Tabuleiros, also known as the Trays Festival. This occasion has the women walking in a parade down main streets carrying half a kilo's worth of flowers and bread on trays.

### The Breathtaking Beaches

Portugal has so many breathtaking beaches to offer, with over one hundred located within its borders. Some of the most beautiful beaches exist in Algarve, Figueirinha, and Comporta. Some of these beaches have pretty cold temperatures but trust me, it's worth it, especially when you are there during sunset.

**Wine. Award-winning Wine**

Wine is one of Portugal's most ancient traditions, so you might assume they've got the art of winemaking down, and you'd be right. Worldwide, Portuguese wine is becoming more well-known and appreciated, as it should be. It's mainly getting praise for the rich quality and explosive flavors it presents. If you consider yourself a wine connoisseur, you must explore the Alentejo and Douro Valley regions for a wine tour. You'll not only get sensational wine, but also some delicious food.

**Portugal Is Inspirational. Just Look at Harry Potter**

If you're a die-hard Harry Potter fan, this might not come as a surprise to you. But Portugal happens to be one of the primary sources of inspiration for the Harry Potter series! Porto, in particular, was where the author spent her days writing at Palácio de Cristal and Café Majestic. Want proof? Well, head to the Livraria Lello, and you might notice some striking similarities between it and the Hogwarts Library.

**So Many Amazing Outdoor Locations**

One of the many amazing things about Portugal is that while it's a small country, it offers almost every kind of outdoor activity, thanks to a diverse range of landscapes. You've got the beaches, perfect for swimming and surfing. Or maybe you want to ski—well then, you head to Serra da Estrela. Want to go camping? If you head to Parque Nacional do Gerês, you can camp under the stars. One of the coolest places to go is the Azores, where the volcanic islands are. You can hike the dramatic cliffs, swim in natural pools and stunning lakes, and enjoy the scenery.

**Fado House**

A quintessential Portuguese experience, a fado house is where you go to understand the heart of the people. At a fado house, you sit back, relax, and listen to melancholic music. Enjoy the incredible food and listen to the musicians whisk you away in their haunting melodies and sensational vocals. Some of the best fado houses are in Lisbon, known as Clube de Fado and Sr. Vinho.

**Gondola Rides**

Venice is known for its gondola rides, but they are far from the only city to offer this popular tourist attraction. In the northern city of Aveiro, Portugal, they also offer gondola rides, albeit on a smaller scale. The waterways are picturesque, offering passengers a relaxing tour of Aveiro.

**Catch a Big Wave**

Portugal is considered a year-round surfing destination. Here, you can catch massive waves without even trying. If you're a surfer looking for a thrill, you must head to Portugal to surf some prime waves. You'll easily have one of the best surfing experiences of your life.

I'll talk more about surfing in depth in Chapter 8: Nazare!

**Madeira**

Once you go to Madeira, you'll never want to leave this

wonderful town. Madeira has charming villages, lava pools, and views to die for. There's so much to love about the town of Madeira. While there, you've got to try the delicious fresh seafood. 'The town's specialty is grilled limpets paired with a stunning—and strong—Madeira wine. It's paradise.

**Portuguese Beer Is Something Else**

Portugal has a long history when it comes to a lot of things, and one such thing is beer. The country has two major breweries that are basically competing against one another. Those breweries are Superbock and Sagres. There's a national debate going over which is better. To help them settle this dispute, you will need to help them out by trying these beers for yourself.

**Instagram-Worthy Locations**

You can say many things about Portugal, but beauty is the first that might come to mind. So gorgeous that you'll want to flood your social media with photos of the amazing things you see while visiting. You'll see buildings covered in picture-perfect tiles, called azulejos by the locals. These tiles cover the façades of buildings. This is only complemented by the intricate cobblestone streets.

**Extremely Affordable for Tourists**

Europe is one of the most desired continents for tourists, but it's also costly, depending on where you go. But that's not the case in Portugal. In fact, it is consistently named one of Europe's best budget destinations. You get that classic

European history and charm at essentially half the price! It doesn't matter where you stay, go, or what you do; your hard-earned money goes much further in Portugal.

**The People**

Portugal has so much to offer, from fantastic food to incredible places. There's no denying it's a gorgeous country, so what could sell it even more? The people. Portuguese people are incredibly hospitable to visitors, which is not always the case in Europe. This is what truly sets it apart. Portuguese people will make it their mission to show you everything their beautiful country has to offer and to ensure you're eating well. It's indescribable how welcoming Portuguese people are.

## INTERESTING FACTS ABOUT PORTUGAL

We're going to take a moment to let all this history and excitement seep in, but first, let's quick-fire some incredible facts about Portugal:

- If you love surfing, Portugal is among the world's best surfing spots. It's the perfect year-round surfing destination, with 800 kilometers of Atlantic coastline and a wonderfully temperate climate.
- Lisbon is home to the oldest bookstore in the world! First established in 1732, Bertrand Bookstore in the Chiado district is a sight to behold. With a mosaic tile exterior, it's well worth a visit.
- Portugal also has one of the world's oldest universities. It was 1290 when the University of Coimbra was established. It's a top-rated tourist destination, so be sure to check it out when visiting.
- The national drink is port, which is also the country's most famous export. That's right, produced in the UNESCO-listed Douro Valley, this sweet, red, fortified wine is very popular in Portugal. Better yet, Douro Valley is the third-oldest protected wine region in the world. So be sure to try some!
- Speaking of port, Portugal is the world's largest cork producer, with over 70 percent of cork exports. They produce tons of cork products like coasters, handbags, etc.
- If you love spice and especially love piri-piri, you can thank Portugal, as they invented the famous chili sauce.

- Thanks to its positioning on the Iberian Peninsula, Portugal's archipelago of the Azores in the Atlantic means it holds the official title of being the westernmost point in Europe.
- Portugal is very green-conscious when it comes to energy. In 2016, they ran the entire country on renewables for five consecutive days! That might not sound that impressive, but it's one of very few to achieve such a feat.
- In Portugal, it's always time for coffee. The drink of choice? An espresso-sized bica served in a tiny cup.
- Portugal has a strange record of having the longest- and shortest-reigning monarchs. The longest was King Henrique, who reigned for seventy-three years, and the shortest was Luis Filipe, who was king for a mere twenty minutes.

## TAKEAWAY

If it wasn't clear already, there are many reasons why you must visit Portugal. The history of this country is expansive. Its illustrious history has given birth to incredible structures, historical landmarks, a vibrant culture, and so much more.

When you take a vacation, you want to go somewhere that has a lot to offer, and in the case of Portugal, there's possibly *too* much to do. You'll have a hard time deciding what stays on the itinerary and what goes.

It doesn't matter if you tour the castles, enjoy the festivals, catch some waves, enjoy the nightlife, or vibe out at a fado house. Portugal is overflowing with incredible opportunities for tourists to enjoy. You've just got to get out there and experience it for yourself. But, of course, we're only scratching the surface. We've got so much more to talk about to get you prepped for the vacation of a lifetime.

# CHAPTER 2
# BOOKING TICKETS

You've heard all the reasons to take a vacation in Portugal. You're probably packing as we speak. Yay! We've convinced you. Now it's time to take the most important step: booking tickets there and back.

> *"There's no such thing as a place better than Portugal."*
>
> UNKNOWN

In this chapter, we will be taking a deep dive into what it looks like to travel to Portugal from around the world. Whether by plane, train, or motor vehicle, we'll provide great tips and tricks to get there for the lowest price and least time. So, let's get into what it means to book tickets to Portugal.

## FLIGHTS TO PORTUGAL: OPTIONS FROM AROUND THE WORLD

Most countries around the world have numerous options for flying to Portugal. During the summer, you'll find that airlines offer more direct flight options than they do at other times of the year. Not all airlines will take you to every destination available in Portugal, with some focusing on one or two locations, so be sure to check if they are going where you need to be.

Let's take a look at what traveling to Portugal from these prominent countries looks like:

**Traveling from the United States**

When traveling to Portugal from the United States, you must decide whether you want a direct flight or if you are okay with a connection(s) along the way. For the most part there aren't as many direct flight options in the US due to its immense size. On average, a flight to Portugal costs $800.

Let's start with a direct option. You can find direct flights from Philadelphia to Lisbon.

There are a lot of connecting options. Delta, in conjunction with their partners KLM and Air France, will get you to Portugal but do have connections in Amsterdam or Paris.

Iberia and British Airways connect through either Madrid or London. Finally, Lufthansa connects in Frankfurt.

American Airlines and Iberia are your best travel options from Boston to Portugal. They have the shortest layovers and reasonable fares.

If you're traveling from Chicago, you want to use Iberia, Aer Lingus, or American Airlines. They have the most reasonable prices with a layover in Madrid, Dublin, and London.

**Traveling From Brazil**

Portugal has a long history with Brazil, as it colonized Brazil in the 1500s. So, if any Brazilians want to travel to Portugal to see some old friends, you have some great options.

From São Paulo to Portugal, you can use Azule Airlines or TAP Air Portugal during the summer for a round trip with no connections.

Year-round trips are aided by airlines like Air France, KLM, and Iberia. There are connections in Amsterdam, Madrid, or Paris, which can last longer than you might prefer. Still, it's worth it once you get to the beautiful country of Portugal.

**Traveling from Europe**

Being in Europe, Portugal is an accessible destination to get to from almost any place in Europe. So, let's take a look at the most popular bases for traveling to Portugal in Europe:

### London

Finding a flight from London to Portugal is easy, and there are many options. Not only are you provided with many options, but it's also easy to get to any airport in Portugal from London. EasyJet seems to be among the most popular options. The lowest price in London for a round-trip flight is roughly £120.

Ryanair can get you from London Luton to Faro direct starting in April every year. They can get you to Lisbon, Faro, or Porto from London Stansted with reasonable pricing. You can find direct flights for as low as £50 one way. These prices are bound to rise in June, but the increase isn't dramatic.

TAP Portugal can get you from London to Porto, Faro, and Lisbon.

British Airways only has flights to Lisbon and Porto. Prices for a direct flight to Lisbon can start at £164 in November, rising to £173 in June.

### Dublin

Looking to escape winter in Dublin? You can get a direct flight from Dublin to Portugal with KLM for much less during the winter months.

Other options include British Airways and Ryanair. British Airways is more expensive and does have a three-hour transfer in London, which is less than ideal. Ryanair prices range from €40 to €250 for a one-way flight from Dublin to either Lisbon, Faro, or Porto (your choice will affect the price).

**Paris**

Among the best options for flying from Paris to Portugal are perhaps EasyJet and British Airways. Flights are also offered by Vueling Airlines, and they can sometimes be cheaper. Summer is when flights tend to be somewhat cheaper, and you could even find a flight for €100 for a round trip.

**Traveling from Asia**

There are numerous travel options available in Asia to get you to Portugal. Let's take a look at the two most popular bases for traveling to Portugal:

**Singapore**

If you're traveling from Singapore, you should consider using Lufthansa Airlines. They offer the best flight option for a Singapore to Portugal flight. It has one stop along the way. Unfortunately, this stop is a three-hour stop, and you won't find better than that. Overall, the journey should take roughly eighteen hours.

Beyond Lufthansa, other options include KLM, Emirates, Finnair, Qatar Airways, and British Airlines.

**Hong Kong**

Flying from Hong Kong to Lisbon is going to be a roughly twenty-hour flight with one stop along the way, which lasts roughly two and a half hours. Airlines to use include KLM, British Airways, and Emirates.

## TIPS AND TRICKS TO FINDING THE BEST DEALS

Let's take a look at some important tips and tricks to help you find the best—and cheapest—travel options to Portugal.

### Who to Fly With

Of course, you want to find the best price, but you also want a trustworthy airline. The great news is that there are so many great airlines in charge of flights to and from Portugal.

Let's take a look at your best options:

- TAP Air Portugal
- KLM
- Air France
- Iberia
- Emirates
- Turkish Airlines
- Ryanair
- EasyJet
- Wizzair

### How to Find the Best Flights to Portugal

There are tons of great services out there that aggregate flight options, showing you different prices and types of flights.

Services like Skyscanner, Skiplagged, and Kayak are great examples of what's out there to help you get yourself on the best possible flight to Portugal.

**Best Time to Book a Flight to Portugal**

What you'll find when you're booking a flight to anywhere in the world, not just Portugal, is that the day and time can make a huge difference in price. But even beyond that, the airport you choose to go tocould also make a slight difference in the cost of your flight.

When it comes to booking flights, you've got so many options to choose from, and they all provide different pricing. Try using flight search engines like the ones we previously mentioned to find the best flights at the most reasonable prices.

There are some basics you should know about when it comes to timing. For starters, try to book in advance. The range of savings to be made on booking flights in advance fluctuates, but it can get ridiculously high. Another thing to consider is flying on less desirable days and months, such as Monday to Thursday, and months like January. It's important to avoid Faro during August as 'it's 22 percent more expensive to fly then!

This isn't to say you can't find savings last minute. It's just not as easy.

## AIRPORTS OF PORTUGAL

Like many countries, Portugal has a wide variety of airports to choose from, which can place you closer to your intended destination. The country has three international airports: Lisbon, Faro, and Porto. There are also dedicated international airports for the autonomous islands of Azores and Madeira, which are pivotal if you're hoping to vacation at these island destinations.

Let's take a look at the core airports in Portugal you'll most likely end up at, depending on your final destination.

**Lisbon Airport**

The first major airport in Portugal is Lisbon International Airport, formally known as Humberto Delgado Airport. It's the country's busiest airport, located just seven kilometers from the capital city. This airport acts as the main international gateway to Portugal, making it a critical airport while also being one of the most likely airports you'll find yourself using.

Lisbon Airport acts as an essential European hub for traveling to Brazil and South America at large. It's actually the largest European hub for South America. It also serves as a European hub for Africa. In Europe, Lisbon Airport ranks as the twentieth busiest airport regarding passenger traffic. The airport features two terminal buildings. The most popular airlines that connect to Lisbon Airport include TAP (the official airline of Portugal, which has its headquarters at Lisbon Airport), Ryanair, Air France, and Easyjet.

In terms of services, you'll find that similar to most international airports, Lisbon Airport features Wi-Fi access, restaurants, cafés, duty-free stores, etc.

**Porto Airport**

The second international airport in Portugal, which is also the second busiest airport, is Porto Airport, formally known as Francisco Sá Carneiro Airport. The airport lies twenty minutes outside of Porto's city center. The airlines connected to Porto Airport include Easyjet, TAP Air Portugal, TAP Express, and Ryanair. Porto is considered a modern and spacious airport, having consistently been mentioned as one of Europe's best airports.

The airport offers numerous shopping options, including clothes, sunglasses, electronics, luggage, souvenirs, a pharmacy, and more. You can also enjoy many food and drink options,, and numerous cafés, bars, and restaurants. They even have regional eateries like La Pausa, Douro, and A Francesinha. So, if you're still hankering for Portuguese food as you're on your way home, stop by for a final taste.

**Faro Airport**

The final international airport is Faro Airport, also known as Algarve Airport. The airport lies four kilometers west of Faro. This airport is extremely popular during the summer, as Faro is a summer tourist destination. It's a reasonably new hub, as it became a hub only in March 2010 due to Ryanair deciding to base seven of its aircraft at the airport.

**Madeira Airport**

Madeira Airport, formally known as Madeira International Airport Cristiano Ronaldo, is also known as Funchal Airport. We get that this might sound a little confusing, so to make it easier, just stick with its common name, Madeira Airport. This is also an international airport, but because it's in an autonomous territory in Portugal, it's not counted among the main international airports in the country.

One thing that you need to know about Madeira Airport is that it's considered one of the world's most dangerous airports. It's not due to crime, but rather a positioning issue. The airport lies between high mountains and the ocean, making it extremely difficult to approach.

It's located thirteen kilometers east-northeast of Madeira's capital, Funchal. Thanks to Madeira's tourism importance and popularity, the airport is the nation's fourth busiest airport. Madeira Airport is the most common for hosting flights to other European destinations.

**The Azores Airport**

Formally named the Ponta Delgada Airport, also known as the João Paulo II Airport, it is Portugal's fifth international airport and services the autonomous territory of the Azores with the airport on the São Miguel island. This island is in the Azores archipelago, composed of nine islands. Each island has its own airport, but the Ponta Delgada Airport is its international hub.

This airport keeps the nine islands further connected, with flights throughout the islands taking place all day. Flights to Madeira and the mainland are also extremely popular. In terms of international flights, you'll most commonly see flights to and from North America and the rest of Europe.

## HOW ELSE CAN YOU GET TO PORTUGAL

Flying isn't the only way to get to Portugal. Let's take a look at some other options to get there:

**Train**

There are trains that will take you from various parts of Europe to Portugal. For example, you can travel from London to Lisbon in twenty-four hours using Eurostar. It requires you to transfer to several different trains along the European stops in Paris and Spain. Fares start at £200 round trip. These aren't your basic trains either, as there are cabins with showers and beds and a restaurant, buffet bar, bar, lounge, etc. In the EU, there are numerous ways to navigate your way to Portugal by using each nation's train networks with lines connecting to other European countries.

### Driving

If you live within the EU, driving from your home nation and getting to Portugal is easy. You can drive from the UK, a roughly 2,000-kilometer- journey. You'll have to make use of cross-Channel services or even the Eurotunnel, and it's not a cheap option when you factor in things like fuel, overnight stops, tolls, meals, etc. But the upside is getting to see France and Spain along the way, making for a stunning road trip with a worthy final destination. Perhaps the biggest downside is the fact that you've got to make this journey again to get home. After a nice vacation, two days in a car isn't the best feeling.

You can take a ferry to Northern Spain to cut down on travel time. This will be more expensive as you'll pay for ferry tickets for all the passengers and your vehicle. Another option is to rent a car while in Northern Spain and return it upon departure.

## TAKEAWAY

So, what should you take away from this chapter? Well, for starters, you've got a lot of options when it comes to getting to Portugal, regardless of where in the world you're traveling from. Of course, some journeys will be quicker, cheaper, and overall easier than others.

Probably the best part of this all are the various modes of transportation some people have when it comes to getting to

Portugal. Planes, trains, driving, and even ferries that take you and your car across the water closer to your destination.

Granted, this can be expensive, so you need to budget your trip accordingly. Great news, that's what we're going to explore next. We'll cover everything you can do to make your money go further on your vacation.

# CHAPTER 3
# BUDGETING

Budgeting is an essential step when it comes to traveling. You need to go in with a firm idea of how much you're going to spend on your trip. This number is bound to change, but if you've budgeted correctly, you've likely planned ahead for any surprises.

In this chapter, I'll break down every aspect of budgeting for your trip and provide some helpful tips on how to save money in certain places. It doesn't matter what type of budget you have. If you can get to Portugal, you can enjoy Portugal.

## CONSTRUCTING A TRAVEL BUDGET

Let's look at each section of a travel budget so you can start getting an idea of how you'd construct your tentative budget. We're going to go section by section. So, let's get started!

**Pre-departure Expenses**

When it comes to pre-departure expenses, we're looking at things like the following:

**Visas**

Not all of these are going to be necessary. Sometimes, you can enter a country visa-free depending on your nationality and the power of your country's passport.

**Medical Protection**

For medical protection, we're talking about things like the shots you're required to have to enter a country (assuming they have required shots), prescription medications, and over-the-counter medications. It's important to also have some form of medical insurance especially if you're prone to health issues.

### Travel Insurance

Some people might choose to travel without travel insurance, and that's a choice you have to make. However, we recommend not risking it. Travel insurance, depending on which one you get, can cover things like loss of money or passport, lost or delayed baggage, trip cancellation, flight delays, personal accidents, medical expenses (sometimes sold separately), and even evacuations. It's better to be safe than sorry.

### Guidebooks and Travel Apps

If you want to make the most of your time in a foreign country, you want to know where to go, what to do, and what to see. In these cases, you'll need things like a guidebook or travel app. These often don't cost much, and they're well worth the small price to make the most of your vacation.

### Gear

This is an optional expense and refers to things like camera equipment, camping gear (if needed), luggage, equipment cases, etc. In some cases, you may already have all these things, which means you won't have to spend extra money!

### Clothing

Once again, this is an optional expense. You may have all the clothes you need for a trip to Portugal or wherever you're going, which means you won't need to spend extra money on new clothes.

**Currency Exchange**

Portugal is an EU country meaning they use the euro as their currency. If you're traveling to Portugal, it's wise to get some euros for your trip. There are places in airports that have currency exchanges.

**Airfare**

In most cases, especially in the case of going to Portugal, airfare is a given. The cost of airfare needs to include getting there and getting back, and these prices vary greatly depending on where you're traveling from, when you're traveling, etc.

**Other Transportation**

While you're there, you're going to need to get around. While walking is a cheap alternative, it's only going to get you so far. So, you will need to use other transportation options in the country. Portugal is fortunate to have a decent public transportation system of buses, trains, streetcars (area dependent), metro/subway (area dependent), bikes (area dependent), and taxi services (including Uber, Bolt, etc.). For this, try to familiarize yourself with the general fares of these services (which we expand on in Chapter 4 - Portugal Transportation) and try to make a flexible budget.

**Lodging and Meal Expenses**

Without researching the area you're traveling to and seeing what kinds of accommodations are available, you'll have a hard time budgeting this aspect of your journey. You need to book accommodation in advance, so you'll be researching this, regardless. The average for a decent hotel is about $65 USD per night, and a hostel is $20 USD per day. Multiply whichever average would apply to you by the number of days you'll be staying there and then increase it by 15 percent for price fluctuations.

For food, work on a $20 per day budget times the number of days you'll be in Portugal and then increase it by 15 percent to accommodate for surprises.

**Special Experiences**

Understand what special experiences exist in the areas where you'll be spending time in Portugal. You don't want too many surprises, as these can be the most costly endeavors. You want to have special experiences, but not when they break the bank. Some tips on this matter include:

- Developed countries will have more expensive special experiences.
- If modern technology, like a helicopter, is involved, then expect it to be more expensive.
- If you're getting prices from travel agents, expect that they're marked up from the price it would be if you organized it yourself.

**Miscellaneous**

When we say miscellaneous, we're talking about the things you buy during your trip—for example, souvenirs, clothes, toiletries, books, beverages, etc.

## EXAMPLE CHECKLIST

| | |
|---|---|
| **Pre-departure Expenses** | |
| Passport, visas, photos | $ |
| Medical Protection (shots, prescriptions, medicine) | $ |
| Guidebooks and Apps | $ |
| Luggage and Daypack | $ |
| New Clothes and Gear | $ |
| Travel Insurance | $ |
| Toiletries | $ |
| **Transportation** | |
| Airfare | $ |
| Airport Parking | $ |
| Checked Baggage Fee | $ |
| Other (trains, buses, etc.) | $ |
| **Communication** | |
| Telephone Fees (SIM, temp phone, etc.) | $ |
| **Meals and Lodging** | |
| En Route | $ |
| Daily Lodging | $ |
| Daily Meals | $ |
| **Special Experiences** | |
| Cultural (festivals, concerts, museums, etc.) | $ |
| Entertainment (clubs, parties, etc.) | $ |
| Adventure (scuba diving, surfing, etc.) | $ |
| **Miscellaneous** | |
| | $ |
| | $ |
| | $ |

| Total Trip Budget | |
|---|---|
| **SUBTOTAL** | $ |
| **TOURIST TAX** | |
| **+15% (Unexpected expenses)** | $ |
| **TOTAL** | $ |

**PLEASE NOTE** - Tourist Tax is $2.20 Per night. It applies to certain municipalities such as Lisbon, Sintra, Cascais, Mafra, Portimão, Santa Cruz, Óbidos, Vila Nova de Gaia, and Vila Real de Santo António for guests over 13.

## TIPS FOR TRAVELING ON A BUDGET

You don't need to be flush with cash to take in and enjoy Portugal for everything that it is! There are tons of ways to travel on a budget. So, let's take a look at some tips for traveling on a budget.

### Choose Your Destination Carefully

It's a fact of life that some places will be more expensive than others. In Portugal, you've got numerous cities, towns, and villages to explore, and each of them is going to be different in terms of price. You'll want to research the areas available and try to understand what might be expected of you financially so you can plan accordingly. Don't worry; even the cheaper places are still well worth the visit!

### Avoid the Tourist Traps

When it comes to traveling, tourist traps are inevitable. A tourist trap can come in many forms, like accommodation in expensive areas, restaurants on the main strip, and something over-advertised. You can find great alternatives that are cheaper and often better—for example, taking a walk around town looking for a hidden gem restaurant. This can open you up to exciting discoveries that don't break the bank.

### Get Travel Insurance

Yes, I've already touched on travel insurance, but it's so important we're going to talk about it again. There is nothing more important than getting some travel insurance if you plan on traveling, especially if you're on a budget! Travel insurance helps in cases of trip cancellations, getting sick abroad, theft, etc. It makes far more sense to be prepared for anything than to risk it!

### Travel Off-Season

Traveling off-season can be a risky endeavor, but it's so rewarding. For starters, traveling off-season is far cheaper, less crowded, and potentially far more relaxing. The trade-off when traveling off-season is that you may end up experiencing weather that's not the best, but that risk can exist during the peak season too! Plan it right, and you'll minimize this risk and save money while having an amazing trip.

### Book In Advance

If possible, avoid relying on those last-minute deals. They're stressful and hard to find. Instead, book as far in advance as possible. When you book in advance, you will find that the prices are far lower than when you book closer to your trip.

**Use Websites to Find the Best Deals on Flights**

There are so many sites and apps out there dedicated to finding you the best deals on just about anything. What you want to focus on is finding the best deals for flights. We've already told you about some amazing apps to look at and consider when searching for cheaper flights.

**Fly Mid-Week**

You'd be surprised at the difference a mid-week flight can make in the price. The weekends are more sought after when it comes to flying, often to accommodate the professional's working schedule. But if you plan it right, you can leave mid-week between Tuesday and Thursday and experience a cheaper flight.

**Pack Well**

Looking to save money? Pack the right way to avoid paying more for unnecessary luggage. The first thing you want to do is pack light! Let's be honest, you're not going to wear half of the clothes you bring with you anyway, so try to pack efficiently for what you'll actually need. Look for opportunities to wear something multiple times. Also, make sure you don't forget anything when packing. If you forget something, it means buying it at your travel destination, and that's likely going to cost you in more ways than you think.

**Be Prepared to Share**

There are tons of accommodation opportunities that cost far less than a hotel, bed-and-breakfast, Airbnb, etc. We're talking about hostels, dorms, and similar locations. There's a slight tradeoff of having to share a bathroom with multiple strangers, but it's extremely affordable.

**Couch Surf, If at All Possible**

When it comes to couch surfing, there are multiple ways you could go about achieving this. For starters, if you know someone in the country you're visiting, then why not stay with them—assuming they don't mind? The other option is making use of couch surfing opportunities promoted online through apps and services. That's right, there are locals out there who offer you the chance to stay in their home for free or next to nothing, which is an extraordinary experience. You get a place to stay and a way to connect with the locals and their culture.

**Travel Overnight**

If Portugal—or whatever country you're traveling to—is far from your home country, why not travel at night? There are several benefits to overnight traveling. For starters, it's slightly cheaper, and when you're on a budget, any savings is a saving overall. The second benefit is that you don't have to worry about accommodation for that first day/night of traveling. You'll get there in the morning, get to your accommodation, and have a whole day to relax or explore. Traveling overnight makes a ton of sense.

**In the Right Area, Take Chances on Accommodation**

This is a risky move, but there are benefits to it if done correctly. If you're traveling to a small town or village, you'll be able to find accommodation where you can book with the owner in person, as needed. This means you can get the accommodation for less because there are fewer fees involved for the owners without using hotel booking services.

**Look into Carpooling Services**

There's actually a thriving carpool service around the world that work off of apps like Bla Bla Car. These services connect local drivers who are already making trips for whatever reason and are offering a seat in their vehicle, where you pay a fee to travel with them. It's a cheaper alternative to services like Bolt and Uber. It's also a great way to meet and interact with locals.

**Read Other Traveler's Backpacking Experiences**

When you're researching your trip, research other people's experiences regarding backpacking. Reading something from someone who's experienced it firsthand means you get a full picture of what's in store, what mistakes to avoid, accommodation opportunities, food, activities, etc.

**Look for Free Activities to Do**

It doesn't matter where you are in the world, there's always something to do for free. You've just got to find those opportunities. It might be a museum, walking tours, parks, beaches, etc. You need to ask around for things to do and seek out those opportunities that cost next to nothing, if not nothing at all.

### Get Yourself a Local SIM

Using data overseas is a budget killer. That is, unless you get a local SIM. When you've got a local SIM card, you can take advantage of the local data packages, which will be far cheaper than paying for Wi-Fi or data roaming. Let's face it, we're a world that is connected by the internet, and not having data can be a problem, especially in a foreign country. Having data means being able to talk to both people traveling with you and those back home, while also having access to navigation systems at all times.

### DIY Excursions

Instead of going on pre-planned excursions, why not figure it out for yourself? You can save so much money, and probably have a better time if you go on these expensive excursions on your own or with your group. To make it even cheaper, take your own food and beverages. Think about it—when you pay for an excursion, most of the money isn't going to the trip but to the guide in charge of the excursion. Cut out the intermediary, and DIY it instead.

### Don't Always Eat Out

I get it. Eating out is easy and less likely to disappoint. But it's also expensive when you're doing it for breakfast, lunch, and dinner. So, to lessen the burden, try to eat more economically.

For starters, find a hotel that has breakfast built into the agreement. Second, consider cooking for yourself. If your accommodation has a place to cook, either in your room or communally, then take advantage of the local grocery stores and get the ingredients to make something simple for lunch and dinner. Nobody is saying avoid eating out altogether, but don't rely on it as much.

**Be Aware of the Potential ATM Charges**

ATMs in foreign countries will drain you financially. This is due to the fees attached to withdrawing and exchanging your money. So what do you do about this? You might think exchanging money beforehand is the solution, but feel it's a risky move. However, it's often cheaper to do exchange money in the country you're visiting. So, instead, if you're going to withdraw money, withdraw as much as you'd be willing to lose. The benefit is that it reduces your use of ATMs; the downside is that it's more money to lose or have stolen.

**Don't Be Afraid to Haggle**

If you've got the confidence, put it to the test and try your hand at haggling. It's not uncommon for local vendors to mark things up for tourists. By assuming this, see if you can get a discount on something you really want to buy. Haggling works best when you're traveling in a group.

### Get Recommendations from the Locals

This is something that can go either way, depending on which country you're traveling to. Locals don't like paying the increased prices tourists will pay, so why not ask where they go in the area for the best food and drinks? You may find a hidden gem that nobody else mentions.

### Bring Your Own Water Bottle and Coffee Cup

This tip isn't for everyone, but don't discount its value. Having a reusable water bottle and coffee cup has its benefits. For starters, if you have a reusable water bottle, you'll significantly reduce the need to buy water while out and about exploring. You can take advantage of free water sources, assuming the water sources are safe for consumption, allowing you to have free water at all times. With the reusable coffee cup, it's possible, but not guaranteed, that you could get discounts, as some places offer discounts if you bring your own cup.

### Walk Everywhere.

It's not an understatement to say that walking is the cheapest form of transportation. If you're on a strict budget, then why not walk to and from your destinations while on holiday? Of course, there are several factors you should consider when you take on the 'walk everywhere' method. For example, is it safe to walk everywhere? Are there any cheap alternatives? What is the distance? What is the terrain like? One thing you shouldn't do if you're traveling on a budget is take things like

Uber, Bolt, or any other taxi services, as they will be expensive.

**Work While Travelling**

We live in a new world where freelancing and remote work are more common than ever. So, take advantage of this and work while you're traveling to make some extra money to spend in the country you're visiting. Beyond remote/freelance work, you can even find work while you're visiting a country. Some hostels offer opportunities to work a little to reduce the rate of your accommodation, or make it downright free! There are a lot of interesting opportunities you can take advantage of to not only stay longer in a country, but also enjoy it more fully.

**Create a Budget and Stick to It**

One of the most important things you need to do when planning to travel on a budget is to actually set a budget. Then, once that budget is set, you get to the difficult part, which is actually sticking to the budget. To avoid any surprises, try to set aside some money in your budget for things you haven't planned for, maybe because you either didn't know about them or only choose to do them when you're there and see them for yourself. Be careful when it comes to a budget; you don't want it to be something that overshadows your trip and makes it less enjoyable.

## HOW MUCH DOES IT REALLY COST TO VACATION IN PORTUGAL?

We've talked about the overall concept of a budget and how you can be frugal while traveling. Now, let's take a look at Portugal itself and what it actually costs to vacation there.

**Average Daily Cost**

The average daily cost per person in Portugal is:

- Budget: $61
- Mid-range: $149
- Luxury: $348

It's important to understand that these are average numbers not including accommodation and transportation. When you travel with more people, there are opportunities to save money in certain areas with group discounts. If you're traveling with kids, you'd be able to lessen their daily expenses as their tickets will be cheaper, they can share hotel rooms, etc.

**Accommodation Budget**

When it comes to accommodation, you're looking at the following rates per day:

- $140 per person for a hotel room
- $279 per couple for a double-occupancy room

These numbers vary depending on where in Portugal you're going to be staying and when. If you're staying during peak season, you'll find these prices may be inflated. Another factor that determines the price of accommodation is the amenities.

### Transportation Budget

For transportation, the overall daily budget is $76 per person for all modes of transportation. Let's take a deeper look at what transportation spending in Portugal can look like.

### Taxi

Depending on the type of taxi you use, the length of your trip, and the time the trip is taken, you're looking at an average of $29 per day or $7 per trip. By law taxis are expected to charge by distance, but ensure the meter starts when your trip does.

### Intercity Transportation

If you're using intercity transportation, that's going to be far more expensive than the daily average of $76, which is for local transportation. You're looking at an average of $97 per trip, depending on the route length, transportation type, and date. A coach bus between cities can be quiet inexpensive for example it's $7 from Braga to Porto.

### Flights

Domestic flights in Portugal vary depending on where you're traveling to. The average for traveling from Lisbon to

Madeira is $103, which is a fair average for most domestic flights. However, flying to the Azores becomes complicated as there are numerous islands in the Azores, and they are cheaper to fly between when in the Azores already; they can be pricy from the mainland.

**Rental Cars**

The cost of renting a car in Portugal varies greatly depending on where you're renting the car from and the area of the car rental service. Overall, the average cost of renting a car is roughly between $40 a day. This can vary greatly depending on the model, time of year, and availability. This can be a cheaper alternative if you're traveling in a group or a family.

**Food Budget**

Your average food budget will be $100 per person per day in Portugal. The cost of meals will vary depending on where you eat and where you are in Portugal.

Here are some more important averages to know when it comes to food and beverages:

- Lunch (for two): $14
- Coffee: $1.53–$2.74
- Pizzeria Lunch (for two): $16

**Entertainment**

The average for entertainment per day is $60. This amount includes things like admission to museums, attractions, day tours, sightseeing, etc. Of course, there are going to be some entertainment opportunities that will exceed this average, as well as ones that are extremely cheap.

### Tips and Handouts Budget

Regarding tips and handouts in Portugal, you will want to have at least an average of $12 set aside. The average amount for a tip in Portugal is between 5 and 15 percent. But we'll get more into the subject of tipping in a bit.

### Scams, Robberies, and Mishaps

Sadly, even Portugal isn't immune to the occasional scam, robbery, and mishap. You want to be prepared for an average daily cost of $6.42 over the course of your trip for things like scams, robberies, and mishaps. This is something you could very well avoid, but it's important to be aware of the potential.

### Alcohol

If you like to drink, prepare to spend, on average, $42 a day on booze. It doesn't matter if it's a drink by the pool in the sun or a drink on a night out with dinner or at an event; you'll want to be prepared. Honestly, this may be on the low end, so prepare to spend a bit more if you're planning on having a great time.

### Water

Depending on your location and travel style, expect to pay, on average, $3.44 a day for water. Great news—the public water in Portugal is considered safe for consumption.

### Portugal on a Budget

There are lots of ways to travel on a budget. Of course, it means making sacrifices. For example, steer clear of the popular coastal towns and populous cities. These tend to be pricier due to their high tourism value. Another tip is to book well in advance for flights and accommodation during off-season periods. Finally, find a cheaper alternative to certain things, like accommodation, by working where you stay for free or more affordable accommodation, going to museums on Sundays when it's free, eating less at restaurants, and more.

You can travel on a budget and still have an amazing experience. Save the expensive parts of Portugal for your next visit when you can save up more in advance.

## TAKEAWAY

If anything should be taken away from this chapter, it's that traveling in Portugal is viable for anyone who can get there. It doesn't matter what income bracket you exist in; there are ways to enjoy this gorgeous country on any budget. Of course, more money means more opportunities, but that doesn't discount the opportunities you get on a lesser budget.

Portugal has so much to offer, and there are so many ways you can make a trip to this country memorable. We will explore all the amazing areas you can travel to and what you can do in them, even on a budget. But first, we've got to dive deeper into the country's public transportation so you know how to navigate regardless of your budget.

# CHAPTER 4
# PORTUGAL TRANSPORTATION

When you're in Portugal, you're going to want to go here, there, and everywhere possible. That sounds easy enough, but the last thing you want to do is spend your vacation walking everywhere or overpaying for transportation.

The good news is, there are numerous transportation options in Portugal, making it easy to travel around the country. In this chapter, we're going to explore what all those transportation methods look like, how to use them, and get a basic understanding of the cost involved.

## PUBLIC TRANSPORTATION OPTIONS OVERVIEW

As a country, Portugal has an incredibly intricate public transportation network that's highly accessible, with numerous options differing in price. It makes connections between major cities. It also connects Portugal to the rest of Europe, with lines extending far beyond their borders.

In Portugal, you'll find that you can travel by plane, train, bus, taxi, streetcar, funicular, and more. You would do well to learn about Omio. This excellent travel website pools the various transportation options and provides a place to purchase tickets. Doing it directly from the transportation companies' websites or mobile apps is cheaper. However, Omio is an excellent alternative if you're looking for a more straightforward solution.

## TRAINS

The first mode of transportation we've got to look at is Portugal's excellent train network. I'll cover connections, tickets, costs, timetables, maps, stations, stops, and international trains.

### Comboios de Portugal (CP)

Like other European nations, Portugal has a connected rail network that's state-owned and managed by Comboios de Portugal (CP), the national train operator. Each year, over 145 million passengers use Portugal's extensive rail network, which extends to much of the nation.

The fastest connections exist between the major cities, such as Porto, Lisbon, Aveiro, Coimbra, Lagos, and Faro. Let's look at some popular train connections you should know about!

### Alfa Pendular (AP)

Mainly running from Lisbon central to Porto, the AP further ventures out into the north to Coimbra, then Braga before heading south to Faro. This line is the most comfortable, fastest (reaching 220 km/h), and most expensive direct line in Portugal.

### Intercidades (IC)

This long-distance service is slightly cheaper than the AP while still being relatively fast, reaching 200 km/h. The IC trains are older and also make more stops along the way than the more direct Alfa Pendular.

### Regionais (R)

The Regionais is the local service. They are slower trains and far more basic than the Alfa Pendular and Intercidades trains. The R will stop at all stations out of Lisbon and Porto's suburban areas.

### Urbano (U)

The Urbano is a commuter-focused urban service for the CP. It serves the areas surrounding Porto and Lisbon.

### Things to Know

On the CP trains, you can bring pets, bicycles, and luggage onboard without paying for an additional separate ticket.

You should download and use the Android or iOS apps to book your ticket, check the timetables, edit itineraries, and stay current on your train details.

**Train Tickets and Costs**

If you're a tourist in Portugal, you're lucky because CP's website/app is straightforward to navigate and buy tickets from. It provides you with up-to-date information regarding train schedules. It's also the fastest way to get a train ticket. If you're not interested in navigating CP's website or app, you can always get tickets in person from the station ticket counters.

Once you've purchased a ticket, it is sent to your phone through the app, SMS, or email. Fair warning, not having a ticket on the train and being caught by the conductor results in a fine of €120.

There are various options for ticket types, like first class, but these are only available on the AP and IC train lines. While they offer slightly better comfort and legroom, they're unlike other trains across Europe because they don't offer complimentary drinks or food. Depending on the length of your journey, upgrading to first class might not be necessary.

A great way to save on your train tickets is to book in advance. Here are all the ways you can save on train tickets:

- 50 percent off if you book five days in advance.
- 65 percent off when you book eight days in advance.
- Kids under the age of four ride free of charge.

- Seniors 65 and over are entitled to a 50 percent discount.
- Passengers 13 and under are entitled to a 50 percent discount.
- Passengers 13 to 25 are entitled to a 25 percent discount.
- There are discounts for groups of four or more which vary in price.

If you plan to travel extensively, consider purchasing a Portugal Rail Pass, which provides unlimited travel for 3 or 7 days from the day of purchase.

**Train Maps and Timetables**

The CP has trains running during the day. If you're exploring late at night, you'll likely have to use the taxis or buses that are still operating.

You'll have access to itinerary planning, conventional timetables, and more online. CP has made it extremely easy to keep up with each line to help you effectively plan around the trains.

**Train Stations and Stops**

As with all countries, the facilities and size of Portugal's train stations vary. Some of the stations are massive beautiful buildings like São Bento Station in Porto, which is filled with art depicting the nation's history. There's also Gare dó Oriente Station in Lisbon which is architecturally impressive. The larger train stations often have restaurants, cafés, bars, shops, and ticketing desks for domestic and international trains. In contrast, the more urban stations are more functionally focused with multilingual staff to aid travelers. Finally, regional stations are simply ticket machines and one platform. You'll know what services and facilities are available at each station through the CP app or website.

**International Trains**

You can enjoy international trains to Spain. You've got some options starting with the Celta Train, which links Portugal's Porto to Spain's Vigo. The other options include Lusitania Overnight Train to Madrid from Lisbon.

Want to get to greater Europe? There are trains to Hendaya, a French town on the Spanish border which is as close as you can get via Portugal. You can book international train journeys through CP or RENFE, Spain's national railway company.

## BUSES

Unlike trains, Portugal's bus network is operated by a series of private operators, which have been segmented into regional companies. They offer an expansive network of routes extending beyond the reaches of the nation's rail network.

There are three intercity bus companies: Rodo-Norte (serves the northern regions), Rede Expressos (serves the nation), and Eva Transportes. These companies offer the most modern and comfortable buses. They've got reliable air conditioning and Wi-Fi. On the longer routes, some provide services like food and drinks. Be careful on weekends as the number of buses available decreases significantly. Always check the schedules to ensure you're not stranded!

Beyond the previously mentioned intercity bus companies which run on the same bus network, here are some that have their own networks, which are also available:

- Flixbus: Portugal to various European destinations like Paris, Amsterdam, Vienna, etc.
- Alsa: the national bus company for Spain, Alsa services routes to Sevilla, Madrid, Barcelona, and even into France.

Besides some remote beaches, nature parks, and hard-to-reach destinations, you should be able to use the buses to get just about anywhere in Portugal. Here are the four different types of buses you will encounter while in Portugal:

- Alta Qualidade: This type of bus offers a deluxe experience, connecting major cities with high-speed travel.
- Expressos: Also connecting major cities, Expressos is a comfortable bus service offering fast travel.

- Rapidas: This local service provides quick regional connections.
- Carreiras (CR): This is the slowest offering for buses, as they stop at most small towns as it's a regional service.

**Bus Tickets and Costs**

Unfortunately, due to there being several service providers, bus tickets and their costs will depend on the company you're riding with. Try to lock onto a single service provider for your time in Portugal, with a backup option in case of an emergency.

If you're using Rede Expressos, you can download their app on iOS or Android. They also have the RFLEX travel program, providing discounts and improved customer service.

Local bus service doesn't allow for pre-booking, so you must rely on bus stops and the schedule. Tickets can be purchased on the bus or from a kiosk (if available).

**Viva Viagem Card**

In Lisbon, you can get the Viva Viagem card, making traveling on the local buses cheaper. The card is inexpensive at €0.50 and valid for a year. You can top up this card and use it as a bus credit card.

**Lisboa Card**

There's also a Lisboa Card which costs €22.00+ (prices vary) and provides free public transportation (bus, metro, streetcar, etc.), free entry to museums and attractions, deals, and discounts.

**Adante Monthly and Andante Tour**

In Porto, they have the Andante Monthly, which works for unlimited use of transportation in designated transportation zones. There's an Andante Tour card for unlimited transportation use for twenty-four hours (€7) or seventy-two hours (€15). With this card, you get unlimited access to the metro, buses, and some of the trains for your selected time.

**Porto Card**

Finally, the Porto Card allows you to enjoy unlimited use of public transportation, discounts on attractions, free access to various museums, and more. The Porto card has several tiers:

**Pedestrian Card:**

While this option doesn't have unlimited transportation, it offers numerous free entry and discount offers to city sights.

- 1-day Porto Card: €6
- 2-day Porto Card: €10
- 3-day Porto Card: €13
- 4-day Porto Card: €15

**Porto Card + Travelcard:**

The Porto card with travel means you can enjoy unlimited city transportation access, free entry to six museums, and 50 percent off for fourteen monuments in Porto.

- 1-day Porto Card + Transport: €13
- 2-day Porto Card + Transport: €20
- 3-day Porto Card + Transport: €25
- 4-day Porto Card + Transport: €33

**Bus Maps and Timetables**

Buses run most of the day, with regular routes from 5:00 a.m. to midnight. There are night buses beyond these hours. Still, they are limited to more popular areas in major cities. The websites and apps of the intercity carriers always have up-to-date information on the schedule of their buses. For local services, check the bus stations for travel routes and timetables.

## TAXIS AND RIDESHARING

If you're looking for something different and less crowded, you might be interested in some of the many different car services in Portugal. This nation has its share of taxis, rideshare services, and more.

One service to consider is TaxiFareFinder, which helps you see how much specific trips might cost. It can be a lifesaver when you're budgeting and planning things for your itinerary.

**Taxi Services**

Retalis is a 24-hour taxi service. Download their iOS or Android app to ensure you always have a last resort. They've got options for 4/6/8 seaters, vans, electric, and reduced mobility. So no matter what, you're covered.

Similar to Retalis, Cooptaxis is another taxi service. It has the nation's most extensive fleet. They also have an app that makes it easy to get a ride.

Uber is a tricky service in Portugal. They've had a tense relationship with the nation for some time. They're now active in most major cities like Lisbon, Coimbra, Porto, Faro, and Braga. However it's limited and at times unreliable.

Other alternatives include Bolt (nationwide) and Cabify (Lisbon, Porto, Madeira, and the Algarve).

**Rideshare**

If you're looking for a cheap alternative with a bit of conversing with locals and potentially other travelers, try a rideshare service. It's like carpooling on vacation. Services like Boleia and BlaBlaCar will help you locate people going to various places in Portugal, who are offering seats in their cars for the journey. You just enter where you are and where you're going, and they see what offers they've got available. It's easy, cheaper, and it can be a fun experience.

## OTHER OPTIONS

Here are some other transportation options available in certain cities:

### Metro

If you want to try Portugal's metro (subway) system, you'll only be able to enjoy that in Porto and Lisbon. These are the only cities in the country with a metro option. They run from 06:00 a.m. to 01:00 a.m. and have various connections to get you across the city and as close to your final destination as possible. Overall, the networks are safe, clean, and efficient. The Lisbon metro has a total of four lines, with fifty-two stations along the way (thirty-one have full accessibility). On the other hand, Porto has a total of six lines, including a direct line to Porto airport.

### Streetcars and Funiculars

Lisbon and Porto, unlike other major cities, have streetcars and the less common funiculars. These are slower, more scenic options for traveling around the city, but they're worth the journey if you're not in a rush. The historic and popular Tram 28 runs through the narrow Alfama streets, which is especially worth seeing.

### Gira Bike

In Lisbon, they've got yet another excellent transportation option: the Gira Bike. Across the city, docking stations allow you to take and drop off these bikes at stations. You're required to download an app on iOS or Android where you can choose the 24-hour offer, allowing unlimited rides (forty-five-minute turns). There's a monthly and annual subscription, but it's only for residents. To pay, you either use Paypal or a credit card.

## TAKEAWAY

It's clear that no matter which part of Portugal you're in, there are plenty of options for getting around. That's part of what makes traveling in this country so great—the sheer sense of how accessible it is as a country. You can explore to your heart's content thanks to well-connected train networks, buses, taxis, and more. Of course, some of these transportation options only exist in certain areas. However, there's still enough to make it easy to get around.

With all this information, it's time to wrap up the pre-trip planning and look at all the other things you need to know before heading off on your Portuguese journey.

# CHAPTER 5
# OTHER PRE-TRIP PLANNING ESSENTIALS

In this chapter, we're going to break down certain things we haven't already covered and expand on some others to further explain the pre-trip essentials. There's no such thing as too much planning. We want to ensure you get to Portugal with everything you need to have an amazing time. That also means understanding the people and cultures you'll experience. So this chapter is going to explore the customs of the Portuguese people, their businesses, and more.

## PORTUGUESE LANGUAGE

You might think that because Portugal is next to Spain, they too speak Spanish. That's not the case, though. For centuries Portugal has had a strong national identity and their own language—Portuguese. Due to Portugal's past as a dominant power in the world and a prolific colonizer (something we'll explore more in Part 2), Portuguese is spoken in a great number of places like Brazil, Angola, Cape Verde, Mozambique, São Tomé and Principe, East Timor, Macau, and Guinea-Bissau.

While Portuguese is the primary language, many Portuguese people do have a basic understanding of English and Spanish, with some being fluent. If these are your primary languages, you may find someone able to help you, but here's what else you can do.

**Phrases That Might Come In Handy**

Try some icebreakers like:

- Olá = Hello
- Adeus = Goodbye
- Com licença = Excuse me
- Bom dia = Good Day
- Boa tarde = Good Evening
- Por favor = Please
- Obrigado = Thank you
- Peço desculpa, mas = I'm sorry, but
- Estou a aprender o Portugues = I am learning Portuguese
- 'yes' is pronounced as Sim
- 'no' is pronounce as Nao
- Boa sorte = Good luck
- Vai mais uma? = One more?
- Bora lá, pessoal! = Come on, guys!
- Fala inlgês? = Do you speak English?

- Você pode me mostrar no mapa? = Can you show me on the map?

These are very basic, but you'll find that locals will appreciate the effort you're trying to make. They will also connect you with people who may be able to help and who can speak English well enough that you understand.

**Learn Portuguese**

You're going away, so why not try to pick up a bit of the language to make it easier while you're in the country? You can use great apps like Duolingo or phrasebooks to help you get the basics down. English is taught in Portugal from the first grade, but it's not something everyone carries with them. You'll find a lot of people might be able to grasp the basics of the language, while others will be fluent. You can also make use of Spanish, as some Portuguese people know that language.

## TYPES OF LODGING

Let's take a look at the different types of lodging and what you need to know about them:

**Pousadas**

$$$$

All across Portugal are things known as pousadas. These are government-owned tourist inns that are established in some of the nation's historic buildings. These can be places like castles, palaces, and convents. You will mostly find these places in areas where suitable accommodation is lacking or non-existent. You may think because they're government-owned and operated that they're less worthy than a hotel, but the quality and service of most of the pousadas are incredible. A few downsides include the waiting list and the cap of a five-day stay in these accommodations. The good news is that honeymoon trips usually have special terms granted.

**Country Homes**

$$$ - $$$$

Another great option is country homes. These include farm estates, restored manor houses, and country homes. Enjoy comfortable accommodation, often in a historic setting with tons of charm. The Viana do Castelo region features the most extensive network of options in this category in Portugal. Other options include Alentejo and Beiras. You can use local tourist offices, which are well-connected when it comes to helping you find the best place to stay. These properties are run privately and always include breakfast, which is often delicious Portuguese cuisine.

**Other Special Accommodations**

While pousadas, country homes, and hotels are among the most known options, they're far from the only options. Here are some other special accommodation options:

**Estalagens**

$$ - $$$

Private version of pousadas. Estalagens are often considered some of the best accommodation offers in terms of price and quality.

**Solare**

$$$ - $$$$

These are relatively new accommodation options, where properties that once belonged to the Portuguese aristocracy are now being renovated and opened as tourist accommodations.

**Residência**

$ - $$

These are a type of boarding houses which offer rooms and breakfasts.

**Pensão**

$ - $$

This is another type of boarding house. Here you can enjoy the lowest rates in the country. However, considering their low prices, don't expect luxurious accommodation. Even a deluxe pensão is equivalent to a standard second-class hotel.

**Reservations**

We've said before that you should take care of accommodation before you travel. This is especially true in peak season. Most accommodation types in Portugal require some form of deposit, usually at least one day's deposit. If you cancel within a week of your trip, you will most likely lose your deposit.

## THE DOS AND DON'TS OF TRAVELING IN PORTUGAL

Here are some dos and don'ts when it comes to traveling in Portugal. You're on vacation in someone else's country, and you want to respect the locals and their nation as much as possible. So, let's see what that looks like:

**Dos**

- Put thought into how you dress and present yourself. The localstend to dress more moderately, with elegance and quality at the forefront of their clothing decisions. Dress formally if you're going somewhere formal, like a church.
- Speak politely and respectfully.
- Show respect to local traditions rooted in Catholicism and Christianity.
- Be kind and compassionate to your Portuguese counterparts.

- Punctuality is important in Portugal, so make sure you're never late.
- Respect the elderly, which means sometimes accepting things that may not seem very respectful back.

**Don'ts**

- Don't wear casual attire in public, as it looks unsophisticated.
- Don't compare Portugal to Spain or even assume similarities. These are two different countries, and they don't need to be compared.
- Be mindful and tactful when discussing things like religion, politics, colonial wars, etc.
- Don't come to Portugal with something to prove. The Portuguese are a modest people, and they don't respond kindly to someone with an inflated ego, who exaggerates themselves and their status or wealth.
- Don't raise your voice in public.
- Don't expect rural areas to be as LGBTQ+ friendly as the country overall. While Portugal is LGBTQ+ friendly, like any country, it's got parts where it's less friendly than others.

## OTHER ESSENTIAL TIPS

Let's take a look at other essential tips for traveling through Portugal:

## Tipping

When it comes to traveling, nothing stumps people more than the practice of tipping people who work in service. In Portugal, there are many things you need to know when it comes to tipping.

### Should I Tip in Portugal or Not?

Overall, tipping isn't mandatory. Locals regularly tip workers in the service industry, like servers and taxi drivers. But even they exclude some types of service workers, like those who work in bars and cafés, who see tips far less frequently. It doesn't matter if the restaurant is family-owned or Michelin star; they tip if they feel inclined. Regarding tourists, it's interesting because more tourist-focused servers at establishments might expect a tip, yet it's still not expected overall.

### Which Businesses Should You Be Tipping?

This is really up to you. We usually focus tipping on businesses that provide a service, such as restaurants, cafés, bars, taxis, hotels, tour guides, etc. If you believe the service you've gotten was tremendous and worthy of a tip, then tip.

### How Much Should I Be Tipping?

The standard when it comes to tipping is 10 percent. The rules are different because tipping isn't necessarily a requirement in Portugal. You can tip between 5-10 percent for a standard tip, go over if you want, and even just round up your bill. You've got options. Just clarify that they can keep the change, otherwise, they may chase you down to return it.

You should stick in the 5–10 percent range for a tip. If you're tipping in a café where they've got tip jars, something between $0.20 and $1 is acceptable. Don't be that person who dumps small change in the tip jar. Instead of looking like you're tipping, it just looks like you're getting rid of change. For taxi drivers, you don't need to put too much emphasis on tipping drivers, but you can tip them between $0.20 and $0.50.

**What Do I Do When I Pay with a Debit or Credit Card?**

There's nothing abnormal about paying with a credit or debit card in Portugal. In this scenario, you can either tip using cash, or if the option is available at the restaurant or venue in question, you should be able to add a tip while paying. The bill will show the total amount and the gratificação (desired tip) section where you can write in the tip you want to give. However, it's important to note that there's no real way of knowing if the tip is going to the server or employer.

**Before Booking**

Before you book your vacation to Portugal, you want to focus on the following tips:

- Avoid the hottest, most expensive, and busiest months of July and August. Off-season Portugal is just as great as peak-season Portugal, except it's kind of better thanks to it being cheaper and less crowded.
- May, June, and September are great months to travel, thanks to weather that's hot but not unbearable.

- Between October and April, the chance of rain does increase dramatically. It also gets relatively cold at night.
- Check the distances and travel times between the places you want to visit, especially if you want to go from region to region. Depending on how long your vacation is, you should spend more time exploring one region properly and visiting another time to see more of the country. You don't want to spend more time traveling than enjoying.
- If you are going to travel while on vacation, consider the fastest transportation options to avoid spending too much time on a plane, train, or car.
- If you're doing the entirety of the planning for your trip, including travel arrangements, make sure you know how to get from the airport to your hotel before you leave. This means you need to understand what the public transportation options are, what you're using, how much it will cost, etc.
- Get a SIM on arrival to ensure you're connected as soon as possible, if you want to make use of the internet or services like Uber, Bolt, etc.

**Discounts**

Portugal has many great options that save you money on numerous things like transportation and activities. You need to familiarize yourself with these ahead of time.

- Lisbon and Porto have their own cards, which are

area-dependent but unlock unlimited transportation, and discounts or free access to certain attractions. Consider these if you're traveling to these areas.
- Look for local tourist websites that help you find the best activities and discounts for these attractions.
- Most major destinations have now introduced a tourist tax of $1.10–$2.20 per night. It's paid for at your accommodation, so consider this when you budget.
- The tourist tax is something you can claim back if you're a non-EU resident in the form of Tax-Free Shopping. Numerous shops in Portugal will have a sign stating they're a tax-free shopping establishment through Globa Blue, Innova, Travel Tax-Free, or Planet. When you pay, you need to tell the retailer you'd like to claim tax back, which will prompt you and the retailer to fill out a form. At the airport, when you're leaving the EU, you will need to get this form approved by customs before you head to an electronic kiosk, which will be the final step of the process.

**Documents to Bring**

Traveling is a documents game. You need several important documents before you can leave or enter a country. Here are the documents you need to remember:

- An up-to-date passport. If you're traveling from outside the EU, your passport must be valid for six months post-travel to the EU. Don't forget to bring some extra photocopies of your passport with you.

- In Portugal, you will need to carry it with you at all times. A copy of your passport will suffice while you keep your physical passport safe in your hotel room.
- No vaccination requirements are needed for traveling to Portugal unless you are coming from a known Yellow Fever zone. This will require vaccination documentation.
- Travelers from the US, Canada, and Australia can travel to EU countries (in the Schengen area) for ninety days visa-free.
- EU citizens don't need a visa to enter Portugal.
- EU citizens with European Health Insurance Cards can bring them to Portugal, which will help reduce the costs of emergency treatment while traveling. These aren't substitutes for travel insurance.
- You need your driver's license to rent a car in Portugal. A license from certain countries (UK, Canada, USA excluded) won't meet Portugal standards, meaning you'll need an international driver's permit. When driving a rental car, you need your license, ID, and the paperwork of the rental car.

**Money**

Here are some things to consider when it comes to money and spending money:

- Try to have some local currency (Euro/EUR/€) when

you arrive in Portugal. However, if you don't, there are ATMs in international airports, making it easy to get euros from your account. Just avoid Euronet machines, which are extremely expensive.

- Smaller establishments may not accept credit cards, and transaction fees can be expensive, so keep this in mind when traveling through Portugal.
- If you exchange your money and get large bills, take them to a bank and try to get them exchanged for smaller notes.

**Packing**

We've gone into detail when it comes to what to pack, but here are a few more tips to consider:

- Comfy shoes are a must, thanks to all the uneven cobblestone pavements.
- Avoid heels as they may make traversing the Portuguese streets difficult.
- Pack lightweight clothes to make it easier to handle the summer heat.
- In winter, pack some heavier pants like jeans, and don't forget a jacket or two.
- Portuguese accommodations won't usually have tea-making facilities, so if you enjoy coffee or tea often, bring along a travel kettle.
- Summer or winter, don't forget to bring sunscreen, an umbrella, insect repellent, sunglasses, etc.
- In significant tourist destinations, you can buy pretty

much anything you might have forgotten to pack or couldn't take with you on the plane.

**Eating Out**

Here are some things you should know before eating out in Portugal:

- Most restaurants will bring out little dishes of olives, cheese, cold meats, and bread. These are like pre-starters, but they're not free. So, don't be surprised when this is on the bill. You can reject this offering by returning it when it arrives, assuming you haven't touched it.
- Fish is something you may find surprising when you get the bill. There are lots of seafood restaurants in Portugal that offer fresh fish. It's charged by weight, and to avoid a nasty surprise, ask your server for an estimate on what it will cost you. There are seafood dishes at fixed prices, so you will have options.
- If you want vegetables or salads, be warned that most mains don't feature either. This is because locals get their greens in the starters. So ask before you order, and if you really want veggies or salad, order it on the side of your main.
- It's customary in most countries for a server to ask for the drink order before the food. In Portugal, food is

the priority. So, you may have to initiate the drink order.

- A lot of restaurants have affordable lunch menus, which are two or three courses at a set price. These can be a great way to save money on lunch and decrease your appetite for dinner. It's a delicious way to economize your eating out experience.
- There's a major difference between Portuguese dining and the dining practices of places like the US. The United States is a place where everyone is always on the go. The bill is promptly served once the meal is over, and customers don't wait around taking in the evening. In Portugal, that's not the case. You eat, you drink, and you take it slow, enjoy the entire meal, and relax.
- Some restaurants and cafés will only accept cash as a form of payment. You can tell if that's the case because they'll have a sign saying 'não temos MB,' or 'não temos multibanco.' These loosely translate to 'we don't take card payments, debit, or credit.'
- Some restaurants and cafés will only allow card payments when the amount is over a certain amount, usually €5. This will usually be made clear through the use of a sign saying 'multibanco acima de €5' (card payments for over €5).

**Festivals and Sightseeing**

Here are some tips to consider when sightseeing or attending festivals:

- At just about any time of the year, a festival occurs somewhere in Portugal. So be sure to be on the lookout for exciting upcoming events you can attend while on vacation.
- If you want to visit a museum, consider going on Sundays, when it's free in the morning. If you've got travel cards in certain places, you get your 50 percent discount or free entrance any time of the week. This also applies to monuments.
- Be warned, most museums are closed on Mondays. So when you're making your plans, be sure to take this into consideration.

## TAKEAWAY

Hopefully, from this chapter, you've taken away the many things to consider before and during your travels. Nobody expects you to be fluent in the language or the locals' ways. Still, by understanding the basics, you're better equipped to experience Portugal in the best possible way.

We're about to go even further, explaining all the fantastic areas in Portugal that you might want to visit. In the coming chapters, we will go place by place to explain what that area is known for, what to do there, where to stay, eat, shop, and so much more!

PART TWO

# CITIES AND PLACES TO SEE IN PORTUGAL

## BITE-SIZED HISTORY: ANCIENT PORTUGAL

Portugal has a long, long history. Humans have occupied the region since 30,000 BC, and that was in the thick of the Ice Age! The original settlers were fishcatchers, hunters, and gatherers.

It wasn't until 5,000 BCE that formal farming practices became known in Portugal. Bronze was officially introduced in 2,000 BCE. Portugal became popular in the trade game in 800 BC when they began trading with the Phoenicians. By 700 BC, Portugal had farming, bronze, and iron, which made them a desirable trading partner. It was in 600 BC that Greece began trading with the Portuguese too.

Everything changed in 210 BC when the Romans began invading. They managed to conquer southern Portugal but struggled with central Portugal due to the Lusitani, a Celtic tribe. In 193 BC, they rejected Roman rule, and thus began a decades-long battle between the Romans and Lusitani. Unfortunately, in 139 BC, the Lusitani ruler, Viriatus, was swiftly captured, leading to the resistance's collapse. Soon after, Portugal was integrated into the ways and world of the Romans. This lasted well into the third century AD.

As we know from history, the empire Rome had built eventually fell into decline. By the fifth century, the grip Rome had on Portugal crumbled. This didn't mean Portugal was free just yet. A people known as the Suevi invaded, and then in the sixth century, another group known as the Visigoths—who ruled Spain at the time—attacked the Suevi. Eventually, they defeated the Suevi. With this victory, the Germanics became Portugal's upper class.

# CHAPTER 6
# LISBON

> "By day Lisbon has a naive theatrical quality that enchants and captivates, but by night it is a fairy-tale city, descending over lighted terraces to the sea, like a woman in festive garments going down to meet her dark lover."
>
> ERICH MARIA REMARQUE, THE NIGHT IN LISBON.

Lisbon is the capital of Portugal. While not an officially documented status, it was declared the capital by Afonso III in 1255 CE. This is one of the world's oldest cities, older than Rome in Italy. Historical records actually state that the only European city known to be older than Lisbon is Athens. As you can imagine, a city this old is filled with history and an unmistakable identity that's persevered and evolved through the centuries to what is modern Lisbon.

In this chapter, we will explore Lisbon and all its history while also understanding what it means to travel there. Through this dedicated chapter on Lisbon, you'll be able to learn about safety, restaurants (and food in general), nightlife, tourist spots, attractions, and even some "hidden gems." Let's dive into the interesting place that is the city of Lisbon.

## OVERVIEW OF LISBON

The capital city of Lisbon lies in the western region of Portugal along the estuary of the Tagus River. Home to the nation's chief port, Lisbon is a cultural, political, commercial, and tourist center, and is the country's largest city. The region is home to over 2.8 million people, while the capital city itself is home to over 550,000. The city's wealth is shown in the incredible buildings, monuments, and living conditions.

## HISTORY AND CULTURE OF LISBON

The history of Lisbon is much like the history of Portugal at large—complicated. Let's look at the highlights.

**Muslim Period and Lisbon's Reconquest**

Due to the Islamic Moors invading Lisbon and the greater peninsula in 711, the country has a great deal of Muslim history attached to it. Today you can still see reminders of the near-century that the Islamic Moors ruled over Lisbon, which they renamed al-Usbuma. While on vacation, you can visit some of these culturally significant places, including:

- Central Mosque
- Comercio Square
- Lisbon Cathedral
- Jeronimos Monastery
- Rossio Square
- Saint George Castle
- Monument to the Discoveries
- Belem Tower

**Lisbon During the Renaissance**

When Alfonso III moved the capital from Coimbra to Lisbon, it solidified Lisbon's importance in the nation's maritime expansion. By the end of the fourteenth century, the House of Aviz came into power. This was the second dynasty of kings. The fifteenth century only saw Lisbon's importance grow. During the fifteenth century, things like warehouses and customs offices were created, and Lisbon became a well-organized port for all areas of overseas trade. The sixteenth century saw Lisbon's the house of India, a trade organisation similar to the East India Trading Company, begin trading with Brazil, Africa, and Asia. Lisbon became Europe's most vital slave trade center, not a title we're sure they're hyping up anymore. Come 1580, the country was conquered by the Spanish King Philip II, and less than a century later, the nation regained its independence.

Of course, we can't forget about Lisbon's horrific earthquake in 1755. This prompted the city to be almost entirely rebuilt. In 1807, Napoleon invaded, but Portugal was soon recaptured by the British. Later on, in 1833, the constitutional monarchy was reinstated until 1910, when the republic was declared.

There are tours available to places that showcase the Renaissance in Lisbon and its role as one of the great nations that pioneered travel over the seas. These tours visit the following locations:

- House of India
- Shipbuilding
- Food and Spices
- The Market and Ribeira Palace
- New Merchant Street

**Twentieth Century Lisbon**

The twentieth century wasn't much kinder to Portugal, or Lisbon, for that matter. It experienced the end of the first republic, the anti-democratic regime taking over, and a military coup in 1974 which resulted in the current third Republic. The nation became a part of the EU in 1986.

## CRIME AND SAFETY

Let's break down the safety of traveling in Lisbon, so you get the full picture of what it's like to visit this lovely city.

**Is Lisbon Safe for Tourists?**

Yes. Lisbon is one of the safest, if not the safest, capital cities in Europe. Most tourists find that they have very few issues when traveling in Lisbon, which is a progressive city that's diverse and liberal. Travelers who are female, older, or traveling solo find it a great place to visit.

It's important to note that Lisbon is still a major metropolitan city, and as a result, it doesn't mean it's 100 percent safe. While overall, it's a safe city to explore, use common sense. Lisbon's biggest issue is the skilled pickpockets that roam the streets and the so-called "drug dealers" looking to dupe tourists by selling them crushed herbs passing for drugs. Overall, however, Lisbon is an extremely safe place to travel to.

**Political and Cultural Climate**

Despite its extremely rocky history when it comes to politics, Portugal, in general, is very stable politically. Even culturally, the people in Portugal are happy, welcoming, and wonderfully pleasant. As a nation, it relies on tourism to bolster its economy. As a result, investments have been made to ensure the country is accessible to tourists. Popular tourist areas have a strong police presence.

**Crime**

As previously mentioned, pickpocketing is one of the most prevalent tourist crimes you'll likely experience in Lisbon. Avoid walking around with items that are valuable and easy to grab. These pickpockets are not your standard pickpockets. They operate at a very high level. They target busy tourist areas and streetcar routes the most. These pickpockets are usually from Eastern European countries, operating in organized gangs, and don't stick to the standards we associate with pickpockets. They are often well-dressed women who blend extremely well with the crowds.

- Tourism Police is the place to go when reporting tourist crimes. This is located in the Praca dos Restauradores Plaza in the Foz Palace. You can contact this office at (+351) 213421623.

  - For insurance claims, you'll need to file a police report, usually within twenty-four hours, at the Tourism Police Station.

Other crimes to be wary of in Lisbon are drink spiking, accommodation scams, and fake drug dealers.

**Local Laws**

One must follow several laws when visiting Portugal and Lisbon city. For starters, always carry identification with you. This can be a photocopy, so you're not putting your passport at risk. Second, while gambling is legal, it's only in official casinos, so make sure your chosen venue is licensed. Finally, if you're under the influence, don't ride e-bikes or e-scooters, as this can result in a fine.

**Travel**

If you're traveling by road, you'll find that during the period from 22 July to 7 August, the border experiences enhanced security with frequent random border checks. The conditions for entering and exiting Portugal can change in an instant. Consider contacting your embassy or consulate to ensure you know what's going on at the border if that's how you intend to travel.

**Areas to Be Wary of in Lisbon**

The safest areas in Lisbon are the tourist destinations, central Lisbon, and the Chiado and Baixa districts. The worst areas are usually to the far northwest of the central city. These are the areas where tourists don't frequent. There are a series of areas that we wouldn't recommend where crime has been known to be slightly more frequent, including the districts of Anjos, Mouraria, and Intendente.

There's an area that is a bit of a mixed bag, the newly transformed Cais de Sodre. This was once the red-light district and is now a nightlife hub. However, its past hasn't necessarily been easy to erase, so you'll still find elements of its history lingering.

## HEALTH

The healthcare system in Lisbon is great for life-threatening emergencies. You are in safe hands. However, you might find the system disorganized and inefficient when it comes to minor health issues. This is largely due to a pervasive problem Portugal has when it comes to staff shortages for non-urgent medical care. Private healthcare options are available but usually require upfront payments and are expensive.

The emergency number in Portugal is 112.

### How to Access the Portuguese Healthcare System

Recently, the Portuguese government announced that the public healthcare system throughout Portugal will be open to everyone, including visitors and expats. EU citizens are entitled to the healthcare system without documentation, but expats need a visa or residency card. Tourists will be provided unfettered access to public hospitals but will incur additional charges.

### Private versus Public

There are few differences between the two options, but they can be what makes up your mind when choosing between one or the other. For starters, public hospitals can have longer wait times. Private hospitals, while convenient, are more costly, depending on your insurance. This is why travel insurance is a must when planning your trip overseas.

**Best Hospitals in Lisbon**

- Centro Hospitalar de Lisboa Central (Hospital Dona Estefania) - Public

  - R. Jacinta Marto 8A, Lisboa, Portugal

- Instituto Português de Oncologia de Lisboa - Public

  - Av. Edmundo Lima Basto, 2790-072 Lisboa, Portugal

- Clínica Central do Bonfim - Private

  - Av. de Fernão de Magalhães 442, 4349-008 Porto, Portugal

**Best Children's Hospitals in Lisbon**

- Dona Estefânia Hospital - Public

  - R. Jacinta Marto 8A, Lisboa, Portugal

- Hospital da Luz - Private

  - Av. Lusíada 100, 1500-650 Lisboa, Portugal

**Pharmacies**

There are numerous pharmacies in Lisbon, most of which are open on weekdays from 9 a.m. to 7 p.m. (1 p.m. on Saturdays), with some closing during the day for lunch. However, each district has a 24/7 pharmacy for emergencies. These are identified with green crosses.

Here are some of the best 24/7 pharmacies:

- Farmácia Ronil - Campolide

 - R. Rodrigo da Fonseca 155, 1070-242 Lisboa, Portugal

- Pharmacy Uruguai - Benfica

 - Av. do Uruguai 18A, 1500-613 Lisboa, Portugal

- Farmácia Holon Campo Grande - Lumiar

 - Campo Grande 414 B, 1700-098 Lisboa, Portugal

- Faculty of Pharmacy, University of Lisbon - Alvalade

 - Av. Prof. Gama Pinto, 1649-003 Lisboa, Portugal

- Octapharma - Produtos Farmacêuticos, Lda - Pontinha

 - Estr. da Paiã 5 c/v, 1675-076 Pontinha, Portugal

## FOOD TO TRY WHILE IN LISBON

Every part of Portugal has specialty dishes that a person should try while in the area. These are some of the dishes Lisbon is known for:

**Bifana Sandwiches**

Made of pork that's been marinated and sautéed in a crispy roll. It's simple and delicious. Some places add more ingredients or offer sides, but you won't be disappointed even if you stick to the simple option. It's a cheap meal that is sure to satisfy you beyond your expectations. These don't require sitting down at a restaurant table, as you can find them in bars and taverns across the city.

**Sardinhas**

Sardines are very popular in Portugal. There are even festivals where locals feast on these delicious fish (See the annual Feast of St. Anthony Sardina in Festivals). Best served in mid-June, they are enjoyed year-round. Many restaurants offer interesting dishes using sardines, some of which are to die for. You can also buy tins of Portugal's famous sardinhas and bring them home with you.

**Pastéis de Nata**

This Portuguese dish is actually popular in many places outside of Portugal. A Pastéis de Nata is an eggy custard tart. They are a bright yellow with a creamy texture invented centuries ago by monks in Belém. All this time later, they're popular desserts around the world, especially in Portugal.

**Chouriço**

We are likely all familiar with chorizo, but chouriço is different. For starters, it's not as spicy and uses subtle flavors of paprika. The core commonality between the two is that they're both pork based. You can find it almost anywhere in Lisbon; they even cook it at the table in some places. It's quite the spectacle. Enjoy chouriço with Portuguese bread (Pão) or add a cheese like Azeitão to take it to the next level.

**Caldo Verde**

Restaurants across Portugal will offer a soup of the day. If you ever hear that day's soup being Caldo Verde, order it. This soup is warm green in color, made with potatoes, olive oil, kale, and salt. When made well, it's a creamy soup, even though cream isn't an ingredient used. You can add some chouriço for extra flavor, which just sends it over the edge. You can buy ready-made caldo verde at Pingo Doce grocery stores.

**Ginjinha**

This is technically a drink, but Ginjinha is a famous Portuguese liquor that's infused with Morello or Ginja cherries. The flavor of the liquor is both tart and sweet thanks to the added ingredients of sugar and cinnamon. Enjoy it as a shot, as a slow-drinking liquor, or in a chocolate cup. It's delicious either way, and there's a reason it's so beloved.

**Piri Piri Frango (Chicken)**

The Portuguese love their spices, and thank goodness for that because the food never disappoints. One dish that makes use of the spice rack is piri piri chicken. This dish blends spices from all over the world to bring you a dish brimming with flavor. Marinated chicken is grilled over an open flame using ingredients like piri piri chilies, lemon juice, salt, olive oil, and various spices.

**Alheira**

Dating back to the Inquisition, Alheira was enjoyed by the Jews as a tasty alternative to sausage. The Jews did this as a ruse to trick the Inquisitors into thinking they weren't Jewish due to them eating pork, but Alheira is a sausage made from kosher proteins like duck, chicken, and veal. The dish has been compared to Kishke due to its stuffing-like texture and has stood the test of time..

**Bacalhau**

Bacalhau is the Portuguese word for cod, and how the Portuguese make it is something else. Cod has variations to make it exciting regardless of how many times you have it. If you want to make bacalhau yourself, you can find it at most markets and grocery stores in Lisbon. Just be prepared; it's daunting in size.

**Azeitão Cheese**

When we think of fancy cheeses, we often think of Italy or France. While their cheese is heavenly, that doesn't mean Portugal doesn't have some skin in the game. The Azeitão Cheese is one of the dozen artisanal cheeses made and served in Portugal. Made from raw sheep's milk in the town of Azeitão just outside of Lisbon, this cheese is ooey-gooey and, most of all, delicious. Pair this cheese with some red wine and salty snacks, and you're in for a treat! This cheese is so soft you'll need a spoon, not a knife.

## RESTAURANTS TO TRY WHILE IN LISBON

There are many amazing restaurants in Lisbon worth visiting. While we'd love to mention them all, we'd be here forever detailing why you should consider them. Here are some of our favorites, and we've chosen restaurants for every type of budget.

*Please note addresses, operation hours, and prices are subject to change.*

**Low Budget Restaurants**

**A Nossa Casa**

*R. da Atalaia 31, 1200-037 Lisboa, Portugal*

$$

If you're a meat lover, A Nossa Casa is the place to go when you're out in Lisbon. In the neighborhood of Bairro Alto, this restaurant has a simple yet delicious menu. You'll find the standard meat and seafood options, but when the food arrives at your table, your taste buds are in for a surprise. While their chicken skewers and freshly steamed razor clams are amazing, the shrimp carpaccio steals the show.

**Operating Hours:**

Monday - Sunday: 6:30 p.m. - 10:30 p.m. (Dinner Only)

**Floresta Das Escadinhas**

*R. de Santa Justa 3, 1100-483 Lisboa, Portugal*

$

Not far from the Arco da Rua Augusta, this simple restaurant is all about meat and fish with a side of boiled potatoes or fries. Floresta Das Escadinhas' show stopper is the sardines, which are their specialty. They also serve a board that has bread, chorizo, olives, and olive oil, all at reasonable prices. Who said you couldn't eat nicely on a budget?

**Boi-Cavalo**

*R. do Vigário 70B, 1100-616 Lisboa, Portugal*

$$

In Alfama, down a cobblestone alley, is an unsuspected venue that offers something unique: experimental contemporary cuisine. Once a butcher shop, Boi-Cavalo is a modern bistro with a menu that never makes it past a week. That's right, if your trip is across two different weeks, you could go twice and have two very different experiences. While options can feel somewhat limited, it's got amazing food, service, and atmosphere.

**Average Budget Restaurants**

**Cervejaria Ramiro**

*Av. Alm. Reis 1 H, 1150-007 Lisboa, Portugal*

$$$

Cervejaria Ramiro is a beloved establishment in Lisbon. This restaurant and beer hall is three stories, and getting in can still be challenging! But after what might be a short wait time, you get to enjoy a unique dining experience. It's an orchestra of chefs cooking, customers enjoying themselves eating and drinking, and a sense of activity in every corner of the establishment. It's almost like a fish market, orchestrated chaos. There's a great wine list, amazing food, and an atmosphere that makes it all worthwhile.

**Operating Hours:**

Monday: Closed

Sunday: 12:00 p.m. - 12:00 a.m.

**D'Bacalhau**

*Zona Ribeirinha Norte, Rua Pimenta 45, 1900-254 Lisboa, Portugal*

$$$

Known specifically for its incredible cod dishes, D'Bacalhau has a lot to offer your taste buds. The menu is loaded with a vibrant array of seafood and meat dishes like burgers, veal, shrimp risotto, grilled octopus, and so much more. At the end of the day, it's the cod that steals the show. This award-winning dish is worth trying at least once in Lisbon. Once you're done, enjoy a stroll on the pier nearby to cap the night off just right.

**Operating Hours:**

Monday - Sunday: 12:00 p.m. - 4:00 p.m. (Lunch)

7:00 p.m. - 11:00 p.m. (Dinner)

Sunday: Closed

**Fine Dining**

**JNcQUOI**

*Av. da Liberdade 182 184, 1250-146 Lisboa, Portugal*

$$$

Perhaps one of the most interesting restaurants on this list, JNCQUOI is located in what used to be a historic theater. Now it's a restaurant, bar, and high-end men's store. It gets stranger because there's a T-Rex replica at the doors welcoming the patrons. So, it's definitely a place to take a look at. Enjoy views of the Avenida while eating incredible dishes. The highlight is the cod, which includes numerous ingredients, making for an interesting and exciting meal.

**Alma**

*R. Anchieta 15, 1200-224 Lisboa, Portugal*

$$$$

If you're looking to spend some money on great food, Alma is a place to add to the itinerary. This establishment boasts two Michelin stars and is in the heart of Lisbon. It's a stunning venue with a beautifully balanced menu of different seafood dishes that take inspiration from not just Portugal, but around the world. If you're a lover of great wine, Alma also has one of the most extensive wine lists in the city. A highlight is the cobblestreet salted cod. It's something they're well known for, and for good reasons.

**Operating Hours:**

Tuesday - Saturday: 12:30 p.m. - 3:30 p.m. (Lunch)

7:00 p.m. - 12:00 a.m. (Dinner)

Sunday - Monday: Closed

**Belcanto**

*R. Serpa Pinto 10A, 1200-026 Lisboa, Portugal*

$$$$

Belcanto has continuously been considered one of the best restaurants in the world. This Michelin-star restaurant is an upscale establishment serving classic Portuguese cuisine. Getting into Belcanto can be a challenge, considering it only has forty-five seats available, so if you're planning a trip, attempt to book in advance. If you can get a table, you'll be treated to a night of elegance in the form of the venue, service, and food.

**Operating Hours:**

Tuesday - Saturday: 12:30 p.m. - 3:00 p.m. (Lunch)

7:00 p.m. - 12:00 a.m. (Dinner)

Sunday - Monday: Closed

**Feitoria**

*Altis Belem Hotel & Spa, Doca do Bom Sucesso, 1400-038 Lisboa, Portugal*

$$$$

Another Michelin-star restaurant, Feitoria, is an upmarket venue located in the Altis Belém Hotel & Spa. They offer a selection of tasting menus paired with various wines to create an unforgettable culinary experience. Combined with the stunning decor and top-notch service, the staff at Feitroia goes above and beyond to make your night something special that you'll remember.

**Operating Hours:**

Exact hours are unknown.

## STREET FOOD TO TRY WHILE IN LISBON

Portugal has plenty of vendors selling delicious street food around the country, and there are a lot of options in Lisbon. Here are some of the street food items you should look out for, and then we'll mention some of the best spots to find them.

**Pao Com Chouriço**

Simply translated, this is bread with chouriço sausage, and while it sounds simple (which it is), it's insanely delicious. You can find this all over Lisbon in cafés and from street vendors. Merendeira offers one of the best pao com chouriço from 11 a.m. to 1 a.m.

**Prego**

A staple in Portugal, prego is a beef dish you can have on a sandwich or served on a plate with some fries, rice, or salad. We recommend taking the sandwich because, combined with the bread, it's more authentic street food. Rui dos Pregos is the best place to go for a prego sandwich. If you want some prego options, try Prego da Peixaria, which has chicken and wagyu options.

**Bifana**

Want something with pork? A bifana is a traditional sandwich in Portugal made with pork filets. Just to emphasize how popular this sandwich is, the local McDonald's has a McBifana—it's just nowhere near as good as the street vendors and cafés make it. Try a bifana from Café Beira Gare, As Bifanas do Afonso, or O Trevo. If you want a vegan bifana, try Ao 26 Vegan Project.

**Salgados**

Now for some savory treats. Salgados come in many options, but the most popular are codfish cakes (pastéis de bacalhau), shrimp turnovers (rissóis de camarão), and croquettes. You will find these in almost every café and the Padaria Portuguesa restaurant chain.

## STREET FOOD SPOTS IN LISBON

Lisbon is filled with amazing places to get some of the best street food in the city. Here are some places to check out:

**Mercado de Fusão**

The Mercado de Fusão market is also known as the Fushion market. Here you can find foods from all over the world. If you're feeling homesick while on vacation, here's where you can get a taste of home. They've got stalls and restaurants offering foods from China, Japan, India, Africa, and many other places around the world.

**Mercado da Ribeira**

This food court is considered one of Lisbon's trendiest spots. While it gained popularity amongst tourists in 2014, locals have been frequenting this market since 1892. It used to be a market dedicated to fresh produce, but then it began integrating food stalls, and that's when it became even more popular. With over thirty food stalls, there are many options for tourists and locals to enjoy.

**Mercado de Campo de Ourique**

This market is smaller than the Mercado da Ribeira, but it's still great to visit. Originally opened in 1934, it sells fresh produce and exotic cuisines. There are plenty of stalls for great street food and ample seating for a comfortable experience. Here you'll find all kinds of food, from Portuguese classics to international options like sushi and so much more.

**Street Food around Portugal**

- Mister Tapas
- Berlineta
- Weeel
- Maria Limão
- Madam Gaugre
- Pizza a Pezzi
- Hamburgueria da Padaria
- Hot Dog Lovers
- Tasca Itinerante

## NIGHTLIFE IN LISBON

Let's break down some of your best nightlife opportunities in Lisbon. We will take a look at bar restaurants, bars, and nightclubs.

*Please note addresses, operation hours, and prices are subject to change.*

**Bar Restaurants**

Want to drink but are also hoping for a bit of food? Here are three of the best bar restaurants in Lisbon:

**Soul Garden**

*Av. José Malhoa 24, 1070-159 Lisboa, Portugal*

True to its name, Soul Garden provides a garden-party atmosphere with smooth, laid-back music. This venue has an authentic alfresco vibe and is a social hub in the summertime.

**Operating Hours:**

Monday - Sunday: 12:00 p.m. - 1:00 a.m.

**The Food Temple**

*Beco do Jasmim 18, 1100-289 Lisboa, Portugal*

This exciting venue is located on the ground level and serves incredible food and drinks, all while having a warm atmosphere with tables built into a staircase. It sounds weird, but The Food Temple is a fantastic place to be in the evenings.

**Operating Hours:**

Monday: Closed

Tuesday - Sunday: 6:30 p.m. - 11:30 p.m.

**Chapitô à Mesa**

*Beco do Jasmim 18, 1100-289 Lisboa, Portugal*

Incredible views of the Lisbon skyline are just the first thing you notice when visiting the incredible Chapitô à Mesa. They serve traditional Portuguese food and have a great bar with live music on the terrace. It's got the makings of a magical night out.

**Operating Hours:**

Monday - Sunday: 12:00 p.m. - 6:00 p.m. (Lunch)

7:00 p.m. - 1:00 a.m. (Dinner)

**Bars**

Looking to drink with friends in the exciting city of Lisbon? Great news, there are a lot of bar options, and here are three of our favorites:

**Pensão Amor**

*R. do Alecrim 19, 1200-292 Lisboa, Portugal*

$$ - $$$

Out in the former red-light district, Pensão Amor is a glitzy and glamorous venue that once was a brothel. It's an interesting venue that which has signs of its former life present in the aesthetic, but that's perhaps what makes it so intriguing as a bar.

**Operating Hours:**

Sunday - Wednesday: 12:00 p.m. - 3:00 a.m.

Thursday - Saturday: 12:00 p.m. - 4:00 a.m.

**Park Rooftop**

*Calçada do Combro 58, 1200-123 Lisboa, Portugal*

$$

In Bairro Alto, atop a car garage, is Park Rooftop. This stunning venue has incredible views of the city, delectable cocktails, and a great atmosphere. There's even a mystical garden, making it even more enjoyable.

**Operating Hours:**

Monday - Thursday: 4:00 p.m. - 2:00 a.m.

Friday - Saturday: 2:00 p.m. - 2:00 a.m.

Sunday:Closed

**CINCO Lounge**

*R. Ruben A. Leitão 17A, 1200-392 Lisboa, Portugal*

$$

With low lighting and a moody atmosphere, CINCO Lounge is a relaxed place to enjoy some drinks in Lisbon. This upmarket bar has some of the best mixologists in Lisbon, with a wide variety of cocktails to choose from.

**Operating Hours:**

Monday - Sunday: 8:00 p.m. - 2:00 a.m.

## Nightclubs

Ready to party? Well, there's a lot to see when it comes to the nightclub scene in Lisbon. Here are some of the best clubs to go to while visiting:

### Ministerium Club

*Praça do Comércio 72, 1100-016 Lisboa, Portugal*

$$$

In the Praça do Comércio, there's a club you'll definitely want to find. Constantly hosting high-profile DJs, Ministerium Club is the place to be when the sun goes down. You'll have to up your wardrobe game to get in, but it's well worth the effort if you do.

**Operating Hours:**

Monday - Thursday: Closed

Friday - Saturday: 12:00 a.m. - 8:00 a.m.

Sunday: 11:30 p.m. - 5:00 a.m.

### LuxFrágil

*Av. Infante D. Henrique a Sta Apolónia Cais da Pedra, Armazém A, 1950-376 Lisboa, Portugal*

$$

LuxFrágil is one of Lisbon's most well-known and popular nightclubs. In Santa Apolónia on the docks, this club has hosted international DJs and music artists. It's also a challenging club to get into. Dress to the nines and pray you get in!

**Operating Hours:**

Thursday - Saturday: 11:00 p.m. - 6:00am

Sunday - Wednesday: Closed

**Musicbox Lisboa**

*R. Nova do Carvalho 24, 1200-019 Lisboa, Portugal*

$$ - $$$

Dance the night away in this club in the Cais do Sodre neighborhood under a bridge. That's right, under a bridge. From the outside, MusicBox Lisboa is low-key, ditching neon lights and flashy signs. On the inside, you get a euphoric energy with a varying mix of music from electronic soul to drum 'n' bass.

**Operating Hours:**

Monday - Saturday: 11:00 p.m. - 6:00 a.m.

## FESTIVALS AND EVENTS IN LISBON

Here's a list of all the different festivals and events that take place throughout the year in Lisbon:

**January**

- **New Year's Concert** - Lisbon's Metropolitan Orchestra plays an incredible concert on the first day of every new year. Tickets range from $5.50 to $20.

**February**

- **Carnival** - During February, Lisbon comes even more alive than any other month. Carnival parties and parades take place with Brazilian carnival costumes, samba music, and many exclusive themed nightclub events. It's an exciting time to visit the city.

**March**

- **Meia Maratona de Lisboa** - This half marathon provides a great opportunity to see the Lisbon skyline from the 25 de Abril bridge over the River Tejo. The marathon ends at the Jerónimos Monastery.

**April**

- **Dias da Música** - Enjoy three days of non-stop music at this famous Centro Cultural de Belém (CCB) springtime festival. All types of music and workshops are available, catering to all ages.
- **Peixe em Lisboa** - If you're a seafood lover, this event is for you. Enjoy some of the best fish and seafood

prepared in numerous ways by Portuguese and international chefs. Taking place in Eduardo VII Park, it's not to be missed.

- **Indie Lisboa** - Eleven-day film festival of experimental film exhibitions, documentaries, shorts, and more. There are also talks, debates, and activities with people from the film industry.

**May**

- **Rock in Rio Lisboa** - This biannual festival happens at the Parque da Bela Vista in eastern Lisbon. Both national and international bands and musicians come to perform at this festival with food stalls and an amusement park.

**June**

- **Santos Populares** - A lot happens in June. You'll see theater performances, street parties, open-air music concerts, and more held on numerous stages across Lisbon. Main festivity areas include Castelo, Alfama, Bairro Alto, and Bica. These events occur across June, but on the twelfth, there's the Feast of St Anthony, which includes a parade and festival of sardines in Avenida da Liberdade.

## July

- **Super Bock Super Rock** - At the eastern waterfront near Parque das Nações, this three-day rock festival features international acts, sun, beer, and fun.
- **NOS Alive** - Three-day music festival located in Oeiras near Belém at the Algés riverside.
- **Delta Tejo** - Ethnic music festival in the Alto da Ajuda district running three days with great music like fado, Brazilian grooves, and more.
- **Festival ao Largo** - Free classic music concerts, ballet, opera, and dance performances taking place outdoors in late July in front of the Teatro Nacional de São Carlos.
- **BaixAnima** - During the weekends from July to September, enjoy free theater performances and live music in the Baixa neighborhoods.

## August

- **Festival dos Oceanos** - For two weeks, the people of Portugal hold this festival that celebrates the oceans. The first two weeks of August, at different places on the waterfront (Parque das Nações and Belém). Enjoy a mixture of theater shows, concerts, conferences, street performances, and exhibitions.
- **Jazz em Agosto** - This annual jazz festival has been going on since 1984. World-famous jazz musicians

come from far and wide to play in an open-air amphitheater.

**September**

- **MOTELx** - Taking place at the Cinema São de Jorge, this international horror film festival is a treat for anyone looking for a little scare.
- **Happy Holi – Colour Festival** - Celebrating color and music, this festival has DJs, dancing, and tons of fun. It gets crowded, especially when they start dispersing the colored powders, but it's great to witness firsthand.
- **Santa Casa Alfama Festival** - This fado music festival takes place in the historic Alfama district. It's a truly Portuguese experience.

**October**

- **DocLisboa** - This film festival runs eleven days and is dedicated to documentaries.
- **Lisbon Marathon** - Starting in Cascais and running twenty-six miles (forty-two kilometers), you enjoy breathtaking (literally) city views along the way. There are other races that are smaller if the main event is too intense for your liking.

**November**

- **Lisbon & Estoril Film Festival** - Known as Leffest, this is one of Portugal's leading film festivals. There are exhibitions from all around the world, and often famous actors and filmmakers make appearances. It's a star-studded event to attend.

**December**

- **Christmas** - This one you should know, but during December, the city is heavily decorated to celebrate Christmas, and it's a fantastic thing to see.

## TOURIST SPOTS AND ACTIVITIES IN LISBON

Let's look at all the places you need to visit and activities you should do while in Lisbon:

**Best Attractions**

Here are some of the best attractions to see when you visit Lisbon:

- **The Castelo de São Jorge** - This beautiful castle still stands above Lisbon and is the location of the Christian crusader's defeat over the Moors in 1147. This was the seat of power in Portugal for over 400 years. Now it's open to the public at $11 for a typical visit of an hour.

- R. de Santa Cruz do Castelo, 1100-129 Lisboa, Portugal

- **The Torre de Belém** - This fort has been a tourist attraction for decades thanks to the Arabic-inspired watchtowers and the carved battlements. Dating back to the sixteenth century, this is a historical sight not to be missed on your trip.

- Av. Brasília, 1400-038 Lisboa, Portugal

- **The Elevador de Santa Justa** - Take this historic elevator up to the top and look out over central Lisbon. You can even visit at night, which is a gorgeous sight to behold.

- R. do Ouro, 1150-060 Lisboa, Portugal

- **Statue of Cristo Rei** - Towering over the Tejo Estuary, this statue inspired Brazil's counterpart of Christ the Redeemer. There are numerous ways to get to the statue, and once you're there, check out the viewing platform overlooking the city and the suspension bridge.

- Av. do Cristo Rei, 2800-058 Almada, Portugal

- **Mosteiro dos Jerónimos** - This monastery dates back to the sixteenth century. Built over fifty years with an unlimited budget, it became something incredible. The intricate detail put into this building is something to marvel at while touring this beautiful tourist destination.

- Praça do Império 1400-206 Lisboa, Portugal

- **Praça do Comércio** - This plaza was once Lisbon's commercial hub for trading spices, exotic items, livestock, produce, and more. Here you'll also find the Arco da Rua Augusta, another historical sight to see while in the area.

- 1100-148 Lisbon, Portugal

- **Padrão dos Descobrimentos** - This is a beautiful monument commemorating exploration from the fifteenth and sixteenth centuries. It stands on the banks of the Trejo Estuary, where many of the expeditions to Brazil and India departed.

- Av. Brasília, 1400-038 Lisboa, Portugal

- **Igreja de São Roque** - On the outside, this building looks like nothing special, but on the inside, you'll find something so extravagant and opulent that it's hard to look away. This church is adorned with gold leaf and fine wood carvings. Commissioned in 1749 and considered one of the most expensive chapels to be constructed in Europe, it still stands proudly today.

- Largo Trindade Coelho, 1200-470 Lisboa, Portugal

- **The Ponte 25 de Abril Suspension Bridge** - Spanning the Tejo Estuary, this suspension bridge is similar to the Golden Gate Bridge in San Francisco. That's probably because the same company built both bridges.

- Pte. 25 de Abril, Lisboa, Portugal

- **Ajuda** - This stunning neighborhood just northeast of Belém is an architectural landmark. This eighteenth-century palace and botanical garden have been perfectly preserved, and it's a sight to behold.

- 213 (Area Code)

- **Palácio Nacional da Ajuda** - Don't just visit the neighborhood but enjoy the tours of the Palácio Nacional da Ajuda. The thirty-five staterooms, the banquet hall, and finally, the grand throne room are things you have to see.

- Largo da Ajuda, 1349-021 Lisboa, Portugal

**Best Activities & Experiences**

Here are some of the best activities and experiences to enjoy while in Lisbon:

- **No. 28 Tram** - This old-school tram (streetcar) doesn't look like much, but where it takes you is what makes it worth it. Running through numerous Lisbon historical neighborhoods, let the 28 Tram be your tour guide.

- Tv. Oliveira à Estrela 19, 1200-747 Lisboa, Portugal

- **The Oceanário de Lisboa** - Enjoy one of Europe's best aquariums. Four massive tanks, each depicting the four different oceans. You'll find a lot of different species of sea life here, with the ability to view them from above and below water level.

- Esplanada Dom Carlos I s/nº, 1990-005 Lisboa, Portugal

- **The Fiera da Ladra Market** - In the Alfama district, the Fiera da Ladra Market happens twice a week. You'll find various curiosities at this market, like lesser antiques, collectibles, and other secondhand items. Even if you don't buy anything, it's still an interesting experience to have while on holiday in Lisbon.

- Campo de Santa Clara, 1100-472 Lisboa, Portugal

- **The LxFactory** - Lisbon is widely known to have a very active and vibrant art scene. The LxFactory is a great example of this. Once an abandoned factory, it is now an art studio with art painted all over the building. With specialty stores, unique stalls, and interesting restaurants, this is a great place to visit and experience.

- R. Rodrigues de Faria 103, 1300-501 Lisboa, Portugal

- **River Cruises and Ferry Rides** - Thanks to the proximity to oceans and other bodies of water, you've got many options for boat tours, ferries, and river cruises. These can be a great way to enjoy a sunny day out in the city.

## HIDDEN GEMS IN LISBON

Lisbon has so many amazing spots that sometimes, certain ones fall through the cracks. Here are some of the hidden gems you should check out:

- **Limão Chill-Out Terrace** - This attractive bar has one of the best views in the city. Enjoy some drinks, food, and take in the view at this relaxing venue. The establishment's decor and design only add to Portugal's vibe.

- Av. Duque de Loulé 83, 1050-089 Lisboa, Portugal

- **Palace of the Marquesses of Fronteira** - Outside of the historic center of Lisbon lies this stunning palace. It's a seventeenth-century building, and inside, it depicts the history of the Restoration War of Independence. What really makes it worth a visit is the grotto-like gardens. You can see the Greek and Italian influences all around the palace, making for an amazing experience.

- Largo São Domingos de Benfica 01, 1500-554 Lisboa, Portugal

- **Quinta dos Azulejos Garden** - This eighteenth century garden is truly hidden and often forgotten. If you're lucky enough to see it, you'll enjoy peace, tranquility, and unbelievable beauty.

- R. Neves Costa 86, 1600-535 Lisboa, Portugal

- **Livraria Bertrand** - This is the world's oldest bookstore, hidden away in the Chiado neighborhood. The whole area feels like a miniature Paris, and this charming bookstore is the glue of the area. Opened in 1732, this incredible bookstore was destroyed in the Lisbon earthquake in 1755 and rebuilt in its current location. Also, check out the world's smallest bookstore, The Livraria Simão.

- R. Garrett 73 75, 1200-203 Lisboa, Portugal

- **Miradouro da Graça** - Instead of heading to the overcrowded miradouros, you can enjoy the Graça neighborhood miradouro, which is far less congested and still has those incredible views.

- Calçada da Graça, 1100-265 Lisboa, Portugal

- **Monastery Sao Vicente de Fora** - Another beautiful monastery, the Sao Vicente de Fora, is often overlooked, but it is home to some of Lisbon's most breathtaking architecture.

- Largo de São Vicente, 1100-572 Lisboa, Portugal

## MUST-VISIT BEACHES IN LISBON

What's a vacation without some time at the beach? Here are some of the best beaches in Lisbon to check out!

- **Praia de Carcavelos, Cascais** - With the longest stretch of sand of any beach on the Estoril Coast, this is a great beach to visit if you want to play some sports outside the water. It's also great for surfing and bodyboarding close to the city.
- **Praia da Ursa, Sintra** - If you're hoping to get away to somewhere tranquil and secluded, this is the beach for you. It's a challenging beach to get to, but worth

it. Be careful at this beach as the currents can be quite strong.

- **Praia da Figueirinha, Setúbal** - Want a beach the whole family can enjoy? Praia da Figueirinha is the best beach for families thanks to its spacious beach, lack of rocks, and shallow and calm waters.
- **Praia do Baleal, Peniche** - Want a little adventure? Here's the beach to be for great surfing, sea caverns, rock climbing, and more. Some great restaurants in the area also serve fresh seafood caught earlier that day.
- **Praia dos Galapos, Parque Natural da Arrábida** - If unrivaled beauty is what you're after, this is the beach for you. Thanks to the white-sanded cove beaches, forested slopes, and beautiful water, it's like visiting a postcard.

## ART AND MUSIC IN LISBON

Lisbon is home to countless museums, street art exhibitions, music festivals, and performances in general, making it a cultural phenomenon. So, while you're visiting, enjoy the cultural offerings, starting with some of our top picks:

**Museums**

- **National Museum of Ancient Art** - This museum showcases pieces that date from the Middle Ages through to the nineteenth century. There are thousands of paintings, furniture pieces, sculptures, ceramics, gold, textiles, silverware, and more, capturing an exciting history of a stunning country.

- R. das Janelas Verdes, 1249-017 Lisboa, Portugal

- **The Geographical Society of Lisbon** - Founded in 1875, the Geographical Society is considered the unofficial HQ of Portugal's Age of Discovery. It's an eccentric site with tons of history seeped into its very foundation. The museum pays homage to the Portuguese time as colonizers and expansionists.

- R. das Portas de Santo Antão 102, 1150-268 Lisboa, Portugal

- **National Azulejo Museum** - A museum dedicated to tiles might not sound exciting, but it's mesmerizing once you visit. Thanks to Portugal's history of being artistic with its tiles, you'll find over 300 different patterns, and it's just stunning.

- R. Me. Deus 4, 1900-312 Lisboa, Portugal

- **Museum of Art, Architecture, and Technology (MAAT)** - The setting of this museum is enough to get you interested in visiting. It's a modern undulating building which is covered in pearly white ceramic tiles. The exhibitions are always changing, and they usually are fascinating.

- Av. Brasília, 1300-598 Lisboa, Portugal

- **Museu do Fado -** Considering Fado's importance in Portugal, it's no surprise that they've got a museum dedicated to the soothing sounds this music provides. This immersive experience showcases the genre's history and the legacy it's created.

- Alfama, Largo do Chafariz de Dentro 1, 1100-139 Lisboa, Portugal

- **Museum of the Orient** - This museum is about showcasing Portugal's influences on Asia. Thousands of pieces chronicle performing arts, sculptures, paintings, ceramics, and artifacts from numerous countries that Portugal influenced throughout the centuries.

- Doca de Alcantara Norte, Av. Brasília, 1350-352 Lisboa, Portugal

**Live Music**

*Please note addresses, operation hours, and prices are subject to change.*

**Fado in Chiado**

*R. da Misericórdia 14, 1200-443 Lisboa, Portugal*

Looking for a taste of Fado music? Fado in Chiado hosts daily Fado shows. It's a great experience if you're looking to truly dive into Portuguese culture. Shows happen at different times of the day, so check online to see what available time slots are available.

**Alface Hall**

*R. do Norte 96, 1200-348 Lisboa, Portugal*

In the middle of Bairro Alto in an eighteenth-century building, the Alface Hall is a hostel and bar that hosts numerous live music events. It's one of the few offerings in the area, so it gets pretty busy. Still, soul, rock, and jazz performances make it an exciting venue.

**Operating Hours:**

Monday - Sunday: 4:00 p.m. - 10:30 p.m.

**Ma Lingua**

*Rua Senhora do Monte 1C, Lisbon 1170-358*

This is an interesting venue. Ma Lingua is in a basement with high ceilings, and the music is more like jam sessions that are rather impressive. You can enjoy dinner with a show and embrace what is a remarkable and unique atmosphere.

**Operating Hours:**

Monday: Closed

Tuesday - Sunday: 6:00 p.m. - 1:00 a.m.

**Zé Dos Bois Gallery**

*R. da Barroca 59, 1200-049 Lisboa, Portugal*

For over three decades, this has been the spot to be when it comes to live music. Hosting exhibitions and events while also providing incredible music, Zé Dos Bois Gallery is the best place to go for a drink and some musical entertainment.

**Operating Hours:**

Monday - Thursday: 6:00 p.m. - 2:00 a.m.

Friday - Saturday: 6:00 p.m. - 3:00 a.m.

Sunday:Closed

**Café Dias**

*R. Pedro Calmon 3B, 1300-516 Lisboa, Portugal*

Out in Santa Amaro, Café Dias is an epicenter for soothing jazz music. You'll constantly find concerts being held at this café/bar venue, with the added benefit of great food and atmosphere.

**Operating Hours:**

Monday - Sunday: 8:00 a.m. - 12:00 a.m.

Sunday: Closed

### Street Art

In Lisbon, there's a lot of street art done in such a unique way that they've got numerous tours available for tourists to see the best of the best. Lisbon Street Art Tours is the go-to company providing these tours around the city, to prominent places that street artists frequent. You can enjoy short tours where you walk or longer tours where you travel to various places. If this isn't your scene, one thing you should definitely do is check out Bordalo II's big raccoon. It's such a cool piece of artwork that everyone can appreciate. You can find it at R. Bartolomeu Dias 43, 1400-038 Lisboa, Portugal.

## WHAT TO DO ON A RAINY DAY IN LISBON

Sometimes, it rains, which is true even when visiting a foreign country. The good news is that there are still things you can do on a rainy day:

- Start the day off with some breakfast at a local café or restaurant.
- Consider as your first activity something like attending a museum while it's nice and quiet.
- After some lunch, enjoy a bit of shopping at the Amoreiras or Centro Vasco da Gama shopping malls.
- For the afternoon, you'll want to try an escape room or maybe watch a movie at a cinema or at your hotel. Some cinemas to try include Cinema Ideal - Misericórdia, Cinema São Jorge - Santo António, and

Cinemas NOS - Carnide, which also have English movies showing.
- The evening will consist of dinner, then a theater trip to the best theater in Lisbon, the Campo Pequeno.
- Enjoy a wine tasting. There are so many offerings in Lisbon for wine tastings, like Adega Belem, Quinta Da Boa Esperanca, and Quinta Da Almiara.
- Feeling adventurous? Hit a local nightclub to finish the night off.

## FUN THINGS TO DO WITH THE KIDS IN LISBON

If you've got kids, you're going to need to do some entertaining things for them. Here are some great activities that are perfect for the whole family:

- **Cable Cars** - Running along the Tagus River, the cable cars are a three-quarter mile journey that consumes only eight minutes of your time, but it's a fun experience with great views and a nice photo opportunity.
- **Tuk Tuk Tours** - There are a lot of Tuk Tuks around Lisbon available for sightseeing tours. They're a great way to view the historical city without it being a boring experience for the kids.
- **Hippo Trip** - This is a unique experience because you start on a bus that turns into a boat, and that's sure to excite the kids. View the city from land and sea while learning about its history from engaging tour guides.

For ninety minutes, you don't have to worry about what to do next to keep the kids entertained.

- Doca de Santo Amaro, Edifício Hippotrip, 1350-353 Lisboa, Portugal

- **Kayak Tours** - Enjoy the coastline of Lisbon by getting you and your family on a kayak tour. They last quite a while and are enjoyable experiences seeing the city from the water.

- R. Jardim do Tabaco N2, 1100-287 Lisboa, Portugal

- **The Adventure Park** - If your kids are filled with energy and have an adventurous spirit, then the Adventure Park is where you should take them. There are zip lines, canoes, treks through the forest, and more.

- Centro Desportivo Nacional do Jamor, 1495-751 Algés, Portugal

- **Museums for Kids** - Your kids might not find all the museums exciting, but there are two that are sure to be interesting for them due to their engaging atmosphere. These two museums are the Lisbon Science Museum and the Electricity Museum. Both museums are interactive and sure to provide fun for all ages involved.

- Largo Jose Mariano Gago Nº 1 Parque das Nacoes (Science Museum)
- Avenida de Brasilia, Lisbon, 1300-59 (Electricity Museum)

## HOW LONG SHOULD YOU STAY IN LISBON?

You should stay in Lisbon as long as you'd like to and can afford to. The truth is that everyone is beginning to notice how amazing Lisbon truly is, and as a result, it's getting busier when it comes to visitors. Plan your trip and ensure you get to as much as the city has to offer in the time you're visiting. We recommend a minimum of three days to get a fair amount out of your visit, especially if you're planning to go to other places in Portugal.

Here's a sample itinerary for you to use when traveling to Lisbon for three days:

**Day 1**

- Arrive and check into your accommodation. Get settled and comfortable in your temporary home.
- Wander outside and take in the sights and sounds of the city from your accommodation.
- Venture to the Praco Do Comercio. Here you can grab a drink, maybe go to one of the local restaurants for some Portuguese cuisine, and enjoy the scenic surroundings.

- Once you've taken all you can of the Praco Do Comercio, you will want to spend the afternoon touring the Alfama neighborhood. It's beautiful on a sunny day and has fantastic spots (Miradouro da Graça, Miradouro das Portas do Sol, or Miradouro de São Pedro de Alcântara for example) to overlook the city.
- In the evening, you will want to enjoy a traditional Portuguese dinner.
- It's been a long day. You're likely going to want to rest up for day 2.

**Day 2**

- Wake up and get ready for another day in Lisbon.
- Enjoy brunch on the city's main street, Avenida. You'll find the best brunch spots on a side street called Zenith.
- After brunch, enjoy a coffee before a visit to the biggest aquarium in Europe: the Oceanário de Lisboa. Even if you're traveling without children, it's worth a visit.
- This is perfect for those kidless travelers. Once you've seen the aquarium, it's time for an evening Bairro Alto Bar Crawl! If you get hungry, don't worry, there are food options almost everywhere.
- If you're feeling adventurous, why not hit one of the clubs or rooftop bars?

**Day 3**

- On your last day in Lisbon, you want to start with breakfast on Pink Street. Enjoy a nice quiet meal on a street fit for BarbieLand.
- After breakfast, grab an electric scooter and head on down to Belem. While in the area, visit the Mosteiro dos Jerónimos and the Torre Belém to enjoy some of the city's history.
- After enjoying some ancient history, take in something more modern with the LX Factory. There's a lot to do at this formerly abandoned factory, which is now art space, a restaurant, and some shops.
- Instead of getting back to your accommodation in a boring way, take one of the many streetcars and enjoy going through some of Lisbon's most beautiful neighborhoods.
- Find a great spot for dinner and enjoy your last evening with some fado music.

## TAKEAWAY

As we're sure it's become clear, Lisbon is a fantastic place to visit. With all the festivals, beaches, museums, restaurants, markets, and culture, it's the place to be. It has so much to offer visitors. It's the cultural hub of Portugal and feeds into the many other cities and towns in the nation. You'll never be without something to do while visiting.

Many people who are touring Portugal start in Lisbon and

head on to Sintra next. The great news is that Sintra is only a forty-minute train ride away. Just make sure you get there early to avoid the chaotic rush. We're going to give Sintra an in-depth look to show you all the amazing things you can do in this next prominent Portuguese city.

# BITE-SIZED HISTORY: THE MIDDLE AGES IN PORTUGAL

The start of the Middle Ages saw Portugal repeating history with yet another invasion. This invasion was by the Moors, hailing from Northern Africa in 711. Southern Portugal was conquered with relative ease, but they struggled in the north.

By the eleventh century, a Visigothic statelet began growing slowly in the north, becoming what we know as Portugal. Under the rule of León's King, Henry was the main count tasked with running Portugal. Upon his death, his wife became regent for their son. When Teresa married a noble of Galician descent, Portuguese nobles feared a union forming with the Galicia, leading to a rebellion spearheaded by Dom Alfonso Henriques, her son. A battle broke out, and they defeated Teresa, making Alfonso Henriques the leader of Portugal. Over time, Portugal gained independence from León, and Alfonso began calling himself the king of Portugal, declaring its independence. Papal diplomats acknowledged Alfonso as king come 1179, legitimizing his claim and making him the nation's first king.

Alfonso set out to recapture territory captured by the Moors, succeeding in Ourique, Lisbon, and beyond. During this time, trade was thriving in Portugal, and the first Cortes, or parliament, met in 1211. Only nobility and clergy were represented at the beginning of the newly established Cortes. Later, King Dinis allowed for the representation of the merchant class.

Between 1348 and 1349, Portugal, like many European nations, was struck by the plague (Black Death). It's estimated it killed more than 33 percent of the nation's population.

The fourteenth century wasn't much kinder to Portugal as they were whisked into a nasty war. This stemmed from concerns that King Ferdinand's daughter, Beatriz—who became queen following her father's death—would unite with the Kingdom of Castile, and Portugal would cease being independent. This was because of her marriage to Juan of Castile. Naturally, this incited a rebellion, and for two years, Portugal and Castile were at war with one another. The end result was the Castilians being routed by the Portuguese army and a new king coming into power.

Come 1386, Portugal and England formed an alliance. Portugal was considered a tremendous maritime nation by the fifteenth century. The following decades saw expansion to the Portuguese kingdom with the capturing of Ceuta, Morocco and the discovery of Madeira and the Azores.

Portugal became known for its navigation prowess. Prince Henry provided tons of money, ships, and resources to captains for exploration of the vast oceans. Thanks to this investment, they traveled far and wide, discovering places new to Europeans like India, which would become extremely important. When Columbus stumbled upon the West Indies in 1492, a dispute between Portugal and Spain broke out over who would invade and colonize these lands. Eventually, a treaty was signed dictating that Spain had a claim to the western side and Portugal had a claim to the eastern side of the Cape Verde Islands.

# CHAPTER 7
# SINTRA

> "Everything in Sintra is divine. There is no corner that is not a poem."
>
> EÇA DE QUEIROZ

Welcome to the "romantic village" of Portugal. Sintra is a UNESCO World Heritage Site filled with charming streets, beautiful buildings, and mystical misty weather. Here, the existence of humanity and nature are almost one.

Sintra is home to over 385,000 people, and while it's in the Lisbon region (fifteen miles outsideLisbon), it couldn't be more different. This major tourist destination has much to offer, like beaches, castles, gardens, parks, and more. Its biggest draw is the natural features that become apparent when you see the municipality—

comprising three parishes—existing on the Sintra Mountains' northern slope. One of the mountain peaks is home to the Pena Palace, built for Queen Maria II during the nineteenth century.

In this chapter, we will explore this romantic setting and discover all the fun things to see and do while visiting.

## HISTORY AND CULTURE OF SINTRA

This stunning municipality is located on the northern slopes of the Sintra Mountains. It comprises three Lisbon Parishes within the larger Sintra Concelho Municipality. This area became known for being a vacation spot for Portuguese royals. Beyond the numerous palaces and buildings for the ultra-wealthy, the Sintra municipality has a less remarkable history than most places in Portugal. It was a relatively normal place in Portugal, home to the rich and powerful but also numerous religious monasteries—one of which was redeveloped by Ferdinand II, known as the Pena Palace. While it's transformed through the ages, you can see signs of almost every period in Portuguese history, with places like the Moorish Castle still standing tall and signs of medieval times in several monasteries. This is one of the many things that makes Sintra such an interesting place to visit.

## CRIME AND SAFETY

Overall, Sintra is generally safe for tourists looking for a nice place to travel to. Sintra's biggest safety issue is theft. While the risk of violent crime is extremely low, the risk of something you own getting stolen via pickpocketing is high. This is because Sintra is a tourist attraction as a whole, which is something pickpockets will consider when choosing where to operate from. It also doesn't help that it's not far from Lisbon, which has a considerable pickpocket problem. Purse snatching can also happen, but this is less common than general pickpocketing.

The second type of theft to take note of is car theft. If you're traveling by car, rented or not, don't leave it open, and don't leave valuables in the vehicle.

## HEALTH

Remember that in the event of a health emergency, you can make use of the Portuguese medical emergency number 112. Other options include seeking assistance from the local authorities or your accommodation.

You're entitled to care from a public hospital using your EHIC card if you're an EU citizen. Of course, this doesn't mean you won't have to contribute anything to medical bills, but being an EU member means it's far less expensive. The public hospital serving Sintra is Prof. Dr. Fernando Fonseca EPE. A new hospital, The Hospital de Sintra, is expected to open in January 2024, meaning if you travel next year, you have another option should you need it.

- Prof. Dr. Fernando Fonseca EPE

  - IC19 276, 2720-276 Amadora, Portugal

- Hospital de Sintra

  - R. Cidade de Loulé, 2725-079 Algueirão-Mem Martins, Portugal

In terms of private hospitals, you've got numerous clinics where wait times are far shorter, and they usually have staff fluent in English (something public hospitals lack). You can enjoy quality yet expensive private care at CUF Sintra, Hospital da Luz, and various others in Sintra and surrounding areas. Once again, we urge you to get comprehensive travel insurance to help cover the bills.

- CUF Sintra

  - Av. Raul Solnado 8 e 8A, 2710-204 Sintra, Portugal

- Hospital da Luz

  - Estr. Real 33, 2710-450 Sintra, Portugal

**Pharmacies**

Most pharmacies in Sintra will operate according to standard hours of operation. However, there are a couple of pharmacies that are 24/7, which are indicated by a green cross.

Here are some of the 24/7 pharmacies:

- Farmácia Sintra IC19

  - R. Francisco Lyon de Castro 27 1C, 2725-397 Sintra, Portugal

- Farmácia Cristina

  - Av. Vitorino Nemésio 14A, 2725-471 Algueirão-Mem Martins, Portugal

## FOOD TO TRY WHILE IN SINTRA

Before we tell you about the amazing restaurants you can visit, let's look at the different foods you'll find In Sintra:

**Fish**

Thanks to perfect positioning and an extensive Atlantic coastline, it should come as no surprise that seafood is a staple in Portuguese cuisine. Portugal has no shortage of variety when it comes to seafood, and they've mastered the art of cooking and enjoying this delicious food. Across Sintra, restaurants serve fish like bass, bream, shellfish, octopus, and so much more. A few famous fish dishes in Sintra include Cataplana, a seafood stew, and Sardinhas Assadas, grilled sardines.

This is just scratching the surface as salmon and bacalhau are also popular, but instead come from the North Atlantic and Scandinavia. One of the most popular dishes is Amêijoas à Bulhão Pato. This decadent dish features clams served in a garlic, coriander, and white wine sauce with crusty bread for dipping and enjoying.

When traveling Portugal and enjoying the seafood along the way, you'll notice that most restaurants and places have very different styles of cooking fish. It makes it that much more interesting to try these dishes when visiting new places.

**Meat**

Portugal is known for having various meat and poultry on their menus. When it comes to steak, you've got options like veal or beef. Sometimes pork even makes an appearance. Negrais, a northeastern town in Sintra, specializes in leitão, which is a roasted piglet.

Speaking of pork dishes, you'll want to try Porco Preto, which is little black pigs fed a strict diet of acorns. It sounds weird, but they are delicious.

Finally, the main type of meat Portugal loves to enjoy is chicken. You can find countless variations of chicken across restaurants in Sintra and Portugal overall. Vegeterians should note that there are lots of options for them too across Portugal, so never fear!

While these are the main types of meats you'll see in Portugal most frequently, that doesn't mean they're the only ones. You'll also find some restaurants serving duck and turkey. However, these aren't staples in a Portuguese menu.

**Sweets and Desserts**

Across Portugal, almost every town and city has a unique dessert that's their own, representing the region and the country simultaneously. Sintra is no exception. The dessert of this municipality is the Queijada de Sintra, also known as a Sintra Tart. The delicious dessert uses a recipe dating back to the middle ages. The tart is filled with curd cheese, egg yolks, ground almonds, cinnamon, and sugar, all cooked in a pastry and covered in icing sugar.

**Colares Wine**

Surrounding Sintra is the Colares Wine Region, among the world's oldest wine-producing areas. After the Douro Valley, it's the country's second-oldest demarcated wine region.

Wine culture in Portugal dates back to the Romans, who introduced it to the country during its occupation. What's interesting about the Colares region is that it's not necessarily the best place to grow and cultivate grapes for wine. It required immense training of the vines to achieve. While the production of wine in the Colares region has sharply declined over the twentieth century, there remain a mere fifty acres of vineyards producing wine.

The wine produced in the Colares region is one of the highest quality wines you'll find in the world, with distinct flavors. The reds are aged long before reaching the market, allowing for these wines' tannic and acidic nature.

## RESTAURANTS TO TRY WHILE IN SINTRA

Here are some of Sintra's best restaurants and cafés, that you will want to try when visiting:

*Please note addresses, operation hours, and prices are subject to change.*

**Incomum by Luis Santos**

*R. Dr. Alfredo da Costa 22, 2710-523 Sintra, Portugal*

$$

If you want to dine somewhere fancy, Incomum by Luis Santos is the place for you. You'll need to dress elegantly if you want to dine at this restaurant not far from the central train station, but the food is gourmet and worth the cost of admission. Dishes like smoked duck carpaccio, stewed octopus, and even desserts like tiramisu are just a sliver of the options at this upper-class dining establishment.

**Operating Hours:**

Thursday - Tuesday:12:00 p.m. - 12:00 a.m.

Wednesday:Closed

**Bar do Fundo**

*Av. Alfredo Coelho, 2705-329 Colares, Portugal*

$$

Looking over the shores of a golden beach, Bar do Fundo has a killer view. The food, thankfully, is just as sensational. Here you can enjoy great dishes that are heavy on rice that's been perfectly flavored, beef steaks, and even light lunch options like avocado toast or pancakes. A great view and amazing food make for one of the best restaurants in Sintra.

**Operating Hours:**

Monday - Sunday: 12:30 p.m. - 10:00 p.m.

**Tascantiga**

*Escadinhas da Fonte da Pipa 2, 2710-557 Sintra, Portugal*

$ - $$

Tascantiga is one of Sintra's best culinary offerings. If you're lucky, you can enjoy outside seating with a fantastic view and delicious food. Even if you aren't lucky enough to sit outside, the food is still the main point of visiting. Some of the dishes worth trying include the tapas, fried cod fritters, mini tenderloin bites, grilled octopus, and more.

**Operating Hours:**

Monday - Thursday: 12:15 p.m. - 4:15 p.m. (Lunch)

7:00 p.m. - 12:00 a.m. (Dinner)

Friday - Saturday: 12:15 p.m. - 4:15 p.m. (Lunch)

7:00 p.m. - 10:00 p.m. (Dinner)

Sunday: Closed

**Romaria de Baco**

*Centro Historico, R. Gil Vicente 2, 2710-568 Sintra, Portugal*

$$$

Hidden away in a side street lies one of Sintra's best restaurants, Romaria de Baco. The venue itself is gorgeous, with some walls covered in stone and a vaulted wood ceiling; it sets the scene for a decadent feast. The food itself is classic Portuguese-style dishes with a modern twist. Considering this restaurant's namesake is the Roman god of wine, try one of their many options or ask a server to pick one for you.

**Operating Hours:**

Monday - Sunday: 12:00 p.m. - 12:00 a.m.

**Casa Piriquita**

*R. Padarias 1, 2710-603 Sintra, Portugal*

$ - $$

While not a restaurant per se, Casa Piriquita is still somewhere you need to visit if you've got a sweet tooth. Casa Piriquita has been operating since 1862 and is a mainstay in Sintra. Here you'll find an array of traditional Portuguese desserts which are to die for. If you make it to this small dessert shop, try the Travesseiro, a light puff pastry filled with secret ingredients and hints of almonds.

**Operating Hours:**

Monday - Friday: 9:00 a.m. - 7:30 p.m.

Saturday - Sunday: 9:00 a.m. - 8:00 p.m.

**Tacho Real**

*R. Ferraria 4, 2710-616 Sintra, Portugal*

$$ - $$$

In the center of Sintra lies Tacho Real, a charming little restaurant serving some of Portugal's best seafood. There are a lot of options when it comes to Tacho Real, but beyond the amazing food, it's the vibe that is true to Sintra's reputation as a romantic village. If you're traveling as a couple, this should definitely be on the list of places you eat.

**Operating Hours:**

Thursday - Tuesday:12:00 p.m. - 3:30 p.m. (Lunch)

7:30 p.m. - 10:00 p.m. (Dinner)

Wednesday:Closed

## NIGHTLIFE IN SINTRA

Unlike its neighbor Lisbon, Sintra isn't known for being a party town or one with a thriving nightlife. Your best bet for nightlife in Sintra is a standard bar, and for that, there are two places worthy of mention, although they're not the only options.

*Please note addresses, operation hours, and prices are subject to change.*

**Adega das Caves**

*R. Pendoa 2, 2710-557 Sintra, Portugal*

$ - $$

During lunch hours, Adega das Caves is extremely busy. However, as night settles in the quiet town, it becomes a completely different place—calm, relaxed, and enjoyable when looking for something to do in the evening. The Adega das Caves specializes in Portuguese wines and beer. Of course, they do sell all the popular liquors too. This bar will keep you entertained until 2 in the morning, when they close.

**Operating Hours:**

Monday - Sunday:12:00 p.m. - 2:00 a.m.

**Taverna dos Trovadores**

*Praça Dom Fernando II 18, 2710-483 Sintra, Portugal*

$ - $$

In São Pedro, 1.24 miles from the center of Sintra, lies Taverna dos Trovadores. This venue is also relatively popular, but more so in the evening. It has that old-fashioned tavern style. Sometimes there's live music only enhancing the vibe. The drink list is expansive, and the clientele varies from locals to those from all around Portugal.

**Operating Hours:**

Monday - Saturday: 12:00 p.m. - 4:00 p.m. (Lunch)

7:00 p.m. - 11:00 a.m. (Dinner)

Sunday: 12:00 p.m. - 4:00 p.m.

## FESTIVALS AND EVENTS IN SINTRA

Take a look at all the festivals and events that take place in Sintra and see if any are happening while you're visiting:

**January**

- **New Year's Bonanza** - Almost all of Portugal goes out of its way to celebrate New Year in style, and Sintra is exactly the same. Parties, food, drinks, and firework shows, in a destination that overlooks the Atlantic coastline and rolling hills, make this a spectacular place to celebrate.

**February-March**

- **Carnival** - Also known as Mardi Gras, this week of

colorful parties, floats, musical concerts, and fancy dress parades takes place in late February to early March. You'll enjoy days of color both during the day and at night, with fireworks capping the night off.
- **Ballroom Masquerade Competition** - Every year, at Pena Palace in March, children and adult dancers come dressed to compete in the masquerade theme.

**April**

- **Holy Week** - As Easter approaches, Sintra yet again becomes a colorful place, with the streets decorated for Holy Week. This is celebrated all over Portugal.
- **CORTEX** - This film festival is where the country's filmmakers gather once a year to showcase projects, host debates, workshops, and more. They've even got Mini Cortex to involve the kids.

**June**

- **The Sintra Festival** - This long festival runs from June to August. It's filled with events along the way, like music performances, dancing, and more. Usually, there's an event a week at minimum. In between events, there are workshops.
- **Festas dos Santos Populares** - Running for most of June (12-29), this festival features carnivals, parades, great food, and activities everyone can enjoy.

### July

- **International Jazz Festival** - Enjoy great music from jazz artists from around the world.
- **Handicraft Fair (Estoril)** - Between July and August is the handicraft fair in Estoril, which is the oldest of its kind in all of Portugal.

### August

- **Ballet Festival** - Slightly overlapping the Sintra Festival is a ballet festival that happens at the end of August when the Sintra Festival is wrapping up.

### November

- **All Souls' Day** - A day to remember those who have passed on. This day is celebrated not only throughout Portugal but in multiple other countries around the world.
- **LEFFFEST** - LEFFEST is Lisbon and Sintra's film festival, bringing together multicultural projects and showcasing impressive productions, facilitating workshops, symposiums, and debates.

### December

- **Christmas** - Of course, we can't forget about Christmas. Portugal goes all out for Christmas, just like they do for New Year. There are many public celebrations during this time, and Sintra becomes a colorful Christmas wonderland.

## TOURIST SPOTS AND ACTIVITIES IN SINTRA

Let's look at all the places you need to visit and activities you should do while in Sintra:

**Best Attractions**

Sintra is just like most places in Portugal, rich with historical landmarks and places for tourists to see. Here are some of our favorite places to visit that you should definitely check out:

- **Pena Palace** - The crown jewel of Sintra, Pena Palace was built in 1838 from the remains of a dilapidated monastery. Built atop a mountain, it overlooks Sintra, the coast, and miles of flatlands. It's a stunning castle and one of the most incredible buildings in all of Europe.

  - Estrada da Pena, 2710-609 Sintra, Portugal

- **Moorish Castle** - This attraction is one of the most interesting. It has similarities to the Great Wall of China, albeit much smaller. Travel back in time 1200 years to the time of the Moors' occupation and enjoy some of the best views in Sintra.

- 2710-405 Sintra, Portugal

- **Cabo da Roca** - This is Europe's westernmost point. This venue isn't much in terms of structure and is more of a natural beauty. This is a fun place to visit if you want to see the edge of Europe.

- Estrada do Cabo da Roca s/n, 2705-001 Colares, Portugal

- **Pena Park** - Just below the beautiful Pena Palace is an enchanting forest. Here you'll find romantic structures like statues of monarchs, viewpoints, Alpine-inspired chalets, and so much more. There's a path that leads to the Cruz Alta, which is also at the highest point—528 meters—in the Serra de Sintra.

- Estrada da Pena, 2710-609 Sintra, Portugal

- **Queluz Palace** - Heavily inspired by Paris' Palace of Versailles, the Queluz Palace was built as a summer home before becoming the permanent residence of the Portuguese Royal Family. As you can imagine, the interior is just as glamorous as the exterior. The gardens are lavish, with statues and fountains just about everywhere.

- Largo Palácio de Queluz, 2745-191 Queluz, Portugal

- **Azenhas do Mar** - This is considered one of the most photographed villages in all of Portugal. It's located just outside of Sintra and is a cluster of Mediterranean homes all whitewashed, built on a cliff right on the Atlantic. It's an incredible place to see.
- **Old Center of Sintra** - This needs to be an early morning venture before the tourists flood the old center. It's a colorful and vibrant place to visit, but unbearable when it's overcrowded. So, get there early.

- 2710-589 Sintra, Portugal

- **Quinta da Regaleira** - This stunning home once belonged to the son of Brazilian emigrants. The family made their fortune in coffee and precious stones, and the Quinta da Regaleira is the product of that wealth. A stunning palace park, Manueline-style masonry, underground tunnels, gazebos, and more make this an unbelievable place to visit.

- R. Barbosa du Bocage 5, 2710-567 Sintra, Portugal

- **Sintra National Palace** - This medieval palace still stands today, making it one of the few that's perfectly preserved. Touring this palace showcases the decadence the royal class lived in with large banquet halls, beautifully painted ceilings, expensive tile work, and stunning architectural features. This is a great place to go during a rainy day in Sintra.

- Largo Rainha Dona Amélia, 2710-616 Sintra, Portugal

- **Sintra Tram** - The Sintra streetcar is a great way to get around town and enjoy the sights and sounds of the various neighborhoods on the way.

## HIDDEN GEMS IN SINTRA

- **Park and Palace of Monserrate** - Deep in the mountains, somewhat removed from the other palaces in Sintra, the Monserrate Palace and Park is often overlooked, which is a big mistake. Save these for a rainy day if you're in Sintra long enough to experience once.

- 2710-405 Sintra, Portugal

- **Convento dos Capuchos** - This sixteenth-century monastery is a short stop but an interesting, one as it showcases how monks used to live in comparison with the luxurious lifestyle of the royals and aristocrats.

- Colares, Portugal

- **Ana's Adventures In Sintra Tours** - More of a hidden gem of a service, Ana's Adventures in Sintra tours are great if you're looking for experienced guides to take you to all the best places. You can walk, drive, or however you want to get around Sintra, with guides fluent in either English, Portuguese, Spanish, or French.
- **Greenwalk** - Another tour company, Greenwalk, offers numerous types of tours with different transportation options like walking, cycling, driving, etc. The guides are well versed in the area and effective in making this a true experience.

## MUST-VISIT BEACHES IN SINTRA

As expected, Sintra is packed with gorgeous beaches to visit. Here are some of our favorites:

- **Praia Grande** - This is Sintra's largest beach and also its most popular. Comprising tall cliffs and miles of golden sand, it's no wonder why it's so popular with locals and tourists alike. To make it even more exciting, the cliffs at the Praia Grande's southern end contain numerous fossils. So, there's something to keep the kids entertained!
- **Praia da Adraga** - Hidden away in a cove, the Praia da Adraga is one of Sintra's most gorgeous beaches. Sometimes the swells get too rough to swim, so it's less popular than some of the other options, but if

you go at just the right time, you'll be able to enjoy the water. Jagged rock formations on both sides of the Praia da Adraga make it dangerous. Don't take your kids to this beach. The beach has wheelchair access and several amenities, including a restaurant.

- **Praia das Maçãs** - Accessible and popular, Praia das Maçãs has something Praia Grande doesn't: shops, restaurants, cafés, and bars. This is because the beach is next to a small town, making it even better than the Praia Grande. Praia das Maçãs translates to the beach of apples, and that's because autumn sees apples falling from the Colares orchards onto the beach.
- **Praia do Magoito** - This beach is similar to Praia Grande. It's large, with a massive coastline, is accessible, has decent facilities, and is never overly crowded. The biggest difference is that Praia do Magoito is considered the beach with the highest concentration of iodine in all of Europe. If you're unsure what iodine is, well, it's supposed to have healing properties.
- **Praia da Ursa** - This is the most difficult beach to get to, but if you're willing to make the journey, it's a worthwhile wild and unsupervised adventure. It takes about 30-60 minutes to reach the beach by foot, but once you get there, the untouched nature of the area is breathtaking.

## ART AND MUSIC IN SINTRA

Sintra is smaller and quieter than Lisbon, but that doesn't mean it doesn't have a vibrant art and culture scene. Here are some of the museums and live music venues you should visit:

**Museums**

- **Museu de Ar (Museum of Flight)** - Easily the most exciting museum in Sintra, the Museum of Flight showcases aeronautical material from the Portuguese Air Force. It's an exciting place to see the history of flight in Portugal.

- 2715-021 Pêro Pinheiro, Portugal

- **News Museum** - Opened in 2016 and inspired by the Newseum in Washington, this museum is all about the news, media, and communication.

- R. Visc. de Monserrate 26, 2710-591 Sintra, Portugal

- **Museu das Artes de Sintra (Contemporary Art Museum)** - This elegant museum is Portugal's first contemporary art museum to showcase a wide variety of paintings, photography, and sculptures.

- Av. Heliodoro Salgado SN, 2710-575 Sintra, Portugal

- **Museu de História Natural (Natural History Museum)** - Located in the Center of Vila Velha de Sintra in a nineteenth-century building is the Natural History Museum of Sintra. Here you'll find a collection of thousands of fossils.

  - R. Paço 20, 2710-602 Sintra, Portugal

- **Museu do Bonsai (Bonsai Museum)** - While it doesn't sound exciting, it showcases hundreds of bonsais cultivated and maintained over many years. It's a beautiful setting with even some fish and turtles making it a touch more exciting.

  - Estr. Chão de Meninos 12 2710, Sintra, Portugal

**Live Music**

**Raiz Sintra**

Volta do Duche nº2, 2710-631 Sintra, Portugal

Looking for live music? One of your best bets is Raiz Sintra. This is one of the few venues that has frequent live performances. Beyond music, you get great food, drinks, and atmosphere.

**Operating Hours:**

Monday - Tuesday: 1:30 p.m. - 11:00 p.m.

Wednesday: Closed

Thursday:1:30 p.m. - 11:00 p.m.

Friday - Saturday:1:30 p.m. - 12:00 a.m.

Sunday: 1:00 p.m. - 11:00 p.m.

**Xentra Bar**

*R. Consiglieri Pedroso 2A, 2710-555 Sintra, Portugal*

Your other option for live music is Xentra Bar, which has live music every weekend. The type of music varies, but it always brings in a crowd and makes the evening in Sintra more romantic, exciting, and enjoyable. To see when they have live music, check their Facebook page.

**Operating Hours:**

Tuesday: 12:00 p.m. - 5:00 p.m.

Wednesday - Sunday: 12:00 p.m. - 2:00 a.m.

## TRAVELING WITH KIDS IN SINTRA

Before we tell you about the fun things you can do with your kids in Sintra, it's important to note that Sintra isn't a baby-stroller-friendly place. So, we suggest bringing along a baby carrier instead.

If you have a Lisbon Card, getting to, from, and around Sintra is covered. Even if you don't have a Lisbon Card, it's not expensive to use public transportation. The best transportation option when it comes to traveling with kids from Lisbon to Sintra is the bus or train. While in Sintra, the bus, streetcars, and taxis are your best bet.

Most of the attractions in Sintra are wonderful places to explore, and kids will have a great time doing so. Whether it's exploring the secret passages in the Quinta da Regaleira or walking the towering walls of the Moors Castle, they will have much to enjoy.

It's important to try to get tickets in advance as sometimes the tourist attractions fill up very quickly.

## HOW LONG SHOULD YOU STAY IN SINTRA?

Sintra is best done as a day trip or a two-day trip. There's a lot to do in Sintra, and a day trip won't be able to cover everything like a two-day trip would be able to achieve. If you're spending the majority of your trip in Lisbon, you can always take numerous day trips to Sintra to enjoy all it has to offer.

Sintra is accessible from Lisbon via train, bus, car, and guided tours. The options are easy to navigate, and a personal recommendation is the train. They have trains leaving every half an hour to Sintra, and you can book your tickets then and there or in advance.

Here's a sample one-day itinerary for you to use when traveling to Sintra:

- See the iconic Pena Palace and Pena Park, which is in the same area.
- Visit the incredible Moorish Castle.
- Check out the unbelievable Quinta da Regaleira and the immaculate gardens.

If you have time, maybe have an afternoon at one of the great beaches in Sintra. Take in the sunset before heading back to Lisbon. If you're staying in Sintra for the evening, then you're more than able to stick around for a bit longer.

*A two or three-day trip to Sintra is more than possible, and encouraged if you have the time to spare.*

## TAKEAWAY

In a nutshell, that's the romantic village known as Sintra. This is a place every tourist coming to Portugal should make an effort to visit. There are so many incredible places to see and things to do. It's unbelievable for such a small area.

In the next chapter, we're going to explore Nazaré. Getting to Nazaré is just as simple as getting to Sintra from Lisbon. You can travel by bus, train, and car. Be prepared. It takes a little while to get to Nazaré via most of these travel options. The bus is the longest transportation option at over two and a half hours, while driving takes one and a half hours. But what awaits you is yet another magical location.

## BITE-SIZED HISTORY: SIXTEENTH CENTURY AND SEVENTEENTH CENTURY IN PORTUGAL

During the sixteenth and seventeenth centuries, Asia was Portugal's gold mine for its supply of spices. At the time, spices were costly in Europe, providing Portugal with an immense economic opportunity. There was a lot of money in the spice trade, and Portugal had cornered the market, dominating the spice trade. This period was massive for Portugal as they began colonizing numerous parts of the world, expanding their influence and power.

In 1510, Portugal annexed Goa, a pivotal region in India. A year later, they took over Malacca, a city in Malaysia. By 1514 they had reached China, and in Macao, they established a trading post. The Portuguese were expedient colonizers, having even colonized Brazil. This string of successes wouldn't last forever, and in 1576 King Sebastião went on an expedition to Morocco, which he led. The expedition turned into an unmitigated disaster. Portuguese died by the thousands, including a vast majority of the nobility and, more importantly, the king. Henrique was his successor, but he died having had no children, leaving a vacuum of power. To fill this void, the Spanish King, King Philip II, laid his claim to the throne, stating he was King Sebastião's nephew. This led to a battle, which the Spaniards won.

Until 1640, both Portugal and Spain shared a monarch. Over time, the union between Portugal and Spain turned sour. As a result, in 1640, a coup was staged in Lisbon by the Portuguese nobles. They quickly disposed of the Portuguese governor and made the Braganza Duke their king. Spain refused to recognize Portugal's independence for twenty-eight years, finally conceding in 1668 when the two nations signed a treaty acknowledging Portugal's independence.

Unfortunately, while finally securing its independence, Portugal was beginning to experience a decline. The Dutch had managed to take over dominance in the global spice trade, and Portugal was suffering as a result.

# CHAPTER 8
# NAZARÉ

> "Nazaré is the most challenging, dangerous wave I've ever surfed. It is the only place in the world in which a giant canyon reaches all the way to the beach."
>
> GARRETT MCNAMARA

Welcome to the quiet fishing village known for big waves. The Nazaré municipality is home to a small population of just shy of 15,000 people, while the town of Nazaré has only some 10,000 residents. This fishing town's history dates all the way back to the seventeenth century and was originally called Nazaréth. While a quiet little town, Nazaré has one big draw that always gets the tourists and locals coming to visit, and that's its big waves.

Yes, this is the place to be if you're looking for the best surfing conditions in the country. Nazaré is also home to the Nazaré Underwater Canyon, which is 140 miles long and has a maximum depth of 16,000 feet. But even for those who don't surf, Nazaré has a lot to offer for a satisfying experience.

## HISTORY AND CULTURE OF NAZARÉ

Nazaré is situated in the far corner of Europe. This stunning beach town is both a fishing village and a tourist resort. It's a simple place with skinny streets in a grid layout, apartment blocks long since sun-bleached, and an expansive beach with parts of it the size of football fields. On the south side, there's a harbor, while on the north side, you've got stark cliffs, with Nazaré lying beneath the two. It's different from other Portuguese towns as it's not populated by the grand monuments or palaces that are frequent in places like Sintra, Coimbra, Lisbon, and so on. Instead, it's a place that expresses its history in other ways. The colorful wooden fishing boats, the traditions like the seven skirts—where women wear colorful layers of skirts and wooden clogs to represent the seven days of the week, seven waves, and seven colors of the rainbow.

Nazaré culture is alive and well. While a tourist town at heart, you can still see the people's roots shining through. Honestly, visiting Nazaré is like touring a living art gallery. Everything is full of life, from the waves on the beach to the people on the streets. You can smell the seafood cooking any time of day and see the funicular leading from the beach to the neighborhood atop the cliffs. Even the boardwalk is a work of art covered in traditional mosaics of black and white stones. This small location is an experience unlike any other in Portugal.

## CRIME AND SAFETY

Regarding crime, Nazaré is a pretty safe place to visit. The only real form of crime is the occasional pickpocketing and general theft. However, it's nowhere near as problematic as it would be in Sintra or, even worse, Lisbon.

The biggest issue with safety has nothing to do with crime but more with the risks you encounter when surfing Nazaré's massive waves. Surfing in Nazaré is a major activity, but there are things to consider when you surf in this beautiful yet dangerous location. For starters, the cliff which flanks the one side of Praia do Norte is something you can get dangerously close to if you're not careful. This is especially true in certain weather conditions like strong winds, storms, etc. There is a professional water safety crew on site ensuring that you are safe at all times. Under their supervision, nobody has died surfing in Nazaré.

To understand the waves in Nazaré, you should watch the documentaries 100 Foot Wave and The McNamara Surf Trip.

## HEALTH

Remember that in the event you require emergency medical attention, you can call the local emergency number 112 or seek assistance from local authorities or your accommodation.

The nearest major hospital to Nazaré is Hospital de Santa André, which is 18.7 miles away in Leiria.

- Hospital de Santa André

- R. de Santo André, 2410-197 Leiria, Portugal

**Pharmacies**

Unlike other major areas in Portugal, Nazaré is void of any 24/7 pharmacies. So make sure you have everything you need during standard operating hours of 8:30/9 a.m. - 8 p.m.

## FOOD TO TRY WHILE IN NAZARÉ

Like any place in Portugal, Nazaré is known for some signature food items which you should try while visiting the area. In Nazaré's case, it's essentially all to do with fruit.

**Ginja de Óbidos e Alcobaça**

Not a full meal but instead a sour cherry, the production of Ginja de Óbidos e Alcobaça is limited to several municipalities in Portugal, including Nazaré, Óbidos, Caldas da Rainha, Cadaval, Bombarral, Alcobaça, and Porto de Mós. Thanks to a hospitable local climate and fertile soil, this fruit achieves a small size, firm flesh, somewhat flattened shape, and crimson red color. The well-balanced flavors of sweet and sour make it remarkably different from other varieties. Why this might sound familiar is because we mentioned Ginjinha liqueur earlier, which is enjoyed throughout Portugal.

**Maçã de Alcobaça**

Nazaré has a wide variety of apples, such as Red and Golden Delicious, Fuji, Royal Gala, Reineta Parada, Granny Smith, and Jonagold. But in Nazaré, the apples are all sweet, juicy, and organic. All of these apples have something different to offer, but at their core, they're all delicious.

**Ginjinha**

Circling back to the Ginja de Óbidos e Alcobaça, Ginjinha is a cherry liquor beloved across Portugal made from these incomparable cherries. A recipe from the ancient Cistercian Monks inspired this delicious ruby red liquor. Ginjinha features no artificial preservatives and serves as either a digestive or apéritif neat in shot glasses. Some places even make use of it in cocktail recipes.

## RESTAURANTS TO TRY WHILE IN NAZARÉ

If you're going to travel to Nazaré, you're going to get hungry. Here is a range of restaurants you should consider when looking for somewhere to eat.

*Please note addresses, operation hours, and prices are subject to change.*

**Maria Do Mar**

*Rua Guilhim 13, Nazaré 2450-223 Portugal*

$$

Considered the "surfer's favorite place to eat," Maria do Mar is known for having great food and highlighting the surfing culture in Nazaré. The walls are covered in pictures of surfers tackling massive waves, and they even have a trophy from the Nazaré Challenge. Besides being a novelty, this family restaurant serves some of the best food in Nazaré. With massive portion sizes, a varied menu, and a great atmosphere, this is a sensational spot to dine at in Nazaré.

**Operating Hours:**

Thursday - Tuesday12:00 p.m. - 3:00 p.m. (Lunch)

6:45 p.m. - 10:00 p.m. (Dinner)

Wednesday: Closed

**Pangeia**

*R. Abel da Silva 50, 2450-060 Nazaré, Portugal*

$$$

First of all, Pangeia is a stunning restaurant. From the decor to the views of the ocean, it's incredible. Beyond its pleasing aesthetics, the food here is to die for. Their specialty is octopus, but just about anything on the menu will satisfy your palate. Some highlights include their seafood stew, Pangeia salad, and garlic chili shrimp. They are also one of the best venues in Nazaré for high-quality desserts. This is an authentic dining experience you won't want to miss.

**Operating Hours:**

Monday: Closed

Thursday - Sunday12:30 p.m. - 3:00 p.m. (Lunch)

7:00 p.m. - 10:00 p.m. (Dinner)

**Blue Jardim**

*R. Gil Vicente 67, 2450-267 Nazaré, Portugal*

$

If you're looking for pizza, Blue Jardim is the place to be in Nazaré. Extremely affordable with great flavor packed into every slice, this restaurant knows how to make a great pizza. The restaurant itself is simple. They've got a lot of food and drink options, outdoor seating, and friendly and knowledgeable staff, making this a great place to spend money on a good time.

**Operating Hours:**

Thursday - Tuesday:12:30 p.m. - 3:00 p.m. (Lunch)

7:15 p.m. - 10:00 p.m. (Dinner)

Wednesday: Closed

**Aleluia**

*Av. da Republica 38, 2450-103 Nazaré, Portugal*

$$

This lovely restaurant overlooks the ocean, allowing that beach town vibe to set in. The atmosphere at Aleluia is friendly, from the staff to the local patrons; it's a great place to come and enjoy some food. They also often have live music, which makes it even better for a drink in the evening. Definitely try their sangrias while dining out at Aleluia.

**Operating Hours:**

Monday- Sunday: 12:00 p.m. - 11:00 p.m.

**Taverna do 8 ó 80**

*Av. Manuel Remígio 8, 2450-106 Nazaré, Portugal*

$$$

One of Nazaré's best offerings is Taverna do 8 ó 80. It's a classic and casual Mediterranean restaurant serving great food and overlooking the Nazaré coastline. While it's more expensive than most other options around Nazaré, it's still very reasonably priced, especially considering you get delicious, hefty meals. The restaurant is stylish, comfortable, and well-staffed to make for an incredible dining experience.

**Operating Hours:**

Monday - Sunday: 12:00 p.m. - 3:30 p.m. (Lunch)

7:00 p.m. - 10:30 p.m. (Dinner)

**Taberna d'Adelia**

*Rua das Traineiras 12, Nazaré 2450-196 Portugal*

$$$$

From the same family that owns Taverna do 8 ó 80, Taberna d'Adelia is a Michelin-star restaurant that's colorful and rustic while being a few steps from the beach. This restaurant also serves Mediterranean food with a higher focus on seafood, serving some of the highest quality fish in all of Nazaré, which is saying something for a fishing town.

**Operating Hours:**

Friday - Wednesday: 12:00 p.m. - 3:30 p.m. (Lunch)

7:00 p.m. - 10:30 p.m. (Dinner)

Thursday: Closed

## NIGHTLIFE IN NAZARÉ

Considering the small-town nature of Nazaré, you're not going to find a thriving nightlife scene in the area. However, there are a couple of bars that are worth visiting if you need something to do in the evenings.

*Please note addresses, operation hours, and prices are subject to change.*

**Farol Gin Bar**

*Praça Sousa Oliveira n° 25, 2459-169 Nazaré, Portugal*

$$

This is one of the most popular venues lining the Praça Sousa Oliveira, and they are big into gin. With over twenty different types of gin to choose from, either on their own or as part of a cocktail, Farol Gin Bar has got lots of options to make for an interesting evening.

**Operating Hours:**

Monday - Sunday: 10:00 a.m. - 4:00 a.m.

**Casa O Santo de Anibal Portugal**

*R. do Juncal 11, 2450-233 Nazaré, Portugal*

$$

If gin isn't something you're all that interested in, then why not try Casa O Santo de Anibal Portugal, Nazaré's best beer house (cervinjaria)? Here you can enjoy various beers, wines, and numerous other types of alcohol while enjoying some delicious seafood snacks. This bustling bar has indoor and outdoor seating and is perfect for relaxing after a long day exploring the town.

**Operating Hours:**

Thursday - Tuesday: 8:00 a.m. - 11:00 p.m.

Wednesday: Closed

## FESTIVALS AND EVENTS IN NAZARÉ

Regarding festivals and events in Nazaré, we need to focus on the most critical time of the year, between October and March. What's the big deal about this time of year? It's surf season—well actually, big wave season.

**WSL Nazaré Tow Surfing Challenge**

The WSL Nazaré Tow Surfing Challenge takes place during the winter in Nazaré. The date of the challenge isn't set in stone and is instead set when organizers believe it's best for the event, which could be anywhere between November 1 and March 31.

**Big Wave Tour**

The Big Wave Tour is also like the WSL Nazaré Tow Surfing Challenge in the sense that it doesn't have a set-in-stone date. However, the date for this event is usually revealed only forty-eight hours before it's expected to take place. Sometimes it's announced a week in advance, but it's always dependent on the conditions of the weather and waves.

To keep up-to-date with these events, it's best to visit the Nazaré Waves website.

## TOURIST SPOTS AND ACTIVITIES IN NAZARÉ

Let's look at all the places you need to visit and activities you should do while in Nazaré:

- **Praia da Nazaré** - This is Nazaré's main beach and essentially the reason the town ever existed in the first place. Once a haven for fishing, it's now a coastline for locals, tourists, and, most importantly, surfers. Here two cultures collide, the locals and their traditional attire and the young tourists and surfers from around the world.
- **Praia do Norte** - This world-famous beach is where a lot of pro surfing pictures originate from, and even though it's extremely popular, it still has that untouched feel to it. Autumn is when the surfers bombard this beach with anxious spectators, while in the summer it's more of an alternative to the Praia da Nazaré.
- **São Martinho do Porto** - While most people are going to come to Nazaré for the incredible waves to try to do some surfing, some might want a calmer beach, and São Martinho do Porto is just that. It's located a few minutes outside of town, but it has some of Portugal's calmest waters thanks to it being a sheltered bay.
- **Miradouro do Suberco** - This viewpoint offers a truly mesmerizing view of the entire town of Nazaré and the ocean. It's a great place to take some pictures to

capture your time in Nazaré.

- Sitìo do Promontório, Largo do Elevador, 2450-065 Nazaré, Portugal

- **São Miguel Arcanjo Fort** - What is a Portuguese town or city without an old fort? Probably not a Portuguese town, but in Nazaré, they've got the São Miguel Arcanjo Fort which dates back to the sixteenth century. It was used to protect the coastline and help guide ships thanks to a lighthouse.

- Estr. do Farol 2450, Nazaré, Portugal

- **Traditional Boats Museum** - Thanks to its extensive fishing history, Nazaré has a museum dedicated to showcasing fishing boats through the ages. This open-air museum is right on the beach and is a great walk through history.

- Av. Manuel Remígio 37, 2450-106 Nazaré, Portugal

- **Sun-Dried Fish Museum** - Before you see this museum, you're going to smell it as you get closer to Praia da Nazaré's central area. Why the smell? Because the Sun-Dried Fish Museum has fish drying in the sun using a centuries-old tradition. It's not widely used anymore except in the case of this open-air museum, which showcases the process and has a building that explores and expands on its history.

- Av. Manuel Remígio 2450, 2450-106 Nazaré, Portugal

- **Nazaré Funicular** - Every fifteen minutes, the Nazaré Funicular departs, climbing up the cliff to Sitio Promontory. Going up, you get some of the most incredible views of the town and accompanying ocean, putting into perspective just how small this former fishing village really is.

  - R. do Horizonte 20, 2450-065 Nazaré, Portugal

## ART AND MUSIC

Unfortunately, due to the small size of Nazaré, there isn't really a thriving and consistent arts and music scene around town. It's best to visit the nearby city of Leiria for art and music events. However, some bars and restaurants around town do occasionally have live bands and musicians performing, so check their Facebook pages to see if any events are coming up while you're in the area.

## WHAT TO DO ON A RAINY DAY IN NAZARÉ

Even on a rainy day, Nazaré has something to offer everyone. Here are the things you can do if the weather isn't perfect for a day by the pool or beach:

- **Capela da Memória** - This small quaint chapel lies on the edge of the promontory and is also known as the Chapel of Our Lady of Nazaré. While modest in size, it's a beautiful chapel decorated with stunning white and blue tiles. It also has a pyramid roof with the tiles continuing on the ceiling. It won't consume much of your day, but it's still a great site to see while in Nazaré.

- R. 25 de Abril 17, 2450-065 Nazaré, Portugal

- **Igreja de Nossa Senhora da Nazaré** - Far bigger than the Capela da Memória, this stunning chapel holds a lot of history for Nazaré. Here, you'll learn of a history dating back to the year 711. The building is large and features two bell towers, Dutch tile that covers the nave, and numerous historical paintings. You can enjoy a fairly decent stay in this incredible chapel, occupying a nice portion of a rainy day.

- Estr. do Farol, 2450-065 Nazaré, Portugal

- **Spa day at Thalasso** - if you're not really interested in sightseeing, then maybe you need a different type of relaxation, and Thalasso is the perfect place for just that. It's a beautiful modern building with high-quality therapies and state-of-the-art equipment like their hydrotherapy machines. The spa boasts a relaxing ocean view with massive windows lining the main spa area, making it extremely tranquil.

- Av. Manuel Remígio, 2450-106 Nazaré, Portugal

## FUN THINGS TO DO WITH THE KIDS IN NAZARÉ

Looking for things to do with the kids that can entertain you both? Nazaré has many great activities and attractions which should satisfy you and your children. Here are some fun things to look out for in Nazaré:

- **Take them on the Funicular** - Connecting lower Nazaré to upper Sitio. It costs about $4.40 a person for a two-way trip, but you get the city's best views and an exciting transportation option.
- **Surfing Lessons** - If you and your kids want to get a taste of the legendary Nazaré waves, then you should head to a surf school. There are two surf schools to consider:

**- Barra Surf Club** - Family lessons cost about $50, while private lessons are roughly $100. Lessons are between 1 and 1.5 hours.
**- Nazaré Surf School** - You can either choose to surf or bodyboard, and they have group lessons at $33 (1 lesson)/$155 (5 lessons)/$265 (10 lessons). Don't book

more lessons than you can attend. You're not there long enough to have too many lessons.

- **Municipal Market** - Right by the beach, the Municipal Market is a must-see for tourists. There's fresh seafood, great food, traditional Nazaré clothes, and friendly locals.

- Av. Vieira Guimarães, 2450-000 Nazaré, Portugal

- **E-bikes** - Travel up to 12.5 miles on one of Nazaré's e-bikes. They've got bikes for all ages, and they make outdoor exploring even more fun for adults and kids. It's a great way to take in those coastal views. Prices range from $28 (4 hours) to $100 (3 days), and there are trailer and baby chair add-ons available.
- **Nazaré Skate Park** - If your kids love to skate, well, there's a skate park with their name on it! You can rent skateboards and gear here and even get lessons.

- 608283, -063734, R. 9 39, Portugal

- **Beach Day** - You're in an area with some of the best beaches in Portugal and the world, so take advantage of them. Take your kids for a lovely time at the beach, for a picnic, some swimming, and, if they can, some surfing.

## HOW LONG SHOULD YOU STAY IN NAZARÉ

In our view, Nazaré is great for a day trip. You can get from Lisbon to Nazaré by train, car, or bus. The bus takes about an hour and forty-five minutes. By car, it's slightly shorter, while traveling by train can take longer. From Porto, you can only travel by car or bus. It's a long drive, regardless of your choice, taking between two and a half and three hours.

The best time to visit Nazaré would be between May and September. The weather is great, and it's not too busy. But from October to March is Big Wave Season, so if that's what you want to see, this is the time to go! Avoid weekends. It gets really crowded.

Here's what you should do if you're visiting Nazaré for a day:

- Explore and enjoy the Sitio Village, which is accessible by car, funicular, or stairs.
- Reach the Nazaré Lighthouse, explore inside, and take in the incredible views.
- Depending on when you're visiting, check out the beaches and try to spot one of the big waves. If you have the time try to enjoy the beach, maybe take a surf lesson.
- Enjoy some of the local food from one of the restaurants I've listed.

- Before leaving, take a walk on the coast and visit the two museums in Nazaré to get a taste of the town's history.

## TAKEAWAY

Nazaré is probably a place you could choose to ignore while on holiday in Portugal, but if you can, it's worth a visit. There might not be a long list of things to see and do like other locations, but it's still a worthwhile place with a great history and some of the best beaches you'll see throughout your trip.

It's time to hit the road because the next stop is Porto. You're going to be traveling either by bus or car, and get ready for an extended time on the road as it takes roughly two and a half hours to get to Porto. Famous for its port wine, it's time to explore Portugal's second-largest city and one of its most interesting.

## BITE-SIZED HISTORY: EIGHTEENTH CENTURY IN PORTUGAL

The eighteenth century brought about some significant victories for Portugal. First, they discovered gold in Brazil, then later found diamonds. The taxes on these minerals helped bolster the country's treasury. In 1703 they signed a treaty for trading with Britain, which boosted wine exports to England, further supporting their financial standing. They also experienced military gains, winning a naval victory over the Turks at Matapan in 1717.

Unfortunately, Lisbon suffered a horrible tragedy in 1755 when it was decimated by a horrific earthquake that killed tens of thousands of Portuguese citizens and destroyed whole sections of Lisbon. The king's chief minister, Marques de Pombal, used the earthquake as a chance to transform the broken city into a more modern one in line with the changing times.

Upheaval was the theme of the eighteenth century, with an assassination attempt on the king resulting in Pombal, the opportunist, using this to execute numerous powerful Portuguese nobles. He took it a step further by expelling the population of Jesuits from the country, seizing their property in the process. It is clear from this period that Pombal was very much in charge, making more decisions than the king himself. He carried out numerous legal reforms, promoted trade, and reformed the country's taxation system. Pombal hoped to turn Portugal into an enlightened despotism.

Things didn't work out for Pombal in the end. In 1777, when the king died, Pombal's enemies saw an opening to punish him, and they took it. They brought Pombal to trial to answer for the prior regime's harsh measures, of which the verdict was guilty. Lucky for him, he escaped punishment due to his age, but he most certainly wasn't popular.

# CHAPTER 9
# PORTO

> "Portugal has a peaceful feel about it. I sit on the terrace overlooking the vineyard there and I feel cut off from the world. You need that sort of thing."
>
> CLIFF RICHARD

Porto is Portugal's second-largest city after Lisbon. Located along the Douro River, the Porto metropolitan area is home to over 1.7 million people. In comparison, the Porto Municipality is home to roughly 231,000 people. If there's one thing Porto is famous for beyond its historical roots and buildings, it's the port wine which was named after Porto.

In this chapter, we will explore this gorgeous city and discover everything it has to offer. From the city's history to all the places to see and things to do while visiting. Let's see what Porto is all about!

## HISTORY & CULTURE OF PORTO

Porto's history dates back to pre-Roman times. Based on historical records, it was determined that Porto was founded in 417. As is the case with Portugal's overall history, the area switched rulers numerous times. Porto has experienced rulers from most of the major players in Portugal during its history, such as the Suevi, Goths, and Moors.

The fourteenth century is when Porto started taking off, thanks to its immense commercial activity and opportunity. This led to massive city development, which happened extremely quickly. Come the fifteenth century, Porto's importance only grew as it became more active in European affairs. Additionally, Porto had become the nation's shipbuilding center. This was largely thanks to its proximity to the Atlantic Ocean and river commerce.

The seventeenth century saw wine becoming an important part of Porto's economic and cultural life. This was a time of immense urban and administrative development in the area, with the baroque style of architecture becoming more prominent in buildings across the city. The development lasted into the eighteenth century.

Culturally, Porto's people are known for being fierce defenders of civil rights, with a famous example being them withstanding a military siege at the hands of the royalist forces between 1832 and 1833. The level of resilience on display in Porto was celebrated throughout Portugal, making it one of Northern Portugal's most impressive cities. As a result of a defiant history, Porto was made a UNESCO World Heritage Site.

## CRIME AND SAFETY

Porto is yet another extremely safe place for tourists to visit in Portugal. This doesn't mean nothing bad ever happens, but from experience, there are a few ways to avoid trouble. Here are some tips for keeping safe and out of trouble in Porto:

- Ensure your wallet is always somewhere safe and hard to reach to avoid pickpockets.
- Never flash your cash or expensive items around when walking the streets.
- If you need to withdraw cash, only visit cash machines and ATMs when it's still daytime. Avoid going at night as the streets aren't as busy.
- Don't be excessive in wearing jewelry, especially expensive jewelry. If you're on holiday, there's no need to carry your finest jewels around.
- If you're traveling in a car, don't leave expensive items in the vehicle unattended.
- If you're in a busy area like a subway, bus, market, etc., ensure you're always aware of your wallet and items. Pickpockets are incredibly good at what they

do, and it can happen in a matter of seconds while you're none the wiser, so remain alert.

**Warnings and Dangers in Porto**

Let's take a deeper look at the crime situation in Porto:

- Overall Risk: Medium
- Transportation and Taxi Risk: Low
- Pickpocket Risk: Medium
- Mugging Risk: Low
- Natural Disaster Risk: Low
- Scam Risk: Medium
- Woman Traveler Risk: Low

## HEALTH

Remember that you can use the Portuguese medical emergency number 112 in a health emergency. Other options include seeking assistance from the local authorities or your accommodation.

There are three major public hospitals in Porto:

- The University Hospital Center of São João

- Alameda Prof. Hernâni Monteiro, 4200-319 Porto, Portugal

- Centro Hospitalar Universitário do Porto

  - Largo do Prof. Abel Salazar, 4099-001 Porto, Portugal

- Hospital da Luz Clinica do Porto

  - R. Beato Inácio de Azevedo 61 85, 4100-284 Porto, Portugal

Porto also has numerous private hospitals, including:

- Hospital CUF Porto

  - Estr. da Circunvalação 14341, 4100-180 Porto, Portugal

- Hospital de Santa Maria

  - Rua de Camões 906, 4049-025 Porto, Portugal

**Pharmacies**

Porto has numerous pharmacies operating throughout the city. You can find the 24/7 pharmacies by locating the green cross in their signage. Some of the 24/7 pharmacies include:

- Pharmacie Barreiros

  - Rua de Serpa Pinto 12, 4050-582 Porto, Portugal

- Pharmacy São João

  - Estrada da Circunvalação nº7698, 4200-162 Porto, Portugal

Most other pharmacies operate from 8:30 a.m. to 8:00 p.m..

## FOOD AND DRINKS TO TRY IN PORTO

There is a ton of great food and drinks you need to try while in Porto. Here are some of our favorites:

**Francesinha**

This is one of Porto's most popular dishes. It's an oversized sandwich, and it's got a lot of ingredients. This sandwich is filled with beef steak, cured meats, ham, and sausages. But that's not where it ends. The sandwich is then covered in copious amounts of melted cheese, beer sauce, and a fried egg.

**Cachorrinho**

A cachorrinho is a Portuguese hot dog that is like a normal hot dog, but will include sausage and cheese in a French roll, which is then grilled in a panini press before being cut into bite-sized pieces.

**Peixe Grelhado**

This isn't necessarily a type of food but more a method of cooking a certain type of food: fish. When you see this on the menu, just know it means there are various grilled fish on the menu, which are lightly seasoned before being cooked over a charcoal grill. This can be any fish, such as sardines, sea bass, sole, turbot, golden bream, etc.

**Pica Pau**

This dish is a traditional Portuguese classic made with red sausage, small pieces of tenderloin steak, fresh sausage, gravy, and garlic. It's often considered a starter or a snack, which doesn't sound right considering the list of ingredients, but it's true.

**Vinho do Porto**

The namesake of the city, Vinho do Porto, is port wine which is very popular in the city. It's made just outside the city in the Douro Valley and is served as a dessert wine. There are numerous types of port, such as white, red, rosé, tawny, etc. All of these different types of ports have something in common; they're all sweeter and richer than your standard bottle of wine. They also have a higher alcohol content, so it's a great way to end a meal.

**Sande de Pernil**

Yet another popular sandwich in Porto is the Sande de Pernil. This sandwich features copious amounts of roast pork and a variation of other ingredients, depending on where you get the sandwich from. The other main ingredient is often a type of cheese. You can get these pretty much anywhere in Porto.

## RESTAURANTS TO TRY WHILE IN PORTO

Porto is home to numerous amazing restaurants, with a list far too long to mention them all. However, these are some of our favorites that are worth a try while in the city.

Please note addresses, operation hours, and prices are subject to change.

**Gazela Cachorrinhos da Batalha**

*Tv. Cimo de Vila 4, 4000-434 Porto, Portugal*

$

At its core, Gazela Cachorrinhos da Batalha is a simple sandwich shop. But they serve some of the best sandwiches in Porto, especially their cachorrinhos. To illustrate their popularity, they've been making cachorrinhos for over fifty years and serve roughly 300 a day. It's a small venue, likely not one you'll sit down and eat at, but it's more about the food, and that's where this restaurant shines.

**Operating Hours:**

Monday - Saturday: 12:00 p.m. - 10:30 p.m.

Sunday: Closed

**Adega Vila Mea**

*Rua dos Caldeireiros 62, 4050-137 Porto, Portugal*

$$

Adega Vila Mea is a family-style restaurant serving a variety of seafood and pork dishes. The venue itself is small, rustic, and has that homey feel to it, making it very intimate. When it comes to the food, they knock it out of the park. It's delicious and perfect for a great dinner. The best meal on their menu is by far the Tras-os-Montes style chunks of pork. Simply divine.

**Operating Hours:**

Monday - Tuesday: Closed

Wednesday - Sunday: 5:00 p.m. - 11:00 p.m.

**Peebz**

*R. da Sra. da Luz 448, 4150-695 Porto, Portugal*

$$

Breaking away from traditional Portuguese food is where Peebz enters the conversation. This burger joint serves different types of hamburgers in a small modern setting. It's an extremely popular venue because the food is delicious. It's nice to have a burger in between the insane amount of seafood and pork on offer in the city.

**Operating Hours:**

Monday: Closed

Wednesday - Saturday: 12:00 p.m. - 3:00 p.m. (Lunch)

7:00 p.m. - 10:00 p.m. (Dinner)

Sunday:12:00 p.m. - 3:00 p.m. (Lunch Only)

**Fava Tonka**

*R. Dr. Alfredo da Costa 22, 2710-523 Sintra, Portugal*

$$

Fava Tonka is one of Portugal's finest vegetarian restaurants in what is a stunning venue basically on the water. The food, while meatless, is divine and worth a try. The venue itself is one of the highlights, thanks to its modern design and earthy decor. Even meat eaters will love it if they give it the chance it deserves.

**Operating Hours:**

Thursday - Friday: 7:00 p.m. - 11:00 p.m.

Saturday - Monday: 12:30 p.m. - 3:00 p.m. (Lunch)

7:30 p.m. - 11:00 p.m. (Dinner)

Tuesday - Wednesday: Closed

**Restaurante Abadia do Porto**

*R. do Ateneu Comercial do Porto 22, 4000-380 Porto, Portugal*

$$

While a lot of the previously mentioned restaurants were small, Restaurante Abadia do Porto is the opposite. This venue is massive, spanning two floors. It's a detriment at times because it can feel like one of those tourist trap venues, but it's anything but a trap. The food and service here couldn't be more amazing if they tried. You'll leave extremely satisfied with the choice of dining in this fine establishment.

**Operating Hours:**

Monday: 6:30 p.m. - 10:30 p.m. (Dinner Only)

Tuesday - Saturday:12:00 p.m. - 3:00 p.m. (Lunch)

6:30 p.m. - 10:30 p.m. (Dinner)

Sunday: Closed

## BEST AREAS IN PORTO FOR QUALITY STREET FOOD

In Porto, the best places to get street food is the markets. Here are two of the best markets, with tons of food on offer from numerous vendors.

**Mercado do Bolhão**

*R. Formosa 322, 4000-248 Porto, Portugal*

$$

Nothing beats a market for street food, and Mercado do Bolhão is one of Porto's finest. Here you'll find a fresh array of fruits, snack foods, seafood, meat, and produce. This market dates back all the way to 1839 and continues to thrive to this day, thanks to great food and things to buy.

**Operating Hours:**

Monday - Saturday: 8:00 a.m. - 12:00 a.m.

Sunday: Closed

**Mercado Beira-Rio**

*Av. de Ramos Pinto 148, 4400-261 Vila Nova de Gaia, Portugal*

$$

The Mercado Beira-Rio is yet another fantastic market to visit. It features dozens of food stalls and vendors selling everything under the sun, from fresh food to trinkets. Some of the popular food stalls include Meat Me, Mais Mar, and for drinks Zero Thirty & Three.

**Operating Hours:**

Monday - Sunday: 11:00 a.m. - 10:00 p.m.

## STREET FOOD SPOTS IN PORTO

Here are some of the best street food spots if you're looking for a quick, yet delicious, bite to eat:

**Café Santiago**

*R. de Passos Manuel 226, 4000-382 Porto, Portugal*

$$

Unlike many venues in Porto, Café Santiago can claim to have a best in the world to their name. The francesinha is on a list of the best fifty sandwiches in the world. It's a remarkable achievement. The amount of effort and care that goes into this sandwich is evident when it's served to you; it's definitely something you need to try while in Porto.

**Operating Hours:**

Monday - Saturday: 12:00 p.m. - 10:45 p.m.

Sunday: Closed

**Majestic Café**

*R. de Santa Catarina 112, 4000-442, Porto, Portugal*

$$$

The Majestic Café is one of Porto's most famous locations. Majestic Café is known for serving high-quality food and desserts and for its stunning venue. It's an incredible space filled with an ornate interior of carved wood, chandeliers, ornate mirrors, and more. Their menu highlights include octopus, smoked salmon, sea bass, and duck magret. On the dessert side, you'll want to try the pasteis de nata, cheese-cake, crème brûlée, or chocolate cake.

**Operating Hours:**

Monday - Saturday: 9:00 a.m. - 11:30 p.m.

Sunday: Closed

**CURB**

*Rua da Torrinha 111, 4050-611 Porto, Portugal*

$

Looking for a great burger at incredible prices? Welcome to CURB. Made with the best ingredients and served in a soft, crispy bun toasted to pure perfection, it's the best burger you'll have in Portugal, and possibly the world. That might be a touch dramatic, but it's not impossible. These burgers genuinely are fantastic, delicious, and packed with flavor.

**Operating Hours:**

Sunday - Monday: Closed

Tuesday - Saturday: 12:00 p.m. - 9:30 p.m.

## NIGHTLIFE IN PORTO

Looking to party? Well, thankfully, Porto has a sizable nightlife scene, so no night has to go by without a little bit of drinking, dancing, and taking in the Portuguese evening.

Please note addresses, operation hours, and prices are subject to change.

**Bars**

Here are some of the best bars to try while in the city:

**Maus Hábitos**

*R. de Passos Manuel 178 4° Piso, 4000-382 Porto, Portugal*

$$

One of the strangest venues in Porto, Maus Hábitos is a bar, pizzeria, and comedy club. Here you'll find any and all experimental events you could possibly wish to see. While it sounds strange, it's a great place to visit and enjoy. You usually never know what you'll get until you're seated in the venue, experiencing it firsthand.

**Operating Hours:**

Monday: 6:00 p.m. - 2:00 a.m.

Tuesday - Thursday: 12:00 p.m. - 2:00 a.m.

Friday – Saturday: 12:00 p.m. – 6:00 a.m.

Sunday: Closed

**Letraria Craft Beer Garden**

*Rua da Alegria 101, 4000-042 Porto, Portugal*

$$

If you're a lover of beer, then Letraria Craft Beer Garden is the place for you. Thanks to a great selection of delicious beers, this venue has become a favorite for locals. It's a no-frills venue with industrial bench seating, a chalkboard wall for the menu, and over 100 ales. Don't worry; they do serve other drinks if ale's not your poison.

**Operating Hours:**

Monday - Thursday: 4:00 p.m. - 12:00 a.m.

Friday: 5:00 p.m. - 2:00 a.m.

Saturday: 12:30 p.m. - 2:00 a.m.

Sunday: 12:30 p.m. - 12:00 a.m.

**Capela Incomum**

*79-81, Travessa do Carregal 77, 4050-167 Porto, Portugal*

$$

An interesting venue to drink in, Capela is a wine bar built inside a former chapel. This venue serves a wide variety of wine from around Porto and the world, as well as various other alcohols. It's a relaxed environment with friendly staff and a nice atmosphere.

**Operating Hours:**

Monday - Saturday: 4:00 p.m. - 12:00 a.m.

Sunday: Closed

### Clubs

Looking for something with a little more action that runs into the early hours of the morning? Here are some of Porto's best clubs:

**MoreClub, Lda.**

*R. da Galeria de Paris 68, 2605-835 Porto, Portugal*

$$

With two dance floors available, MoreClub, Lda. is a great place to come and party. You'll find it's spacious, the drinks aren't expensive, and the party goes all night, almost every night! It gets busiest after 2:00 a.m., so if that's what you need to have a good time, pre-game at some of the bars mentioned above.

**Operating Hours:**

Monday - Saturday: 11:00 p.m. - 6:00 a.m.

Sunday: Closed

**Plano B**

*R. de Cândido dos Reis 30, 4050-151 Porto, Portugal*

$$

When you get to Plano B, you're in for a treat. This venue has dance floors spread over three floors playing all kinds of music to satisfy all musical tastes. Just about everything happens in Plano B from thumping club music to art and theater. It's a strange and wonderful place.

**Operating Hours:**

Sunday - Wednesday: Closed

Thursday - Saturday: 10:00 p.m. - 6:00 a.m.

**Beach Clubs**

Despite a beautiful coastline, a beach club in Porto is not always the easiest thing to find. Thankfully, they do have a couple of great options up north:

**Praia da Luz Beach Bar**

*R. Cel. Raúl Peres, 4150-155 Porto, Portugal*

$$$

Praia de Luz is an in-betweener. It's not necessarily a bar or beach club. It's a simple café and restaurant that transforms at night into a thriving party. You can enjoy cocktails in the afternoon, maybe some dinner, and then as the night progresses, the DJ starts slowly introducing a different vibe, and it's electric.

**Operating Hours:**

Monday - Sunday: 9:00 a.m. - 2:00 a.m.

**Melanina Beach Club**

*Rua Padre Amaro, Praia Pedras do Corgo S/N, 4455-109 Lavra, Portugal*

$$

Melanina Beach Club is among the best venues in the region for so many reasons. It's classy, always vibing, constantly hosting beach parties, and isn't overboard expensive. Be sure to dress appropriately, i.e., beach chic, as they're strict about the dress code at Melanina.

**Operating Hours:**

Monday: Closed

Tuesday - Thursday: 12:00 p.m. - 9:00 p.m.

Friday - Saturday: 12:00 p.m. - 2:00 a.m.

Sunday: 12:00 p.m. - 9:00 p.m.

## FESTIVALS AND EVENTS IN PORTO

Here are some of the festivals and events that happen in Porto throughout the year:

**February**

- **Porto International Film Festival** - Enjoy international filmmakers' various experimental fantasy and horror films. It's a fun festival that has featured famous directors like Luc Besson, the Coen brothers, and more.

**March**

- **Porto Interceltic Festival** - European performers gather to perform Celtic music for the masses over ten days all over Porto.

**April**

- **Easter** - During the Easter period, Porto transforms. The city literally showcases its religious roots and traditions by decorating and celebrating accordingly. There are concerts, dance shows, plays, and lots of traditional foods.

**May**

- **Porto Burning of the Ribbons** - More for the students than anything else, the Burning of the Ribbons is all about welcoming new and old students to university life. There are concerts and celebrations just about everywhere. The entire population of Porto gets involved.

**June**

- **Serralves em Festa** - In Parque de Serralves, during the early days of June, a forty-hour non-stop festival occurs. Music, dancing, shows, exhibitions, and more take place on the property.

- **Book Fair** - A wonderful festival celebrating literature. Often you'll find authors visiting and hosting panels, meet and greets, and more.
- **Festa de São João** - Easily Porto's most popular festival is Festa de São João. A crazy, unfiltered night of fun, where the streets are filled with people drinking, dancing, barbequing, and performing.
- **Regata dos Rabelos** - Wooden sailboats once used to ferry wine across the Douro once again set sail. There are competitions, great food, and, most importantly, wine.
- **Rhythms of the World Festival** - This music festival showcases Brazilian and Portuguese culture through music, exhibitions, gastronomy, workshops, circus acts, and more.
- **NOS Primavera Sound** - This three-day music festival takes place in Parque da Cidade do Porto and features local and international artists. The NOS Primavera Sound Festival has had famous acts like The National, Pixies, and more.
- **São Pedro da Afurada** - To celebrate the patron saint of fisherman, Saint Peter, Afurada parties up a storm with fireworks shows, processions, street parades, and so much more.
- **Grande Prémio do Porto** - This festival is for everyone who loves car racing. Drivers run the Boavista Circuit driving in classic stunning vintage sports cars. The event is semi-annual, so it's not guaranteed to be running when you visit next.

**July**

- **The City of Porto's International Folklore Festival** - This festival brings local and international acts together to tell stories, perform music, and more.
- **Porto Wine Fest** - This is Porto's largest wine festival, held on the Gaia River Bank. Beyond copious amounts of wine, there are also activities, showcases, gastronomic events, and more.

**August**

- **Ritual Rock Nights (Noites Ritual Rock)** - This festival is a series of rock concerts by local bands held at the Palácio de Cristal Gardens.

**September**

- **Festival Internacional De Marionetas Do Porto** - This won't be everyone's cup of tea, but if you're interested in a puppet festival, Porto has you covered.
- **Vinho Verde Wine Fest** - This wine festival is held annually at the Porto Customs House. There are exhibitions, tastings, commented wine tastings, gastronomy, and so much more.
- **Red Bull Air Races** - An impressive air show hosted by Red Bull, this is an event that's a lot of fun to attend. It showcases pilots performing daring stunts and showcasing their talents in the sky.

- **Porto Blue Jazz** - A wonderful music festival to attend is the Porto Blue Jazz Festival. It features some of the biggest names in the genre, making for a great evening of wonderful music.

**October**

- **Porto Half Marathon** - Looking to exercise while on holiday? That's great—Porto has a half marathon in October that's perfect for you.
- **Festival da Francesinha** - In October, various restaurants celebrate food by showing the reinvention of the iconic Porto meal Francesinha.

**November**

- **Porto Marathon** - October was about the half-marathon, but November welcomes a full marathon. This is a popular event, bringing in local and international competitors.

**December**

- **Feira do Artesanato do Porto** - Mid-Christmas season brings about the winter crafts fair, showcasing work from Portugal and around the world.
- **Christmas** - The Christmas season brings about a visual transformation of the city, with lights and decorations everywhere. Celebrations are held almost

every night all over the city. It's a wonderful time to visit.

- **Corrida de São Silvestre** - Yet another race is the Corrida de São Silvestre, which is held in the space between Christmas and New Year.
- **New Year** - Enjoy traditional fireworks and parties across Porto with thousands of people ready to ring in the new year.

## TOURIST SPOTS AND ACTIVITIES IN PORTO

Let's take a look at some of the best tourist spots and activities you can find:

- **Cruise Down the Douro River** - This is an unforgettable experience not to be missed while visiting Porto. Traveling down the Douro River gives you some of the most incredible views of the city, showcasing not just the city itself but also its natural beauty, rich cultural heritage, and landscapes. It's absolutely worthwhile.
- **Church of Santa Clara** - Considered one of Porto's architectural treasures, the Church of Santa Clara is one not to be missed. It's a stunning building from the fifteenth century covered in intricate stonework and impressive attention to detail. The church also features the tomb of Queen Saint Elizabeth.

- Largo Primeiro de Dezembro, 4000-404 Porto, Portugal

- **Igreja do Carmo** - This church dates back to the eighteenth century and offers a unique design covered in stunning tiles, carvings, and decorated elements, making it impressive from the outside alone. But inside is just as impressive. There's gilded woodwork, painted ceilings, altarpieces, and more which are absolutely breathtaking.

- R. do Carmo, 4050-164 Porto, Portugal

- **Serralves Museum** - Enjoy a day of viewing contemporary art at the stunning Porto Serralves Museum. Located in Serralves Park, you can enjoy a healthy mix of art, nature, and great architecture. It's an authentic cultural experience.

- Rua D. Joao de Castro 210, Porto 4150-417 Portugal

- **Liberdade Square** - Portugal is great at many things, and one such thing is public squares. This is one of the more important public squares, representing the city's journey toward independence. It's a stunning public space surrounded by impressive buildings. In its center is the King Pedro IV monument, which is incredible in its own right.

- Avenida dos Aliados Downtown, Porto 4049-066 Portugal

- **Porto Cathedral** - If there's one thing there's no shortage of in Porto, it's stunning churches and cathedrals. The Porto Cathedral is yet another example of impressive architecture and construction. Over the centuries, this twelfth-century cathedral has undergone renovations leading to a mix of various styles being incorporated.

- Terreiro da Sé, 4050-573 Porto, Portugal

- **Wine Cellars in Vila Nova de Gaia** - What is visiting Porto without visiting the vineyards and trying out the local wine? It's not a trip to Porto. The wine cellars are located in Ribeira de Gair, just opposite Porto. Not only will you enjoy great wine, but also impressive views of the city.
- **Sao Francisco Church** - This incredible church is one of the city's few pure examples of Gothic architecture. It was built in the thirteenth century as part of the Saint Francis Convent. In the eighteenth century, the interior underwent renovations and took on a baroque style.

- Rua do Infante D. Henrique, 4050-297 Porto, Portugal

- **Palácio da Bolsa** - You haven't seen opulence and style until you've seen the Palácio da Bolsa. It features incredible neoclassic architecture and is adjacent to the Sao Francisco Church, making it convenient to explore both. Originally, this building was a stock exchange built on the site of a former convent, and took over seventy years to complete.

- R. de Ferreira Borges, 4050-253 Porto, Portugal

- **Ribeira** - The Ribeira is Porto's medieval historical district. It's located near the river and is an incredible area to tour. You'll see numerous instances of historic architecture and monuments. There are also many restaurants in the area, and this is where river cruises depart to the wine cellars found in the Vila Nova de Gaia.

- Rua Cais da Ribeira Praca Ribeira, Porto 4050-510 Portugal

## HIDDEN GEMS IN PORTO

While there are a lot of tourist attractions, Porto has plenty of hidden gems that often get overlooked. Here are some of our favorites:

- **Livraria Lello** - I've already briefly mentioned Livraria Lello. It's one of the world's most famous bookstores, a running theme for Portugal. This is the bookstore where the author of Harry Potter visited and wrote some of the hit book series. She was even inspired by the bookstore itself, which you might find obvious once you visit yourself.

- R. das Carmelitas 144, 4050-161 Porto, Portugal

- **Casa da Musica** - This building is hard to miss, so how much of a hidden gem it is might be debatable. But what makes it a standout is not just the innovative design but also the concerts held in this venue almost every night of the year. You'll enjoy a night of incredible music by orchestras, solo artists, and bands.

- Av. da Boavista 604-610, 4149-071 Porto, Portugal

- **Clérigos Tower Museum & Church** - The Clérigos Tower was created in the eighteenth century and stands seventy-six meters tall. Here you'll find a rich history in the museum, a stunning church, and the best panoramic views in Porto.

- R. de São Filipe de Nery, 4050-546 Porto, Portugal

- **Jardins do Palacio de Cristal** - Enjoy panoramic city views at the Crystal Palace Gardens, designed in the nineteenth century. This site was created with impressive gardens featuring statues, fountains, lush lawns, colorful flowers, and more. There was once a palace, which no longer stands, but the gardens and tower are more than enough.

- R. de Dom Manuel II, 4050-346 Porto, Portugal

- **World of Discoveries** - If you want to learn more about Porto's rich maritime history, you must visit the World of Discoveries. It's an incredible museum that is situated along the Douro River and offers an interactive experience to explore the unique and rich history of Porto.

- Rua de Miragaia 106, 4050-387 Porto, Portugal

- **Capela do Senhor da Pedra** - You might be sick of churches and chapels, but this is something special. This tiny chapel is located on the shores of the Atlantic Ocean and is almost in the water itself. It's a really great spot to visit, and it's one very few people seem to get to.

- Sr. da Pedra 11, 4405-712 Gulpilhares, Portugal

## MUST-VISIT BEACHES IN PORTO

Here are some of the beaches you should try to visit while in Porto:

- **Praia dos Ingleses** - One of Porto's most popular beaches is Praia dos Ingleses. It features a long, stretching promenade with numerous restaurants, cafés, bars, and shops. The water is calm, the sand is white, and overall it's just perfect.
- **Praia da Aguda** - Located in the Aguda fishing village, the Praia da Aguda is a stunning beach. It's one of the calmer beaches, with numerous fishercatcher's houses along the coastline, some cafés, holiday homes, and a small harbor.
- **Praia do Homem do Leme** - This is one of Porto's most family-friendly beaches. The beach is filled with golden sands, calm waters, two playgrounds, and cafés. The beach is very accessible, so if you're a family looking for a great day at the beach, this is the one for you.
- **Praia do Molhe** - The beach is beautiful, but it's by no means the main attraction. The incredible golden, neo-classic pergola is a sight to behold. The beach is accessible via a staircase along the pergola and features relatively calm waters and rock formations.
- **Praia do Carneiro** - Yet another striking beach, Praia do Carneiro is located near the Douro River's entrance and has a fort nearby that was originally built to protect the river's mouth. Enjoy relaxing walks along the beach and impressive views when the waves get intense and crash against the lighthouse.

## HOW LONG SHOULD YOU STAY IN PORTO

If you want to have a good experience in Porto, you should attempt to stay at least two days in the city. This gives you a decent amount of time to explore the most important parts of the city and its numerous offerings.

Getting there is easy thanks to the international airport available. You could fly directly to Porto from almost any country that offers direct flights, such as the US, Canada, Australia, the UK, etc. If you're already in Portugal or the EU, you can get there via car, bus, or train. When you're in Porto, traveling around is relatively easy. There's a host of public transportation options like streetcars, metro, and buses. You can also walk most of the city or take conventional options like taxis or an Uber.

The best time to visit Porto is April, May, September, and October. While summer is often viewed as the best time to visit, it's extremely populated with tourists during the season, so it can become a bit much.

Here's a sample itinerary for a two-day trip to Porto:

**Day 1**

- Visit the beautiful Avenida dos Aliados.
- Look out over the city at Vitória Viewpoint.
- Explore Ribeira Waterfront Boulevard.
- Enjoy a Douro River Cruise.

- Take a break at the Gardens of Infante Dom Henrique.
- Visit the Monument Church of St. Francis.
- See one of Portugal's many beautiful bookstores: Livraria Lello.
- See the sunset at the Foz do Douro beach.

**Day 2**

- Tour the splendid and small Chapel of Souls.
- Go try the many types of amazing foods at the Bolhão Market.
- Visit yet another stunning church, the Church of St. Ildefonso.
- Unless you arrive or leave Porto by train, you must visit the historic São Bento Railway Station.
- Tour Sé do Porto and take in the stunning city views from the terrace.
- Go on the Gaia Cable Car.
- If you have time, visit the Porto Wine Cellars.

## TAKEAWAY

It's understandable why Porto is such a popular tourist destination. There are so many things to see and do in this historic Portuguese city. You can enjoy an eventful time, great food, a good vibe, and so much more. It's simply a must-see destination if you're planning on visiting Portugal.

We've seen all that Porto has to offer, and then some. Now it's time to take a trip to the Algarve region, where we'll explore Faro and Lagos. You'll want to hop on a plane or train to get to the Algarve as fast as possible because it's far from our current destination of Porto. By train, you're looking at a six-hour journey. By plane, it's a bit over half the time at three and a half hours. Let's get over to Faro and see what's happening in the Algarve region.

# BITE-SIZED HISTORY: NINETEENTH CENTURY IN PORTUGAL

Heading into the nineteenth century, Portugal experienced something it was all too familiar with—an invasion. This time the French invaded the country in 1807, and the court, including King Joao VI, left for Brazil swiftly. This didn't last long, as a rebellion broke out in 1808, starting in Spain before spreading to Portugal. The British got involved in 1809, which led to conflict for three years, resulting in the French being evicted from Portugal by 1811.

The year 1820 saw a war from within, with a revolution breaking out. The king still resided in Brazil at the time, which made it easy for numerous military officers to seize power. With a newly formed "constitutional Cortes," a fresh constitution was established. However, the constitution offered to the people wasn't popular with the clergy and conservative landowners.

The king eventually returned upon the Cortes' request. While he accepted the updated constitution, the Queen did not. Also happening at this time, their son, the prince, stayed put in Brazil, and eventually, Brazil broke from Portugal after a three year war, ultimately gaining their independence. This was a significant blow to Portugal.

When the king died, his son Pedro—who was ruling over an independent Brazil—was expected to take over, but Pedro had zero intention of returning to Portugal. Eventually, Pedro abdicated his claim to the throne, leaving it to his only child, Maria, who was seven years old. This meant that her uncle, Miguel, took on the role of regent until she was old enough to take the throne. While originally willing to rule until Maria was of age to take over, he eventually chose to seize power, making himself the king with unlimited power, thus discarding the constitution, which limited the monarchy's power.

Unsurprisingly, this led to a revolution, but was more localized to the Azores. At the same time, things weren't going well in Brazil, with the emperor falling from power. Pedro fled to Portugal, declaring himself regent instead of Miguel. Unlike Miguel, Pedro had the support of the rebels and the rebel army. The fight between the two powers lasted three years, resulting in Miguel being exiled and Pedro taking the throne.

The fighting and the instability of the previous several years divided the country. The divide was between two factions. Those who preferred having the monarchy remain but be stronger, versus those who disputed the monarchy, wanting a constitution that was liberal. Yet another rewritten constitution was introduced in 1838 to appease one side. Still, it was opposed by the others, resulting in a civil war that ran between 1846 to 1847. The only reason it was a brief civil war was because external powers got involved.

As the nineteenth century went on, the industrial revolution began, and while most of Europe was transforming into industrialized nations, Portugal stagnated, remaining an agricultural country low in wealth. During this time, the monarchy's popularity continued to wane as republican sentiment grew. In 1891, Portugal experienced yet another revolution. It was brief and defeated swiftly, but it was far from over.

# CHAPTER 10
# FARO

> "Any Portuguese town looks like bride's finery – something old, something new, something borrowed, and something blue."
>
> MARY MCCARTHY

We've officially entered the Algarve region, home to the beautiful cities of Faro, Lagos and numerous historical villages and towns. Faro is the Algarve region's capital city and the southernmost city in all of Portugal. Tourists love Faro for numerous reasons, including the fact that English is widely spoken in the area, and for its undeniable beauty. Home to roughly 61,000 people, Faro wasn't always as important as it is today. Lagos used to be the region's capital. Unfortunately, when the earthquake of 1755 struck and essentially leveled the former capital city, Faro was chosen to take over, and its capital city status hasn't changed since.

In this chapter, we will explore the charming city of Faro, its history, and everything it has to offer tourists. Let's start with a little look at Faro's history.

## HISTORY AND CULTURE OF FARO

Like many cities in Portugal, Faro's history is one filled with conquests, Portuguese royalty, disasters, and historical significance.

### Capital of the Moorish Kingdom

It was in the eighth century when the Moors came to town and conquered Faro. For over 500 years, the Moors would control numerous parts of Portugal, with Faro becoming the capital of the independent Moorish Kingdom. During their occupation, they improved the city walls and built many historic structures that still stand to this day.

### Conquest of Faro

In 1249, King Afonso III conquered Faro from the Moors and integrated it into a united Portugal. As the tale of this conquest goes, the city was well-defended, with city walls and a large wooden city door used to get in and out. Afonso III and his men brought a lot of wood, which they burned by the front door, eventually destroying it. Upon the city doors' destruction, the Portuguese entered the city and recaptured the territory.

Like many conquered cities throughout Portugal, the Portuguese replaced the main mosques with Christian churches. In Faro, the mosque was changed to a gothic Christian church called Santa Maria Cathedra. Moors residing in the now-Portuguese city were allowed to stay. They were also granted civil rights and the ability to continue their economic activities.

### The Earl of Essex and the Bishop's Library

In 1577, Faro became a bishop's seat for the first time since pre-Moorish occupation. In 1596, a time when several Spanish kings ruled over Portugal, an army of 3,000 English soldiers came to Faro and sacked the town. At the helm of this attack was the Earl of Essex. The soldiers burned buildings and took control of the bishop's library, taking the contents back to England, where they were later held at

Oxford. Among these books was one of the first books ever printed in Portugal, a Torah in Hebrew.

In response to the attacks, Faro rebuilt and grew from the tragedy, with numerous new religious buildings, an improved defensive wall, and more. The wall, known as Cerca Seiscentista, was built to defend Faro during the time of the Restoration War, which raged on for twenty-eight years.

Come the eighteenth century, Faro was experiencing immense economic wealth. This was largely thanks to gold found in Brazil, which Portugal had colonized in the sixteenth century. This economic wealth was showcased in numerous buildings around the city, like baroque churches, palaces, and attractive houses.

**Earthquake of 1755**

The Algarve region was hit hard by the earthquake of 1755. Faro, while damaged, was far less impacted than cities like Lagos. This was thanks to the geographical features of the area, like the Ria Formosa lagoon's sandy banks, which helped protect the city. The result of the destruction in Lagos led to Faro being declared the new capital of the Algarve region.

From the destruction of the earthquake came rapid large-scale city restoration projects. Thanks to the wealth of the Portuguese Catholic Church, bishop Francisco Gomes de Avelar led the charge to rebuild and create new buildings, at the same time creating much of what became the basis of modern Faro.

## CRIME AND SAFETY

Faro is known as being a relatively safe city that has few instances of crime. It's yet another case of a Portuguese city being safe overall. Still, with that distinct reminder, it doesn't mean you should let your guard down.

The safety of Faro in the evenings in Faro has been questioned on more than one occasion. The city is well lit at night, so overall, it's not necessarily dangerous, but still be careful. Some buses have late-night routes. Be sure to look for these and find out more about these options from your accommodation to ensure you safely travel around Faro late at night.

## HEALTH

Remember that you can use the Portuguese medical emergency number 112 in a health emergency. Other options include seeking assistance from the local authorities or your accommodation.

There is one major public hospital in Faro:

- Centro Hospitalar Universitario do Algarve

  - R. Leão Penedo, 8000-386 Faro, Portugal

The University Hospital in Faro is among the biggest hospitals in all of the Algarve region. Specialized healthcare is offered in this hospital, which ranks as one of the best in the region.

**Pharmacies**

In Faro, there are numerous pharmacies to choose from. Almost all the pharmacies operate from 9 a.m. - 8 p.m.. However, there's also a 24/7 pharmacy option:

- Penha Pharmacy

  - Estr. da Penha nº 52, 8005-135 Faro, Portugal

You can always tell which pharmacies are 24/7 as they'll have a large green medical cross marking them.

## FOOD TO TRY WHILE IN FARO

While you're in the city of Faro, you should indulge in some local delicacies. Here are some dishes you definitely should be trying:

**Cataplana**

When we talk about cataplanas, we're referring to stews. In the Algarve region, a cataplana is often seafood based. Some common cataplanas include cataplana de carne de porco com amêijoas (pork cataplana with clams)., cataplana de peixe (fish cataplana), cataplana de marisco (seafood cataplana), and cataplana de peixe e marisco (fish and seafood cataplana). A personal favorite is the pork and clams cataplana. It shouldn't work, but it is incredible.

**Oysters**

It's no secret that Portugal and seafood go hand-in-hand. Oysters are particularly popular in Faro, seeing as they come from the Ria Formosa, not far from the city. You will find most restaurants serve them, and they are truly a delicacy in the region.

**Javali**

The further inland you go in the Algarve region, the more meat-focused the dishes become. One dish that's enjoyed throughout the Algarve is javali, which is wild boar. There's no one particular type of javali dish, but if you see it on the menu, you should try it.

**Leitão**

This stunning pork dish is made using a piglet that's between four and six weeks old. The meat is spit-roasted over a wood fire creating one of the most tender, succulent, delicious dishes you'll ever have. It's not necessarily a regional classic, but it's still served throughout Faro.

## RESTAURANTS TO TRY WHILE IN FARO

Looking for somewhere great to eat while in Faro? Here are some of our favorite restaurants in the city:

Please note addresses, operation hours, and prices are subject to change.

**Pigs and Cows**

*R. Baptista Lopes 57, 8000-225 Faro, Portugal*

$$$

Pigs and Cows is one of the interesting restaurants on offer in Faro when it comes to a dining experience. Combining traditional local cuisine with French cooking techniques and a host of flavors from around the world, you've got a sensational combination creating some of the best food in the city. You'll find P&C in the north of the old town. The atmosphere is intimate in a small dining room where you can watch the food being made, thanks to an exposed kitchen. The dishes are varied and go beyond just pigs and cows, with a standout being the duck confit and Creole octopus rougaille.

**Operating Hours:**

Monday - Wednesday: Closed

Thursday - Sunday: 6:30 p.m. - 11:30 p.m.

**Tertúlia Algarvia**

*Praça Dom Afonso III 15, 8000-167 Faro, Portugal*

$$

Boasting a stunning location, Tertúlia Algarvia is known for its serious approach to local cuisines. One of the most renowned dishes to come out of the Tertúlia Algarvia kitchen is their cataplana. This fish stew is generously stuffed with cockles, octopus, sweet potatoes, and more, creating one of the best cataplanas you'll eat in Faro.

**Operating Hours:**

Monday - Sunday: 10:30 a.m. - 11:00 p.m.

**Alameda Restaurant and Rooftop**

*Rua da Policia da Seguranca Publica 10, 8000-151 Faro, Portugal*

$$$

Almeda has the distinction of being one of Faro's most beautiful restaurants. It's located on the outskirts of the old town. It serves up one of the best culinary experiences thanks to a playful approach to texture and flavor. The dishes are as stunning to look at as they are to devour. You can dine inside the lovely dining room or eat alfresco on their rooftop with a decent view to accompany your meal. They offer a tasting menu, which is what I'd recommend to get a nice variety of beautifully constructed dishes, some of which feature oysters and octopus.

**Operating Hours:**

Monday: 7:00 p.m. - 12:00 a.m.

Tuesday - Wednesday: Closed

Thursday - Saturday:7:00 p.m. - 12:00 a.m.

Sunday:1:00 p.m. - 3:00 p.m. (Lunch)

7:00 p.m. - 12:00 a.m. (Dinner)

**2 Irmãos**

*Praça Ferreira de Almeida 15, 8000-156 Faro, Portugal*

$$$

2 Irmãos has been around since 1925, making it one of Portugal's oldest restaurants. If you're looking for an authentic Portuguese dinner, you couldn't get more traditional than 2 Irmãos. It's a gorgeous restaurant that features some classics like wooden beams, azulejo-tiled walls, and a lot of color. Some of the standout dishes include grilled octopus and Iberian pork cheeks.

**Operating Hours:**

Monday - Saturday: 10:00 p.m. - 11:00 p.m.

Sunday: Closed

**Mavala Osteria Italiana**

*Largo da Madalena 10, 8000-134 Faro, Portugal*

$$

Hidden away in a Faro backstreet, Mavalo Osteria Italiana is a favorite amongst the locals. Owned and operated by born-

and-raised Italians, you'll find an authentic Italian experience with delicious food that's authentic, simple, and packed with unexpected flavors. A dish you have to try is the prawn and pistachio pasta, which is divine. Surprising but divine.

**Operating Hours:**

Sunday - Monday: Closed

Tuesday - Saturday: 12:00 p.m. - 3:00 p.m. (Lunch)

7:00 p.m. - 11 p.m. (Dinner)

**Pizzeria Bell'Antonio**

*R. Conselheiro Bivar 52, 8000-343 Faro, Portugal*

$$

Looking for quick food that's still delicious? Pizzeria Bell'Antonio is a great option for some of the best pizza in the city. Service is fast, the food is great, and you can either sit down or enjoy takeout, making it extremely convenient.

**Operating Hours:**

Monday - Sunday: 12:00 p.m. - 11:00 p.m.

**Paparazzi**

*R. Baptista Lopes 52, 8000-343 Faro, Portugal*

$$$

While Pizzeria Bell'Antonio serves some of the best pizza in Faro, the honor of best pizza might have to go to Paparazzi.

They've often got specials going, so if you're feeding your entire family, you'll get a great deal on food that nobody is going to be disappointed in. If you're a vegetarian, this is a great restaurant for you as they've got a lot of options.

**Operating Hours:**

Monday - Saturday: 12:00 p.m. - 2:30 p.m. (Lunch)

7:30 p.m. - 10:30 p.m. (Dinner)

Sunday: Closed

## NIGHTLIFE IN FARO

Faro, being the capital of the Algarve region, is sure to have numerous places for you to go get a drink and dance the night away. Here are some of the best bars and nightclubs in Faro.

Please note addresses, operation hours, and prices are subject to change.

**Bars**

Here are some of the bars you can find:

**Columbus Cocktail & Wine Bar**

*Praça Dom Francisco Gomes, 8000-168 Faro, Portugal*

$$$

Easily one of Faro's most attractive offerings, Columbus Cocktail & Wine Bar is a stunning venue with an incredible atmosphere. The drinks are amazing, they often have live music performances, and overall it's just a spectacular spot to spend an evening.

**Operating Hours:**

Sunday - Thursday: 12:00 p.m. - 2:00 a.m.

Friday - Saturday: 12:00 p.m. - 4:00 a.m.

**Game Over Faro**

*R. do Montepio 28, 8000-410 Faro, Portugal*

*$$*

If you're looking for something a little different, Game Over Faro offers an interesting take on a lounge bar. Come for the drinks and stay for the assortment of arcade and console games. With a nice variety of games to play, it's definitely a fun experience waiting to be had.

**Operating Hours:**

Monday: Closed

Tuesday - Sunday: 6:00 p.m. - 2:00 a.m.

**O Castelo**

*R. do Castelo 11, 8000-149 Faro, Portugal*

$$ - $$$

Take the party to the beach with O Castelo. This stunning venue, located on the beaches of a lagoon, provides a spectacular view for any time of the day. Perfect for sunset and even better when the sun goes down, this bar turns into something of a dance club, making it a great place to grab drinks, relax, and party.

**Operating Hours:**

Monday - Sunday: 10:30 a.m. - 2:00 a.m.

**Bar CheSsenta**

*R. das Orquídeas 23, 8005-196 Faro, Portugal*

$

Bar CheSsenta is a rather small venue located down a narrow cobblestone street that offers a great time. Frequently hosting live musicians, karaoke events, and tons of drink specials, it's a bar for anyone and everyone.

**Operating Hours:**

Monday - Sunday: 4:00 p.m. - 4:00 a.m.

**Nightclubs**

Here are some of the nightclubs you can find in Faro:

**Call In Faro**

*R. de Sao Pedro 9, 8000-078 Faro, Portugal*

$$$

Call In Faro is one of the strangest venues in Faro. For starters, it's got a great name, but it's also got some of the strangest operating hours we've ever experienced. At its core, it's a bar, but the later it gets, the more the dance club aspects of this venue come alive. This is a great place to come and party!

**Operating Hours:**

Sunday - Monday: Closed

Tuesday - Saturday: 10:00 p.m. - 4:00 a.m.

**Prestige**

*Largo da Madalena 11, 8000-134 Faro, Portugal*

$$

Another great club in Faro is Prestige. The only problem is, it's only open three days a week, which sucks. But when it's open, it's a proper party. Great music from local and sometimes international DJs, cheap drinks, and a great vibe make this a place to spend the early hours of the morning.

**Operating Hours:**

Sunday - Wednesday: Closed

Thursday: 9:00 p.m. - 2:00 a.m.

Friday - Saturday: 11:00 p.m. - 4:00 a.m.

## FESTIVALS AND EVENTS IN FARO

Here are some of the festivals and events that happen in Faro throughout the year:

**March**

- **Procisao do Enterro do Senhor** - Held before Easter on Good Friday; this religious procession happens all over Faro.

**June**

- **Feira de Arte e Artenasanato** - This art fair is all about showcasing local handmade products. It's a great way to see local artisans, enjoy great food and drinks, and have a cultural experience.

**July**

- **Arte Viva** - During the Arte Viva festival, the entire city of Faro breaks out into performances, art shows, and music. Lasting most of the evening, this is when Faro truly comes alive.
- **Concentracao Internacional de Motos** - One of the world's biggest motor festivals, the Concentracao Internacional de Motos is always a great time with beer, live music, demonstrations, bikers, and more.

**October**

- **Feira de Santa Iria** - This religious festival is a celebration with markets, music concerts, rides, food, drinks, and more.

**December**

- **Christmas** - Yet another place in Portugal that knows how to celebrate Christmas, Faro is a great place to be for the holiday season, thanks to a cheerful environment, micro-festivals, and great food.
- **New Year** - Are you looking to party hard to end the year and start a new one? Faro is a great option for New Year, thanks to numerous live performances and parties held to celebrate another year.

## TOURIST SPOTS AND ACTIVITIES IN FARO

Let's look at all the places you need to visit and activities you should do while in Faro:

- **Museu Municipal** - Residing in a former convent from the sixteenth century, the Museu Municipal is a cultural showpiece. The museum showcases the history of the region, covering periods like the Romans, Moors, and beyond. It goes up to the nineteenth century and has numerous artifacts, galleries, and more.

- Largo Dom Afonso III 14, 8000-167 Faro, Portugal

- **Santa Maria Cathedral** - Once an Arab mosque, it was reconstructed in the thirteenth century and throughout Faro's history to include numerous architectural styles, including Gothic, baroque, and Renaissance features. The building looks haphazard from the outside, thanks to the constant changes, but that doesn't change how stunning it is on the inside. The level of detail is something to be admired.

- Largo da Sé 11, 8000-138 Faro, Portugal

- **Cidade Velha** - One of the most popular things to do is to tour the compact old town, which features medieval buildings and Roman foundations. This area is doused in Portugal's long and complicated history, giving you a glimpse of what Faro once was.

- R. DomingosGuieiro 19, 8000 Faro, Portugal, 8005-408

- **Igreja da Nossa Senhora do Carmo (Capela de Ossos)** - In the heart of Faro's city center lies the Carmo Church, built in the eighteenth century. It's a striking building with a twin-towered façade sporting a baroque architectural style. Every inch of this building is impressive and just reminds you of the effort put into religious buildings throughout Portugal's history.

- Largo do Carmo 21, 8000-148 Faro, Portugal

- **Milreu and Estoi** - Not far outside Faro lie Milreu and Estoi, two Roman sites of great importance in Algarve history. These ruins date back to the first and second centuries and express what once was an expansive villa complex and a central courtyard.

  - 8005-411 Estoi, Portugal

- **Faro Jewish Heritage Center** - The Faro Jewish Heritage Center is a great place to understand Jewish history in Portugal. This center features a museum and Jewish cemetery, restored over time, with gravestones dating back to 1838.

  - R. Leão Penedo, 8000-386 Faro, Portugal

- **Parque Natural da Ria Formosa** - The entire Algarve region is filled with natural beauty, and Parque Natural da Ria Formosa has a taste of that on display. This nature reserve covers over thirty-seven miles of coastline and has marshlands, lagoons, islets, channels, and salt pans. It's a great place to explore.

  - 8700-225 Faro, Portugal

- **Teatro Lethes** - Prior to 1845, this beautiful building was a Jesuit college before becoming a music and concert hall. Over time, renovations were made to widen the auditorium and improve and expand seating. The unfortunate aspect of the Teatro Lethes is that it is often closed due to a lack of funding and shows. Hopefully, when you visit, it's open, so you can see an amazing showcase in this incredible building.

- R. de Portugal 58, 8000-281 Faro, Portugal

- **Land Train** - Head to the marina, where you'll depart on this tourist train that takes you around Faro. This attraction allows you to see the most prominent landmarks and attractions in a unique way. It's a roughly 45-minute round trip and a great activity if you have kids.

- Praça Dom Francisco Gomes 12, 8000-269 Faro, Portugal

- **Forum Algarve** - While you're likely more interested in visiting one of the many historical landmarks, there's nothing wrong with wanting a morning, afternoon, or day of shopping at the Forum Algarve. This mall hosts 120+ shops with most major brands present, along with over twenty restaurants spanning numerous global cuisines.

- N125 Km 103, 8009-126 Faro, Portugal

## HIDDEN GEMS IN FARO

- **Alameda João de Deus Garden** - This small city park is a great place to take a load off after venturing around the city. You'll be in great company as this park is filled with peacocks. It's a unique experience.

- 8000-544 Faro, Portugal

- **Segway & Quad Tours** - Enjoy a great experience seeing various parts of Faro in style. You can take a Segway tour through Ria Formosa Natural Park thanks to AlgarveBySegway. Another option is quad biking on numerous tour options with Rooster Quad Tours.
- **Ilha Deserta** - Thanks to Animaris Tours, you can enjoy a day on Ilha Deserta, an uninhabited island that's great for a day in the sun. Animaris Tours gets you there and back and makes your time on the island comfortable and relaxing.

- R. Cmte. Francisco Manuel 41, 8000-138 Faro, Portugal

- **Parque Ribeirinho de Faro** - Another great park to visit is Ria Formosa. You'll find fantastic bird observation platforms, wildlife, an adventure playground, bathroom facilities, and a park café here.

- Parque Ribeirinho de Faro, Faro, 8005, Portugal

- **Centro Ciência Viva do Algarve** - The Live Science Center is a great option in Faro if you're traveling with children. You'll all be able to have fun at this extremely interactive venue that's all about technological and scientific awareness. That might not sound fun, but they've cracked the code to make it an engaging and enjoyable experience.

- R. Cmte. Francisco Manuel s/n, 8000-250 Faro, Portugal

- **Ilha de Faro** - Ilha de Faro is the westernmost island, only accessible by car through a single-lane bridge. It's challenging to get to during summer, thanks to traffic. But once you get there, you can enjoy a white sand beach, crystal clear water, and a great place for watersports like windsurfing.

- Ilha de Faro, Faro, Portugal

## MUST-VISIT NATURE AND BEACHES IN FARO

- **Praia do Ancão** - Situated halfway between Quarteira and Faro, this beach is an area populated by resorts. It forms the western boundary of Ria Formosa Park. This pristine beach is complemented by numerous facilities, making it a comfortable beach to visit. Some areas of this beach are restricted to resorts, but as a result of this, there are parts of the beach that never get too crowded.

- **Praia da Ilha da Culatra** - This smaller beach is located near the Ria Formosa reserve and is only accessible by ferry. As a result, it's never busy, making for a great reason to visit. Accompanied by a small beach town, the Praia da Ilha da Culatra is a simple yet enjoyable beach.
- **Praia de Garrao** - Another beach located in the resort area is the Praia de Garrao. It's beautiful, with a great coastline, golden sands, and calm waters. With great amenities in the area, like rentals, a beach café, and restaurants, it's yet another beach worthy of enjoying.

## HOW LONG SHOULD YOU STAY IN FARO

To fully experience Faro, you should stay at least three days. That's enough time to visit the bulk of the tourist attractions, get into some activities, and have a day at the beach. You can make it longer, like a full week, spending your entire vacation in the Algarve capital. There's enough to do and see to make it a worthwhile vacation.

To get there, you can use the Faro International Airport. Other options include driving, going on a bus, or taking a train. While in the city you'll be doing a lot of walking. You can also make use of taxis and buses.

**Day 1**

- Visit the Cidade Velha to see old-town Faro.
- After a short bus ride to North Faro, you'll want to visit the Igreja da Nossa Senhora do Carmo.
- Visit the Faro Jewish Heritage Center to explore Jewish history in Portugal.

**Day 2**

- Enjoy a day at the beach, either Ilha de Faro, Praia do Ancão, Praia da Ilha da Culatra, or the Praia de Garrao.

Or…

- Take a boat trip with Animaris Tours to Ilha Deserta.

Or…

- Go on a Segway or quad bike tour. If you're not interested in these options, you can always just visit and explore the parks on foot.

**Day 3**

- Visit Milreu and Estoi to explore the ruins of a Roman villa.
- Get back to the city and ride the land train.

- Check out the Santa Maria Cathedral.
- Visit the Forum Algarve and shop, eat, and explore at the mall.

## TAKEAWAY

Faro may not have always been the capital of the Algarve region. Still, when it took on the role, it took it seriously and became a must-see destination. With a rich history, great food, and awesome landmarks and natural features, there's never a moment where you'll have nothing to do.

The Algarve region is home to two major tourist destinations. We've explored Faro, and now it's time to take a drive, train ride, or bus to our next destination: Lagos.

# BITE-SIZED HISTORY: TWENTIETH CENTURY IN PORTUGAL

The twentieth century might be Portugal's most pivotal moment in history. 1908 saw the assassination of King Carlos, and by 1910 the republican revolution resumed, led by both the navy and the army. King Manuel II deserted Portugal for Britain, and by 1926 the Portuguese army took control of Portugal. This was the result of decades of dissatisfaction over the standard of living.

The revolution brought about change, but it's hard to decipher whether it was positive or negative. A Combra University lecturer, Oliveira Salazar, took on the role of finance minister in 1928. In 1932 he became Portugal's prime minister. A new, publicly approved constitution was brought into effect thanks to a referendum. However, it soon became clear that Salazar was a dictator. He had his own secret police, the press was ultimately censored, and even political parties became illegal.

While there are many negatives to be drawn from Salazar's time in power, it wasn't all negative. As prime minister, Salazar spent a lot of money improving Portugal by investing in public works like roads, bridges, public buildings, social programs, etc. Industries grew as they caught up industrially. Unfortunately, poverty remained a pervasive issue. The 1960s brought new problems to the African colonies when guerilla warfare began spreading. Portugal's resources were spread thin with quelling the rebels in Africa while focusing on home issues as well.

In 1968, due to his failing health, Salazar resigned begrudgingly. Marcelo Caetano replaced him, but discontent was growing in the ranks of the army, and on April 25, 1974, a coup was afoot. Supporters of the latest revolution wore carnations of red and white; as a result, it became known in history as the Carnation Revolution. This revolution had the most positive results, with democracy being restored. Portugal became part of the EU in 1986, and in 1999, they were one of the first countries to adopt the euro.

# CHAPTER 11
# LAGOS

> "Wet or fine, the air in Portugal has a natural happiness in it."
>
> HG WELLS

Staying in the Algarve region, we turn our attention to the alluring city of Lagos. With over 2,000 years of history, this ancient maritime town is an incredible place to visit while in Portugal. Existing at the mouth of the Bensafrim River and along the Atlantic Ocean, there's a lot to see and do in this city of only 33,500 people. Famous for its walled old town, striking cliffs, and beautiful beaches, Lagos is a destination you won't want to miss.

In this chapter, we will explore the city of Lagos and everything it offers tourists. Let's take a deeper look, starting with the history of the city.

## HISTORY AND CULTURE OF LAGOS

Similar to Portugal's national history, Lagos' history is long, complicated, and interesting. The first known settlement was the Phoenicians. Eventually, the Romans came in and took over, naming the settlement Lacóbriga, which would eventually become the current name of Lagos. After the Romans were the Moors; this set up a back-and-forth of power. Before any conquests were attempted, the Moors fortified their settlement of Zawaya (meaning lake or lago) with a wall that still exists today.

### Conquest of Lagos

In 1189, European crusaders, with the aid of the Portuguese army, conquered the town of Zawaya (formerly Lacóbriga). They achieved a stunning victory, even capturing Silves in the process. Not even two years later, this would be reversed when the Moors reconquered the towns. It would only be in the thirteenth century that the Moors would be driven out.

Lagos' unique natural harbor made it an incredibly important place for discoveries. The famous Henry the Navigator lived in Lagos and was even the governor of the Algarve region.

### Age of Discoveries

One of Portugal and all of Europe's most important periods in history was the Age of Discoveries. Lagos played an outsized role in this history. Lagos became the center for those looking to explore the seas in the fifteenth century. It was a launching point, and in 1415, over 200 ships commanded by Henry the Navigator set out from Lagos to conquer an important city in Morocco, Cueta. It was an important trade city, and it began the age of exploration and expansion for Portugal, as they would begin conquering numerous lands beyond their borders.

In 1434, a captain had dared do something no European had ever tried before, sailing around Cape Bojador in West Africa. This was the start of the discovery of the African coast by Europeans and, unfortunately, the slave trade in Portugal and numerous parts of the world. At the center of the slave trade and African trade was Lagos, making it the most important city in all the Algarve. You can still see the old slave market in Lagos' old city center.

The only reason Faro is now the Algarve's capital is because Lagos was essentially destroyed in 1755 by a terrible earthquake.

## CRIME AND SAFETY

As it stands, Lagos ranks as a relatively safe city in Portugal. It's not as safe as some cities and towns we've previously discussed, but it's not overly dangerous.

The best advice we can give when traveling in Lagos is to be slightly more guarded than you would be in other parts of Portugal. Overall, we didn't feel unsafe while visiting Lagos, but that didn't mean we let our guard down. Also, be very careful walking alone at night.

## HEALTH

In case of emergencies, you can use the Portuguese medical emergency number 112 in a health emergency. Alternatively, you should seek assistance from the local authorities or your accommodation.

There is one major public hospital in Lagos:

- Hospital de Lagos

  - R. Dr. António Guerreiro Tello, 8600-315 Lagos, Portugal

**Pharmacies**

Lagos has many pharmacies operating throughout the city. In Lagos you will find one 24/7 pharmacy:

- Farmácia Ribeiro Lopes

  - R. Garrett 22, 8600-740 Lagos, Portugal

Otherwise you can make use of the numerous other pharmacies during standard operating hours of 8:30/9 a.m. - 8 p.m.

## RESTAURANTS TO TRY WHILE IN LAGOS

Thankfully, Portugal is consistent when it comes to food, and Lagos is no exception in offering excellent traditional Portuguese food. Here are some of the best restaurants to try in Lagos:

Please note addresses, operation hours, and prices are subject to change.

**Quintal do Peixe**

*Bairro 1º de Maio 19, 8600-315 Lagos, Portugal*

$$

Enjoy a nice casual meal at Quintal do Peixe. It's a charming seafood spot in Lagos that offers fresh and delicious food. Stocked with stunning local wines and beers (as well as international offerings), this seafood restaurant is worth visiting while touring the area. The golden fish burger is one of their best offerings.

**Operating Hours:**

Monday - Sunday: 12:00 - 10:00 p.m.

**Jukebox Tapas & Meals**

*R. Soeiro da Costa 40A, 8600-624 Lagos, Portugal*

$

While Jukebox Tapas & Meals isn't the nicest-looking restaurant in Lagos, it's still a great spot for some quality, inexpensive food. All the classics are here, like meatballs, piri piri prawns, fried chorizo, pork cheek, and more. There's something for everyone, from sandwiches and burgers to tapas.

**Operating Hours:**

Monday: Closed

Tuesday - Saturday: 6:30 p.m. - 10:00 p.m.

Sunday:6:00 p.m. - 10:00 p.m.

**Bar Quim**

*Q.ta da Praia 15, 8600-315 Lagos, Portugal*

$

Another inexpensive dining option is Bar Quim. Located on the beachfront with some tables existing on the sand, it's a beautiful place for a delicious meal and maybe some drinks. Of course, the biggest downside of Bar Quim is that it closes relatively early, but get there in the late afternoon, and you're in for a great time. The house special is the prawns, which come in a pan with garlic, coriander, olive oil, and some lemon, which pairs well with some rustic bread for the leftover sauce. It's a house specialty for a reason—it's delicious.

**Operating Hours:**

Monday - Saturday: 9:00 a.m. - 7:00 p.m.

Sunday: Closed

**Avenida**

*Av. dos Descobrimentos 53, 8600-645 Lagos, Portugal*

$$$$

Looking for something a bit more upscale? Well, Avenida—a Michelin Star restaurant—is the place to be for a fancy dinner. Be warned, they've got a strict dress code of smart casual and don't allow kids under twelve. The experience you get at Avenida is unforgettable. First of all, it's a lovely restaurant located in the Hotel Avenida. Second, the food is to die for. Their catch of the day and six-course tasting menu are among the highlights. Sadly it's not a lunch spot, but perfect for dinner or a nice breakfast.

**Operating Hours:**

Monday - Sunday: 8:00 - 11:00 a.m. (Breakfast)

7:00 - 10:00 p.m. (Dinner)

**Tasca Jota**

*R. Salgueiro Maia 8, 8600-620 Lagos, Portugal*

$$$

Serving up traditional Portuguese food with a modern twist, Tasca Jota is yet another great offering in the Lagos food scene. The restaurant is a combination of wooden beamed ceilings and stone floors, all complemented by a friendly, knowledgeable staff. Despite being helmed by a young team, the food and service are excellent. Some of the highlights include tapas, their signature dish of pork belly, and their homemade bread.

**Operating Hours:**

Monday - Sunday: 12:30 - 11:00 p.m.

## STREET FOOD IN LAGOS

If you're lucky enough to travel to Lagos in July, check out the annual Lagos Street Food Festival. It's an event not to be missed that offers tons of great street food options, drinks, entertainment, and more. For the days it's on, it runs from noon to midnight, and it's a constant party of food and drinks with great live music. Best part? It's free to enter. Of course, the food will run up the bill, but it's worth it if you can attend.

## NIGHTLIFE IN LAGOS

Lagos has a thriving nightlife scene, from great bars to more vibey clubs, that can keep you entertained. No matter what you're looking for, Lagos has you covered!

Please note addresses, operation hours, and prices are subject to change.

**Bars**

Here are some of the bars you can find:

- **Rua 25 de Abril Bar Crawl** - A Lagos hotspot for

nightlife is the beautiful Rua 25 de Abril street, where countless pubs and bars are waiting for you. You can find just about any type of vibe on this street, from the casual bar to an epic party. Get ready for a night of drinking, dancing, and ultimate enjoyment.

The bars to enjoy the most include:

**Mynt Bar**

*R. 25 de Abril 103, 8600-763 Lagos, Portugal*

$ - $$

Mytn Bar on R. 25 de Abril street is among one of the most popular bars in the area, thanks to their cocktails which are among the best in Lagos. The vibe is great and can often get a bit wild, and thanks to long operation hours you can enjoy most of the night in this great venue.

**Operating Hours:**

Monday - Sunday: 6:00 p.m. - 2:00 a.m.

**Zanzibar Lagos**

*R. 25 de Abril 93, 8600-763 Lagos, Portugal*

$

Get ready for massive cocktails at insane prices. Zanzibar in Lagos on R.25 de Abril street is incredible for so many reasons. It's a friendly establishment with a great atmosphere and low prices for quality cocktails. This is one of the best venues, not just on R.25 de Abril street, but in all of Lagos for a great night out.

**Operating Hours:**

Monday - Saturday: 7:00 p.m. - 4:00 a.m.

Sunday: Closed

**Aficionado**

*R. 25 de Abril 55, 8600-315 Lagos, Portugal*

$$

Aficionado is yet another popular venue on R.25 de Abril street with an extensive drinks list, great sangrias and cocktails, and a chilled party atmosphere that lasts into the early morning. They constantly have specials early in the evening and throughout the day to keep your party going all night long.

**Operating Hours:**

Monday - Sunday: 11:00 a.m. - 2:00 a.m.

**Nightclubs**

Here are some of the best nightclub options:

**InsideOut Bar**

*R. Cândido dos Reis 19, 8600-315 Lagos, Portugal*

$$

If you're looking for a place to get wild and enjoy cheap

drinks, InsideOut Bar is the club for you! This is by far Lagos' busiest venue for a party, but it's so worth it because the music is amazing, and they are open until the early hours of the morning.

**Operating Hours:**

Monday - Sunday: 9:00 p.m. - 4:00 a.m.

**Bon Vivant**

*R. 25 de Abril 105, 8600-306 Lagos, Portugal*

$$

A definite standout in Lagos is Bon Vivant, a rooftop party where resident DJs take over. You get killer city views, drinks, and great music.

**Operating Hours:**

Monday - Sunday: 4:00 p.m. - 4:00 a.m.

**Duna Beach Club**

*Pinhal da Meia Praia, 8600-315 Lagos, Portugal*

By day, this beach club is for relaxing. By night, Duna for partying. When the restaurant closes, the DJ takes over and brings an excellent beach party vibe.

**Operating Hours:**

Monday - Sunday: 12:30 p.m. - 17:00 p.m. (Lunch)

8:00 p.m. - 12:00 a.m. (Dinner + afterparty)

**Other**

- **Sunset Cruise** - If you want something more intimate, a sunset cruise is your best bet. See Lagos from the water during sunset for an incredible city view.

## FESTIVALS AND EVENTS IN LAGOS

Just like any place in Portugal, Lagos is filled with festivals and events that you can attend while visiting. Here are some of the most prominent festivals and events in the area:

**February**

- **Carnival of Loulé** - Much like the Carnivals thrown across Portugal and made famous in Brazil, this is Lagos' take on the event. Three days of parades, floats, a Gala Ball, and more. Be prepared to dress accordingly.

**August**

- **Lagos Sunset Color Party (Youth Party)** - Enjoy a party with great music, food, and color. You pay a small fee to get in and get a colorful powder bag which you release whenever you want throughout the event, creating a splendid sight of colors. It's a delightful experience.

**August**

- **Fashion Fair** - A fun experience to have is attending the Lagos Fashion Fair. See up-and-coming designers showcase beautiful clothes in a multicultural environment.

**December**

- **Christmas** - Like any town or city in Portugal, Lagos takes Christmas very seriously. The city becomes a colorful Christmas wonderland. There are festivals celebrating the occasion, making it even more special.

- **New Years** - Time to ring in the New Year with a party which Lagos is more than happy to provide.

## TOURIST SPOTS AND ACTIVITIES IN LAGOS

Let's look at all the places you need to visit and activities you should do:

- **Ponta da Piedade** - Portugal is home to some of the world's most beautiful beaches, and Ponta da Piedade is no exception. It's a bit of a trek getting to and from this beach, thanks to the imposing cliffs and long staircase, but it's worth it!

- **Old Lagos** - The old city center for Lagos, here you'll find a bevy of historic buildings from the past still somewhat contained in the sixteenth-century walls. You can learn more about Lagos' history, both the good and bad.

- R. Lançarote de Freitas 7, 8600-586 Lagos, Portugal

- **Igreja de Santo António** - Across Portugal, magnificent churches and cathedrals are waiting to be seen by tourists looking to take in the history. Igreja de Santo António is one such church. It's a national monument with two bell towers, gilded woodcarvings, and paintings.

- R. Gen. Alberto da Silveira 1, 8600-594 Lagos, Portugal

- **Museu Municipal Dr. José Formosinho** - With a detailed account of Lagos' history, this museum can teach you everything you need to know about this historic part of Portugal and its overall history. They even have a scale model of the city, which we thought was pretty cool.

- R. Gen. Alberto da Silveira 1, 8600-594 Lagos, Portugal

- **Zoo de Lagos** - The Lagos Zoo hosts over 350 species, most of which are birds in incredible aviaries. There are a lot of parrot species to see here. Some other animals include various monkey species, wild cats, turtles, tortoises, goats, lemurs, sheep, and more.

- Medronhal, Quinta Figueiras, 8600-013 Lagos, Portugal

- **Forte da Ponta da Bandeira** - Dating back to the seventeenth century, this fort was low profile from when the artillery was sophisticated for its time. It's a great place to visit to take in some views of the rocky coast.

- 8600-563 Lagos, Portugal

- **Marina** - The Marina has a lot to offer tourists. You can go dolphin watching, whale watching, go on boat tours, engage in water sports, and more.
- **Centro Ciência Viva de Lagos** - In the center of Lagos lies the Science Museum. This excellent museum details the efforts and discoveries which led to the Age of Discovery in Portugal.

- R. Dr. Faria e Silva 34, 8600-734 Lagos, Portugal

- **Praia de Dona Ana** - This is the closest beach to Lagos' old city center. It's a stunning beach with incredible cliffs, golden sands, and calm waters. The beach is also very spacious, which makes it even better.

- 8600-315 Lagos, Portugal

- **Praia do Camilo** - Neighboring Praia da Piedade, this beautiful cove at the foot of striking cliffs offers calm waters, natural tunnels, and coves. It's a bit of a walk down as you'll need to take the 200-step staircase down to get to the golden sands.

- 8600-544 Lagos, Portugal

## HIDDEN GEMS IN LAGOS

While there are many places tourists love to frequent, some seem to go under the radar. Here are some of our favorite hidden gems:

- **Benagil Caves** - This is an incredible place to see when in Lagos. You can see them from a coastal hike above, on a boat tour, or go inside on foot.

- 8400-401 Lagoa, Portugal

- **Monchique** - Visit the town of Monchique, which is almost stuck in time. Rich with culture and history, it's a beautiful place to visit. While you're there, you might as well go to Foia, which is ten minutes away and is the highest point in the entire Algarve region, and has impressive views of the surrounding areas.

- **Rota Vicentina** - If you're looking for an epic hike, the Rota Vicentina is the perfect coastal hike to take. Spanning over 280 miles, you'll see the most dazzling views of the coast.

- Av. Teófilo da Trindade Nr 6, 7630-124 Odemira, Portugal

- **Sagres** - This village on the Algarve's western edge is made better by raging seas, massive cliffs, and a windswept landscape. It's a popular destination amongst brave surfers, but the village is a great place to visit and see.
- **Cabo Sao Vincente** - Not far from Sagres is Cabo Sao Vincente. It lies in a rather dramatic and barren region. It's a small village, but its positioning makes it incredibly beautiful.

## HOW LONG SHOULD YOU STAY IN LAGOS?

While this question's answer is entirely up to you, we think you should spend at least three days in Lagos to fully experience everything the area offers. Over the past few decades, Lagos has become a true tourist destination and resort town, all without losing the city's traditional charm and historic value.

For the most part, this is a city where you do a lot of walking around. You can take taxis or rent a car, but otherwise, there aren't public methods of transportation to get around. To get to Lagos, you're either going to take a bus or train unless you're traveling in a rented car.

Here's a sample itinerary for a three-day trip to Lagos:

**Day 1**

- Visit the stunning center of Lagos, where you'll find numerous historic buildings and monuments.
- Visit Forte da Ponta da Bandeira.
- For the afternoon, after the historic center and some lunch, we suggest heading to Ponta da Piedade to explore the area by foot or take a boat tour (which leaves from the Marina).

**Day 2**

- Visit Zoo de Lagos and see all the roughly 350 different types of animals.
- Go on a coastal hike and take in the gorgeous sights of Lagos' natural side.
- Spend the afternoon relaxing on the beaches of Lagos.

**Day 3**

- Visit the village of Burgau, Sagres, or Praia da Luz, which are all charming villages on the outskirts of the

city. Depending on your time management, you might even be able to visit them all.
- If you have time, go surfing, dolphin watching, or jet skiing.

## TAKEAWAY

The Algarve Region has so much to offer tourists. Lagos and Faro are the perfect places to get a taste of the region, thanks to their access to surrounding historic towns and villages. You'll be able to explore a lot of the region by using these two destinations as hubs and taking some day trips here and there.

Our next destination takes us all the way to the other side of Portugal. Traveling by train takes over eight hours; traveling by car is better, but not by much, at nearly six hours. Still, the oldest city in Portugal is the other side of that journey: Braga.

# CHAPTER 12
# BRAGA

> "Portuguese is cheerful and sweet, like a language of birds."
>
> PAULO RÓNAI

From the Algarve to the other side of the country in northern Portugal lies Braga. This is Portugal's oldest and perhaps its most interesting city, home to over 193,000 people. Why is it so interesting? Well, for starters, it's the happiest city in Portugal and the third happiest city in Europe. That's an incredible achievement. Braga's history is extremely interesting, considering it's the oldest city in the country; it goes without saying there's a lot of history within the walls of this city.

In this chapter, we will explore Braga and everything it offers tourists. Maybe along the way, we'll piece together why this is the happiest city in Portugal.

## HISTORY AND CULTURE OF BRAGA

Braga has over 2,000 years of history, meaning it has many stories to tell. Originally founded in 16 BCE by the Romans, the city was called Bracara Augusta to honor the Roman emperor Cesar Augusto. Of course, there were inhabitants in the region long before the Romans came to town.

Throughout the history of Braga, it was conquered and reconquered numerous times before D. Agonso IV, the king of Leon, donated Braga to his daughter as a dowry. You can see much of this rich history on just about every street, from the monuments to the churches and cathedrals. Countless architectural styles from throughout history are on display.

Braga is particularly known for its religious tourism. Not only is this the oldest city in Portugal, but it's among the oldest Christian cities in the world. Holy Week in Braga is celebrated by Christians far and wide as they pour into the city to celebrate.

There are countless places in Braga where you can further explore the rich history of the city:

- Museum of Costume Dr. Gonçalo Sampaio

  - Rua do Raio, nº2, 4710-925 Braga, Portugal

- Palácio do Raio - Interpretive Center Memories of the Mercy of Braga

 - Braga Norte 920, 4700-327 Braga, Portugal

- Museum of the Biscainhos

 - R. dos Biscaínhos s/n, 4700-415 Braga, Portugal

- Monastery of S. Martinho de Tibães

 - Monastery of S. Martinho de Tibães

- Museum Pio XII

 - Largo de Santiago 47, 4700-039 Braga, Portugal

## CRIME AND SAFETY

Braga is considered a safe city to visit in Portugal. Considering they're so happy, you'd hope that translates into low crime stats. Portugal is lucky when it comes to crime and safety because it's relatively safe overall, making it a great place for tourists to vacation regardless of where they choose to visit.

Like any city in Portugal, you want to still be on your guard. Crime is low in general, but it's far from non-existent. So, just be cautious of certain situations and avoid leaving valuable items unattended.

## HEALTH

Remember that you can use the Portuguese medical emergency number 112 in a health emergency. Other options include seeking assistance from the local authorities or your accommodation.

There is one major public hospital in Braga:

- Hospital de Braga

  - R. das Comunidades Lusíadas 133, Braga, Portugal

**Pharmacies**

Numerous pharmacies in Braga operate along standard business hours of 8:00 a.m. - 8:30 p.m. (sometimes later). There's also one 24/7 pharmacy should you need something in an emergency.

- Farmácia Braga

  - Av. Frei Bartolomeu dos Mártires, 4715-384 Braga, Portugal

## FOOD TO TRY WHILE IN BRAGA

Braga is home to several dishes which are special to the city. Here are some of the dishes you should seek out and try while visiting:

**Pudim À Abade De Priscos**

Portugal is home to numerous desserts that have originated within its borders. Pudim à Abade de Priscos is a Braga original. The dessert is a simple yet rich crème caramel pudding served best with black coffee or espresso.

**Fidalguinhos**

This is another dessert popular in Braga. It's a cookie, but it's not just any old cookie. The Braga original features a cross-legged design, which was done intentionally to represent noblemen who didn't need to work to get ahead in life back in the day. This cookie is crunchy, delicious, and addictive.

**Bacalhau À Braga**

A popular dish in Portugal is cod (bacalhau). One of the popular variations of bacalhau is serving it with sliced potatoes, roast peppers, onions, and olive oil. The potatoes are cooked to resemble crisps, and they make the dish just that much better. While these ingredients don't seem like they should work together, they do.

**Tibias de Braga**

Another regional sweet treat, Tibias de Braga, is more difficult to find compared to Pudim À Abade De Priscos and Fidalguinhos. This dessert gains its name from its distinct look, which resembles the tibia bone. The pastry is a crunchy dough filled with sweet cream and sprinkled with sugar. If you can find one, you'll die and go to heaven.

## RESTAURANTS TO TRY WHILE IN BRAGA

While visiting Braga, you're going to get hungry. Thankfully, Braga is home to some incredible restaurants ready to take you in and feed you some amazing traditional food. Here are some of our favorites:

Please note addresses, operation hours, and prices are subject to change.

**Dona Júlia**

*Estr. Via Falperra EN 309, 4715-390 Braga, Portugal*

$$$

At Dona Júlia, you get a rather interesting experience. Each room in the restaurant is a different color, with there being Red, Blue, and Green rooms, along with a terrace. This restaurant was built into an existing structure, so they ran with this. They made it exist perfectly in the space and combined a rustic and modern design. The food is fresh and consists of numerous dishes. You'll be hard-pressed to find something unenjoyable on the menu.

**Operating Hours:**

Monday: 12:30 p.m. - 3:00 p.m. (Lunch)

7:30 p.m. - 10:30 p.m. (Dinner)

Monday: Closed

Tuesday - Saturday: 12:30 p.m. - 3:00 p.m. (Lunch)

7:30 p.m. - 10:30 p.m. (Dinner)

Sunday: 12:30 p.m. - 3:00 p.m. (Lunch Only)

**Michizaki**

*R. Dom Frei Caetano Brandão 169, 4700-031 Braga, Portugal*

$$

If you're tapped out when it comes to Portuguese food and want something different, then you need to head to Michizaki. This traditional Japanese restaurant is as far away from Portuguese food as you can get. Offering interesting, fresh, and delicious dishes, it's so much more than sushi on offer.

**Operating Hours:**

Sunday - Monday: Closed

Tuesday - Thursday: 12:00 p.m. - 2:30 p.m. (Lunch)

7:00 p.m. - 10:00 p.m. (Dinner)

Friday - Saturday: 12:00 p.m. - 2:30 p.m. (Lunch)

7:00 p.m. - 10:30 p.m. (Dinner)

**Centurium**

*Av. Central 134, 4710-299 Braga, Portugal*

$$

Looking for something classic and chic? Centurium is a stunning restaurant serving beautiful traditional Portuguese dishes ranging from seafood to various types of meat. The servings are generous and delicious, with a sizeable selection of Portuguese wines. You can find Centurium next to the city's historical center, open for lunch and dinner.

**Operating Hours:**

Sunday - Monday: Closed

Tuesday - Saturday: 12:00 p.m. - 3:00 p.m. (Lunch)

7:00 p.m. - 10:00 p.m. (Dinner)

**Retrokitchen**

*R. do Anjo 96, 4700-867 Braga, Portugal*

$ - $$

If you want something exciting and unpredictable, you need to venture to Retrokitchen. It serves traditional Portuguese food, but the menu constantly changes, so recommending a dish is futile. It's a simple-looking restaurant that you'd likely walk past if you weren't being told to try it. There's a distinct vintage feel to the venue with wooden chairs and tables, yet the decorations take a more modern approach.

**Operating Hours:**

Sunday - Monday: Closed

Tuesday - Saturday: 12:30 p.m. - 2:30 p.m. (Lunch)

8:00 p.m. - 11:00 p.m. (Dinner)

**Restaurante Bem-me-quer**

*Campo das Hortas 6, 4700-210 Braga, Portugal*

$$ - $$$

At Bem-me-quer, you get one of the most aesthetically pleasing restaurants and a taste of traditional Minho food. The restaurant is cozy and rustic, with striking surroundings only aiding in the overall beauty of the venue. The food and service are amazing, among the best in the city. It's easily one of Braga's finest venues.

**Operating Hours:**

Monday - Wednesday: 12:00 p.m. - 3:00 p.m. (Lunch)

7:00 p.m. - 10:00 p.m. (Dinner)

Thursday: Closed

Friday - Saturday:12:00 p.m. - 3:00 p.m. (Lunch)

7:00 p.m. - 10:00 p.m. (Dinner)

Sunday:12:00 p.m. - 3:00 p.m. (Lunch Only)

**Insólito**

*R. Cândido de Oliveira 1115, 4715-213 Braga, Portugal*

$$

One of Braga's finest, Insólito is well known for its numerous cod dishes and excellent presentation. Every day, they offer up different dishes off-menu that are amazing and don't disappoint. The menu is filled with great options, too, with seafood and meat options ready to be devoured. The restaurant has a very standard look about it, with nothing overly extravagant on display, but the food more than makes up for it thanks to its stylish and well-thought-out presentation.

**Operating Hours:**

Monday: Closed

Tuesday - Sunday: 12:00 p.m. - 3:30 p.m. (Lunch)

7:00 p.m. - 11:00 p.m. (Dinner)

## STREET FOOD IN BRAGA

When it comes to street food in Braga, many of the restaurants above could apply. However, here are some places where street food is truly served:

**Praça - City Market**

*Praça do Comércio, 4700-370 Braga, Portugal*

$ - $$$

If you're looking for an authentic street food offering in Braga, then Praça City Market is the place to be. It's got tons of great food stalls, fresh produce, and drinks. There are even shops that sell wine for $1, and it's great wine, not the kind of wine you'd expect to get for a dollar.

**Operating Hours:**

Sunday - Monday: Closed

Tuesday - Friday: 7:00 a.m. - 5:00 p.m.

Saturday: 7:00 a.m. - 2:00 p.m.

**Mercado Bacalhoeiro**

*R. Dr. Carlos Lloyd Braga 47, 4715-363 Braga, Portugal*

$ - $$$

Another market you can try is Mercado Bacalhoeiro. It's nowhere near the same as Praça - City Market, considering it's far smaller with fewer options. However, it's still a great place to visit for good food, fresh goods, and great products.

**Operating Hours:**

Sunday - Monday: Closed

Tuesday - Saturday: 10:00 a.m. - 7:30 p.m.

## NIGHTLIFE IN BRAGA

Braga is sure to have numerous places for you to get a drink and dance the night away. Here are some of the best bars and nightclubs in Braga.

Please note addresses, operation hours, and prices are subject to change.

**Bars**

**Sé La Vie**

*R. Dom Paio Mendes 37, 4700-424 Braga, Portugal*

$$

This café bar is perfect for a relaxed night of drinking and socializing. They've got an extensive drinks menu and often have live music. The vibe of this venue is very alternative, with Sé La Vie's interior looking like it's a proper tavern while the venue itself is modern.

**Operating Hours:**

Sunday - Thursday:2:00 p.m. - 12:00 a.m.

Friday - Saturday:2:00 p.m. - 2:00 a.m.

**Café-Concerto RUM by Mavy**

*Travessa do Carmo Edifício Gnration, 4700-370 Braga, Portugal*

$$

If you're looking for somewhere to start and end the night,

Café-Concerto RUM by Mavy is a great place to try. It's always got a youthful crowd within its multicolored walls. They've constantly got live music acts playing the night away. You'll find they've also got a great selection of drinks and food, none of which is overpriced. Overall, this is a great venue for a fun night out.

**Operating Hours:**

Sunday - Wednesday: Closed

Thursday: 9:00 p.m. - 2:00 a.m.

Friday - Saturday: 11:00 p.m. - 4:00 a.m.

**Colinatrum**

*R. Damião de Góis 11, 4700-028 Braga, Portugal*

$$

Drinks with a view? Yes, please! Colinatrum is one of our favorites, thanks to its stunning countryside views. It's a simple wood and glass café that's great for cocktails, late-night bites, and late-night drinks. It's the perfect place to enjoy a drink and feel totally at peace.

**Operating Hours:**

Sunday - Thursday:9:00 a.m. - 12:30 a.m.

Friday - Saturday:9:00 a.m. - 2:00 a.m.

**Domus Vinum - Wine Bar & Tapas**

*Largo Nossa, Largo da Sra. da Boa Luz 12, 4700-248 Braga,*

*Portugal*

$$ - $$$

Come to Domus Vinum if you want a vibey yet classy wine bar. The patio is lit by lanterns, Brazilian beats bring in that atmosphere, and the selection of wines is among the best in the city. If you want to add food to the equation, try the Spanish and Portuguese tapas; it's delicious.

**Operating Hours:**

Monday - Sunday: 7:00 p.m. - 2:00 a.m.

**Nightclubs**

Here are some of the nightclubs you can find in Braga:

**Lagers**

*R. da Cintura 49, 4720-333 Ferreiros, Portugal*

$$

Lagers is a great place for drinking and dancing. This venue opened in 1982, becoming the city's first modern nightclub and an instant success. Several stages are available with different types of music for everyone to enjoy. The only real downside of this venue is that it's only open two nights a week. You need to know that Lagers can host a ton of people, over 1,000, to give you an idea. So get ready for an experience unlike any other.

**Operating Hours:**

Sunday - Thursday: Closed

Friday - Saturday: 11:00 p.m. - 6:00 a.m.

**Lustre**

*Praça Conde de Agrolongo 115, 4700-312 Braga, Portugal*

$$

One of Braga's finest venues for a night of unrivaled fun is Lustre, the disco bar. This club has proper 70s decor, keeping with its funky theme. The DJs always play the best music to dance to, the drinks aren't expensive, and the vibe is off the charts. It's almost impossible not to have a great time dancing the night away at Lustre.

**Operating Hours:**

Sunday - Wednesday: Closed

Thursday: 9:30 p.m. - 2:30 a.m.

Friday – Saturday: 9:30 p.m. – 6:00 a.m.

## FESTIVALS AND EVENTS IN BRAGA

Here are some of the festivals and events that take place across Braga throughout the year:

**April**

- **Semana Santa (Holy Week)** - Holy Week takes place during Easter and is one of the city's largest events all year. It's a ten-day celebration filled with processions, activities, performances, exhibitions, and more.

**June**

- **Braga Romana** - This is one of their most important festivals, celebrating the city's heritage and its people. This festival sees Romana markets recreated along with processions and various entertainment performed in the style of their ancestors back in Roman times.
- **Sao Joao Festival** - The Sao Joao Festival marks midsummer and honors St John the Baptist. It's not a festival unique to Braga and is celebrated throughout Portugal and worldwide. You can expect a massive street party and feasts lasting all night.

**July**

- **MIMARTE** - This is Braga's theater festival, lasting the first half of the month with a heavy focus on street theater. Performances take place all over the city, showcasing Braga's artistic talent. Performances also take place at the D. Diogo de Sousa Museum, the Arcada, and Rossio da Sé.

- **The Braga International Folk Festival** - This three-day festival brings the city together to hear the tales of Braga's rich history. It's done with a musical edge, making it more engaging and enjoyable.

**September**

- **BragaJazz** - Enjoy some of the finest jazz in Portugal at BragaJazz, a festival that brings musicians from all over Portugal together to perform beautiful music for the people.

**October**

- **Music in the Fall** - Another music festival, Music in the Fall, takes place at several cultural buildings and is a collection of shows, musical performances, and exhibitions.

**December**

- **Christmas** - Braga goes all out for Christmas with decorations and parties galore. If you find yourself there the Christmas season, know you won't be disappointed.

- **New Year** - Just because Braga isn't the biggest city in Portugal doesn't mean they don't know how to party on New Year's Eve. The night is filled with music and dancing as everyone celebrates the end of one year and the start of another.

## TOURIST SPOTS AND ACTIVITIES IN BRAGA

Braga is home to numerous amazing tourist attractions that you should definitely try to visit while in the city. Here are some of the highlights:

- **Museum of Sacred Art** - This museum is home to a rich collection of religious artwork and other treasures. It's a great place to experience some of the history of the city and Portugal overall. It's located in the Braga Cathedral's treasury. Perfect for a two-in-one visit.

- 4700-424 Braga, Portugal

- **Braga Cathedral** - This imposing cathedral is a must-see in Braga. The Gothic architecture is incredibly detailed, and the Manueline towers have a galilee (porch) that offers impressive city views.

- R. Dom Paio Mendes, 4700-424 Braga, Portugal

- **Bom Jesus do Monte** - You'll spend a lot of time just looking at this impressive religious sanctuary in awe. The monumental staircase is breathtaking, both metaphorically and physically. Every inch of this sanctuary is beautiful and just a treat to tour.

- Estrada do Bom Jesus, 4715-056 Tenões, Portugal

- **Sameiro Sanctuary** - A short walk from Bom Jesus de Monte brings you to the stunning Sameiro Sanctuary. This shrine was built in the eighteenth century and was dedicated to the Virgin Mary. It features an insane view of the city, while the shrine itself boasts stunning archways and a massive altar. It's one of the most impressive shrines you'll ever see in all your travels.

- Av. Nossa Sra. do Sameiro 44, 4715-616 Braga, Portugal

- **Fonte do Ídolo (Idol Fountain)** - If you're looking for more Roman-era monuments, then Idol Fountain is perfect. The monument has been said to have likely originated in the first century BCE and became an important water source for the local population. There are numerous statues and signs that this was once part of a much larger complex. It's an interesting site to visit, without question.

- R. do Raio 379, 4700-924 Braga, Portugal

- **Capela São Frutuoso de Montélios** - This chapel is one of Portugal's oldest surviving Christian buildings and was originally constructed in the seventh century. The Moors destroyed it, and it was rebuilt in the tenth century. It's a unique building for numerous reasons. One is that it features pre-Roman architecture, which is rare. It's a stunning building and a great way to explore the city's history further.

- Caminho da Ordem, Braga, Portugal

- **Ponte da Barca** - Looking for a picturesque town? Then Ponte de Barca is perfect to visit. This market town features an incredible fifteenth-century bridge that really allows you to make an entrance. There are so many amazing things to see in this small town, like churches, monuments, architecture, and so much more.

- Located in Peneda-Gerês National Park

- **Lindoso** - In Lindosa, you'll find the ruins of an ancient castle and a collection of tomb-like stone granaries. They look like really extreme coffins and are raised above ground on granite legs. You can find tons of these on the slopes below the castle ruins and the small village below.

- 4980-020, Portugal

- **Bravães** - One of the most gorgeous things you'll see in the area is the Bravães Romanesque gateway. It's located in a village with numerous examples of Roman architecture and carvings. It's incredible and perfect for some amazing photos.

- Three miles West of Ponte da Barca

- **Antigo Paço Episcopal** - Once the palace of archbishop Antigo Paço Episcopal, the palace dates back to the fourteenth century and was enlarged several times between the seventeenth and eighteenth centuries. While a tourist attraction, it's not actually open to the public. Instead, it's university offices, a library, and archives. It's still a fantastic building to look at, even if it's from the outside.

- Praça Mun., 4820-142 Braga, Portugal

## HIDDEN GEMS IN BRAGA

Even Braga is home to some hidden gems that everyone seems to overlook when visiting the city. Here are some you need to know about:

- **Mosteiro de Sao Martinho de Tibaes** - This breathtaking monastery features some of the best examples of rococo interior architecture and a level of luxury not seen in many churches previously mentioned. It's located just outside of Braga, which is why it often gets missed when people are touring the city. Don't make the same mistake.

- R. do Mosteiro n.º 59, 4700-565 Mire de Tibães, Portugal

- **Castro de S. Lourenco** - This interesting ancient settlement on a hill offers a unique view into the history of early settlers. It's not much, and you'll likely only visit for a little over an hour, but it's fascinating to explore and understand Castro de S. Lourenco.

- Rua de São Lourenço, 4740-001, Portugal

- **Ecopista da Linha do Tâmega** - Ecopista is home to numerous hiking and cycling trails for you to explore nature in the Arco de Baúlhe area. It's a popular destination with locals, and it's time you see what all the fuss is about. Spoiler alert: The fuss is that this place is beautiful and peaceful.

- Arco de Baúlhe, Portugal

- **Toboga** - If you're looking for some great activities to take part in, then Toboga has exactly what you need.

They offer canyoning, e-bike, and guided tours across Braga.

- R. do Ribeiro, 4715-428 Braga, Portugal

- **Sanctuary of Penha** - Not only is the Sanctuary of Penha a symbol and beacon of faith for Guimarães near Braga, but it's also one of the most beautiful places in the region. A small chapel, exquisite architecture, and charming gardens make this one of the best religious spots to visit.

  - Varanda de Pilatos, Guimarães, Portugal

## MUST-VISIT NATURE AND BEACHES IN BRAGA

You'll find that in Braga, there's an endless supply of incredible green spaces and riverside beaches. We'd be here all day if we went through them all, but here are a few of the must-visit spots in Braga:

- **Peneda-Gerês National Park** - Without a doubt, one of the most—if not the most—beautiful national parks in Portugal. Peneda-Gerês is an incredible place to visit, home to endless nature, wildlife, lakes, and even historical sites. You cannot visit Braga without taking a visit to the Peneda-Gerês national park.

- **Parque de Lazer da Ínsua** - A great beach park to visit with the family, Parque de Lazer da Ínsua exists on a river, making it an ideal place to walk, explore, relax on the beach, and more.

- **Leisure and Picnic Park of Cunha** - If you're looking for a place to play beach volleyball, basketball, or football, this is the perfect park to do any of these activities and then some. They've got great facilities on site, like a bar, grills, tables, chairs, and just about everything you'd need for a great day at the park.
- **Monte do Picoto Park** - The park with the most activities might be Monte do Picoto Park. Here, you can enjoy paintball, mountain biking, mini-golf, shooting, tree climbing, and so much more. This is an extremely family-friendly park and is sure to keep everyone entertained.
- **Riverside Beach of Navarra** - This park is great for relaxing on the beach and has tons of opportunities for the kids to have some fun, too. From playgrounds to water activities, there's a fair amount to be enjoyed at the Riverside Beach of Navarra.

## HOW LONG SHOULD YOU STAY IN BRAGA

When it comes to how long you should be staying in Braga, I'd argue two days should suffice for a worthy visit. Getting to Braga is not that simple, but not as complicated as you'd think. Your options are train, bus, taxi, or driving in a rental car. However, options like train and bus can result in having to get on multiple journeys to reach Braga, depending on where you're departing from.

When you're there, you'll find that public transportation isn't the same as it is in cities like Porto, Lisbon, etc. You'll be doing a lot of walking, which is fine considering Braga's a very walkable city. You can take a bus around the city if you'd like. Depending on how long you're staying, you can get a tourist pass for unlimited travel. These provide unlimited trips and can come in handy when you're staying two or three days.

Here's what a two-day trip to Braga would look like:

**Day 1**

- See the insane Bom Jesus do Monte and marvel at its architectural design.
- Visit the Sameiro Sanctuary not far from Bom Jesus do Monte.
- Visit Peneda-Gerês National Park.

**Day 2**

- Enjoy Braga's city center.
- Tour the Braga Cathedral and Museum of Sacred Art.
- Visit the Capela São Frutuoso de Montélios.

## TAKEAWAY

Braga is one of Portugal's most historically significant cities and is worth visiting to understand the country's history better and to experience one of Europe's happiest places to be. It's an extremely interesting place that will leave you forever changed.

From Braga, we're heading to another pivotal city in Portugal's history: Coimbra. We will explore the university city and see what it can offer tourists, who most certainly aren't visiting to enroll at Coimbra University. So let's hop in our car, on a train, or on a bus, and travel a few hours down the coast to the river city of Coimbra.

# CHAPTER 13
# COIMBRA

> "Braga prays, Porto works, Coimbra studies, and Lisbon has fun."
>
> PORTUGUESE SAYING

A riverfront city and the nation's former capital, Coimbra is known in Portugal as the University City. Coimbra is a historical center in Portugal thanks to the heavy presence of archaeological structures which date back to the Roman and Moorish times.

Home to nearly 150,000 people, Coimbra is a diverse city with many students roaming the streets. Thanks to the rich history found on just about every street, the city has a lot of unique places to visit to indulge in the nation's earliest history.

Visiting Coimbra is an incredible experience thanks to everything it has to offer visitors. It's home to one of the world's oldest universities, Portugal's second-biggest library, and Coimbra fado music. In this chapter, we will explore Coimbra and all it offers to those wishing to visit this stunning riverfront city.

## HISTORY AND CULTURE OF COIMBRA

Once home to kings and queens, Coimbra has a rich history. It's the third largest city in Portugal, and while it's now known as the city of scholars and students, it was once the center of culture in all of Portugal.

**The Romans**

Nobody is saying that Coimbra's history starts with the Romans. Still, more often than not, we note the Romans as being the first significant instance of habitation in Coimbra. The Aenminium settlement was initially 10 kilometers south of modern Coimbra in the town of Conimbriga. Conimbriga was abandoned in 468 in the search for higher ground and people settled in Coimbra. Today, remnants of the Aenminium settlement in Conimbriga can still be seen in the archaeological remains.

The Romans played an important role in Portuguese history. In Coimbra, you can still see some of the numerous Roman monuments from their time in Portugal.

Visit the following monuments for a taste of Roman history in Portugal:

- The Aqueduto de São Sebastião: The last remaining Roman aqueduct. Many future aqueducts were built in its likeness.

  - Alameda Júlio Henriques 1887, 3000-393 Coimbra, Portugal

- Conimbriga: The ruins of this former Roman city still very much exist. You can visit the museum, see the ruins, and enjoy the historic atmosphere.

  - Conímbriga 3150-220 Condeixa-a-Velha, Portugal

**The Moors**

In 713, Coimbra was conquered by the Moors and became the thriving commercial center for trade between the Christian North and Islamic South. The Moors oversaw the city to gain tremendous wealth. Today, you still see the many contributions they made to the city. Mostly you see the street planning, arches, and the Arco de Almedina, which was once the city's main entrance. While Coimbra now is very different from the times of the Moors, even modern Coimbra owes much of its design and layout to when the Moors presided over the city.

Visit the following monuments for a taste of Moorsish history in Portugal:

- Arco de Almedina: It's not the most exciting monument, but it's ancient and impressively still standing, now integrated into the city.

  - 3000-180 Coimbra, Portugal

- Unlike The Romans, the Moors left a far more profound mark on the overall city of Coimbra. You'll find remnants of their presence far more frequently around the city, even in its very layout.

**The Jews**

The existence of Jews in Coimbra predates the Moors and even the Romans. However, they took up greater prominence during the Moors' occupation, considering the Romans banished them to the Iberian Peninsula during their rule in Coimbra. It's unsure whether the coexistence of the Moors, Jews, and Christians existed, but what we do know is that Jews were a well-integrated and essential part of Portuguese society.

The Jews often acted as translators between the Moors and Christians during the Moorish occupation. The Jews had a difficult time in Portugal when the Moors' reign ended and the Medieval Inquisition began. Jews were executed, their homes and heritage destroyed, and if they were lucky, they were allowed to leave the country alive or be forced to convert to Christianity.

Visit the following monuments for a taste of Jewish history in Portugal:

- Casa da Judiaria Velha: This is the first and oldest Jewish quarter in Coimbra. It dates back to the twelfth century.

- Rua nossa, R. Sra. da Boa Morte 24, 3500-197 Viseu, Portugal

- Patio of the Inquisition: This building was prominent during the Inquisition, as it was where over 11,000 Jews' fates were decided.

- Rua Pedro Rocha, Coimbra 3000-330 Portugal

**Modern Coimbra**

Today, Coimbra is like many modern European cities. It's retained many of its historical elements but has modernized in various ways through architectural expansion and contemporary influences. Thanks to the influx of students, both from Portugal and internationally, the city has grown in population, size, and prominence. Now, Coimbra is home to fantastic restaurants, bars, cultural events and galleries, making it a great place to visit all year round.

**UNESCO World Heritage**

While in Coimbra, you need to visit Coimbra University, which became a UNESCO World Heritage Site in 2013. The city of Coimbra was built on the mountains and hills the Romans found when they moved from Conimbriga. This meant that when the university was built, it was surrounded by a beautiful landscape, historic buildings, natural monuments, ancient villages, and more.

## CRIME AND SAFETY

The great news about Coimbra is that it's a highly safe place to explore. It's considered 1.5 percent safer than Lisbon and 18 percent safer than Porto, and those are considered safe cities. Coimbra is among the safest cities in Portugal, so put your mind at ease. Of course, this isn't to say crime doesn't exist; it's just less likely. The pickpocketing issue isn't anywhere near the problem it is in Lisbon, but it can still happen to you.

## HEALTH

Emergencies can happen regardless of how careful you are while traveling. You need to know what to do in case of an emergency. For starters, you need to know that the emergency number in Portugal is 112. You can also seek assistance from the local authorities and your accommodation.

In Coimbra, the primary hospital is Coimbra University Hospital. This is one of the country's best and most prominent hospitals, delivering high-quality patient care.

There is one major public hospital in Coimbra:

- Centro Hospitalar e Universitário de Coimbra

  - Praceta Professor Mota Pinto, 3004-561 Coimbra, Portugal

**Pharmacies**

Coimbra has many pharmacies operating throughout the city. Unfortunately, there are no 24/7 pharmacies available. So ensure you make all pharmaceutical purchases during standard operating hours of 8:30/9 a.m. - 8 p.m.

Finally, it's important to note that pharmacies in Coimbra are not 24/7.

## TRANSPORTATION

Coimbra is connected by an excellent bus network which can get you to just about any part of the city. Considering Coimbra's size, it's easy to walk around, but be warned that the hills can get intense. This is why it's not regarded as great for cycling.

Other modes of transportation include taxis and rideshare services. Still, these can get pretty pricey if you're one or two people traveling.

## FOOD TO TRY WHILE IN COIMBRA

Like every part of Portugal, Coimbra is known for its specific delicacies that you should try while in the area. Here are some of the most popular dishes in the University City of Coimbra.

**Pastel De Tentúgal**

One of the most popular sweets in Coimbra comes from the small village of Tentúgal, just 20 kilometers outside of Coimbra. These sweets, known as Pastéis de Tentúgal, are predominantly light and flaky pastries. The filling is made using sugar and eggs, with the outside of the pastry covered in powdered sugar.

**Pastel De Santa Clara**

Similar to the Pastéis de Tentúgal, the Pastel De Santa Clara is also a light, flaky pastry. However, the filling has the inclusion of almonds instead of just eggs and sugar. They come in numerous shapes and sizes and most often have a half-moon shape. They are considered the truly Coimbra version of the Pastéis de Tentúgal.

**Leitão Assado À Bairrada**

Coimbra is in leitão country, so you'll find that the most popular style of cooking is leitão style. More specifically, the Leitão Assado à Bairrada style. Most of the restaurants in Coimbra specialize in this style of cooking. So what is the Leitão Assado à Bairrada style? It's fatty foods that are delicious, salty, and great with a glass of wine.

## RESTAURANTS TO TRY WHILE IN COIMBRA

Coimbra is home to some amazing Portuguese restaurants that offer a variety of dishes. Here are some of the ones you need to keep an eye out for while you're visiting!

Please note addresses, operation hours, and prices are subject to change.

**Dux**

*R. General Humberto Delgado nº 448, Coimbra*

$$$

At its core, this is a traditional tavern. However, the owners of Dux restaurants have made them more modern in some of the elements. Dux boasts a stellar wine list populated with countless wines from around Portugal and the world. When it comes to the food, you'll find many traditional dishes and some that are more known internationally, like chicken tempura and numerous others. High-quality food, drinks, and atmosphere, what more could you ask for!

**Operating Hours:**

Sunday - Thursday: 12:30 - 3:00 p.m. (Lunch)

7:30 - 11:00 p.m. (Dinner)

Friday - Saturday:12:30 - 3:00 p.m. (Lunch)

7:30 - 12:00 p.m. (Dinner)

**Nacional**

*Rua Mário Pais, 12, 1.º, Coimbra*

$$$

In Coimbra's historic center, you're going to find Nacional in a building that looks super unimposing. Inside this unassuming building, you will be treated to an extraordinary culinary experience. Nacional is famous for its high-quality regional cuisine offerings. Some of the highlights include Nacional's old-fashioned duck and monkfish fillets.

**Operating Hours:**

Monday - Saturday: 12:30 - 2:30 p.m. (Lunch)

5:30 - 10:00 p.m. (Dinner)

Sunday:Closed

**Tapas Nas Costas**

*Rua de Quebra Costas, 19, Coimbra*

$$

A favorite among tourists, Tapas Nas Costas specializes in snack-like dishes. The restaurant itself is stunning, with walls of stone, comfortable chairs, and an exceptional ambiance. If you're lucky, when you go to Tapas Nas Costas, you might get to enjoy the live music coming from the streets. Some highlights from their menu include duck dumplings, codfish, and lamb. They've also got a great wine list, so you'll have a well-rounded experience.

**Operating Hours:**

Monday - Saturday: 12:30 - 2:30 p.m. (Lunch)

5:30 - 10:00 p.m. (Dinner)

Sunday:Closed

**Zé Manel dos Ossos**

*Beco do Forno, 12, Coimbra*

$

Operating for over fifty years, Zé Manel dos Ossos exists down a narrow alley in Baixa, almost hidden away. But thanks to an incredible reputation, it's always busy. It's a rather small venue with only seven tables, and often people line up to dine in this historic establishment, a testament to their craft. The food is delicious, and it's complemented by a warm ambiance.

**Operating Hours:**

Monday - Saturday: 12:30 - 2:30 p.m. (Lunch)

5:30 - 10:00 p.m. (Dinner)

Sunday:Closed

**Marquês de Marialva**

*Largo do Romal 16, Cantanhede, 3060-129, Portugal*

$$$

The attractive and fancy Marquês de Marialva is a restaurant to check out while in Coimbra. It resides in an old house that was restored to accommodate a stunning restaurant. There are a total of three separate dining rooms that all feature a classic and rustic decor. One of the dining rooms has an open fireplace, making for an inviting environment. The food is traditional Portuguese with a focus on the Coimbra region. The highlight from the menu is the baked cod done "lagareiro" style.

**Operating Hours:**

Monday - Saturday: 12:15 - 2:45 p.m. (Lunch)

7:15 - 21:45 p.m. (Dinner)

Sunday:12:15 - 2:45 p.m. (Lunch only)

## NIGHTLIFE IN COIMBRA

Thanks to a thriving student population, Coimbra's nightlife scene is vibrant and varied. You'll find a healthy mix of intellectual cafés, cocktail bars, clubs, and more.

**Bars**

If you want to get a drink with your friends and just relax, Coimbra has numerous bars perfect for such an activity:

**Coimbra Ó Porto**

*Urbanização Quinta da Várzea II, Lote 14, Loja 9, 3045-000 Coimbra, Portugal*

$$

If you want the best selection of Portuguese wines and brewed beers, Coimbra O Porto is the place to be. They've got a great tapas menu to go along with the drinks, keeping you well-fed and hydrated.

**Operating Hours:**

Monday - Saturday: 4:00 p.m. - 12:00 a.m.

Saturday:4:00 p.m. - 10:00 p.m.

Sunday:Closed

**Passport Lounge**

*R. da Couraça Estrela 13, 3000-433 Coimbra, Portugal*

$$

This rooftop bar is the perfect place for an evening drink. Overlooking the city and Mondego River, Passport Lounge a great place to go before dinner to get some amazing pictures and delicious drinks.

**Operating Hours:**

Monday - Thursday: 5:00 p.m. - 1:00 a.m.

Friday - Saturday:5:00 p.m. - 2:00 a.m.

Sunday:5:00 p.m. - 12:00 a.m.

**Sapientia Boutique Hotel**

*R. José Falcão, 3000-062 Coimbra, Portugal*

$$

Located in a beautiful boutique hotel, Sapientia offers great views, buckets of champagne, and the best sangria in Coimbra. See the courtyard of the University, the Mondego River, the Joanine Library, and more from this rooftop bar.

**Operating Hours:**

Monday - Sunday:12:00 p.m. - 11:00 p.m.

**Nightclubs**

If you want to dance the night away in the city of students, you're in luck. While Coimbra has a variety of clubs, these are our picks for the ones you won't want to miss:

Please note addresses, operation hours, and prices are subject to change.

**NB Club Coimbra**

*Rua Venâncio Rodrigues 9, 3000-409 Coimbra, Portugal*

$$

One of Coimbra's most popular clubs, NB Club Coimbra is known for its great dance floors and music selections. It's also known for keeping the party going till early in the morning. Some Coimbra students leave the club and head straight for classes. So, if that's not an indicator of how great the parties are at NB Club Coimbra, we don't know what is.

**Operating Hours:**

Monday:Closed

Tuesday:11:59 p.m. - 7:30 a.m.

Wednesday:Closed

Thursday - Sunday:11:59 p.m. - 7:30 a.m.

**In Club**

*R. Ten. Valadim 22, 3000-399 Coimbra, Portugal*

$$

Certainly not as great as NB Club Coimbra, In Club is a decent alternative. The drinks are well-priced, and the vibe is good and gets better with every passing hour. They've got a great selection of music and decent-sized dance floors. If anything, this can be a great start before heading to NB Club Coimbra later.

**Operating Hours:**

Monday: Closed

Tuesday - Sunday:10:30 p.m. - 4:00 a.m.

**Other**

Here are some other options you might want to consider that are outside of the realm of clubs and traditional bars:

**Café Santa Cruz**

*Praça 8 de Maio, 3000-300 Coimbra, Portugal*

$$ - $$$

The perfect place for intellectuals to go and hang out. Serving some of the best coffee in Coimbra, Café Santa Cruz is all about the atmosphere. They often have live music nights and other events, always keeping it fresh and interesting.

**Operating Hours:**

Monday - Saturday: 8:00 a.m. - 12:00 a.m.

Sunday:8:00 a.m. - 8:00 p.m.

**Praxis**

*Rua António Augusto Gonçalves lote 28/29, Santa Clara, 3040-320 Coimbra, Portugal*

$$

This gastro-brewery is a great spot for a summer evening. If you're looking for great food and a wide selection of beers, Prexis is the place for you.

**Operating Hours:**

Sunday - Thursday: 11:00 a.m. - 11:00 p.m.

Friday - Saturday:11:00 a.m. - 12:00 a.m.

**À Capella**

*Pátio Vitória 53, 3000-121 Coimbra, Portugal*

$$

Enjoy live music from some of the best Fado musicians in the country at À Capella. You can eat great food, enjoy the wonderful vibe, and relax while the music plays the night away.

**Operating Hours:**

Monday - Sunday: 6:00 p.m. - 1:00 a.m.

## FESTIVALS AND EVENTS IN COIMBRA

Just like any place in Portugal, Coimbra is filled with festivals and events that you can attend while visiting the area. Here are some of the most prominent festivals and events in the area:

**April**

- **Semana Santa (Holy Week)** - Taking place around Easter, this is the biggest religious event you'll find in Coimbra. Filled with celebrations and ceremonies, it's a lot of fun to experience.

**May**

- **Queima das Fitas (Burning of the Ribbons)** - Starting on May's first Friday and lasting eight days, the Burning of the Ribbons is an event organized and led by students. It's a party every day.

**June**

- **International Jazz Festival** - A weekend of live music by some of the world's best jazz musicians.
- **Coimbra Arts Festival** - This is almost an ongoing festival that takes place for a few months, where there are weekly fado concerts, conferences, cooking demonstrations, cinema screenings, theater shows, art exhibitions, and more.

**September**

- **Festa das Latas** - A whole week of cultural events, including concerts, sports matches, cultural activities, exhibitions, and more. This event is for welcoming new students to Coimbra University, and in a way, Coimbra, but essentially anyone can enjoy the festivities. One thing you shouldn't join in on is the festivities' end, because students dress up as animals and then are "baptized" by older students. It gets a bit wild. I've seen it once, and that was enough for us.

**December**

- **Christmas** - Celebrating in style, Coimbra becomes a wonderful place during Christmas, with decorations, festivals, parties, and markets marking this special time of year.
- **New Year** - End the year and start the next in style. Coimbra is known for its incredible New Year's Eve parties with dazzling fireworks and lively entertainment. It's a party that takes over the streets, leading to a thriving celebration.

## TOURIST SPOTS AND ACTIVITIES IN COIMBRA

Here are some of the best attractions to see when you visit Coimbra:

- **Velha Universidade de Coimbra (Old University)** - It's without a doubt the number one thing you should be going to see in Coimbra, as it's the central point to this city's existence. Transferred from Lisbon in 1537, this is one of the oldest universities in Portugal.

- Paco das Escolas, Coimbra 3000-370 Portugal

- **Arco de Almedina** - This will be a quick but important visit. The Arco de Almedina is part of the gateway to the original city. It has incredible historical significance, so much so that the city was built around it to include it for history to always remember.

- R. do Arco Almedina 45, 3000-116 Coimbra, Portugal

- **Conímbriga** - The ruins of the old Roman settlement before they moved to what is now Coimbra; Conimbriga is an important place in Coimbra's history. Now it's a great site to visit to explore that history. It's Portugal's most extensively excavated site from the time of the Romans.

- Conímbriga 3150-220 Condeixa-a-Velha, Portugal

- **Parque Manuel Braga** - This stunning park on the water's edge of the city is a great place to explore and take in some nature. There's also a Museu Da Agua which occasionally hosts exhibits, book fairs, and art exhibitions.

- Av. Emídio Navarro, 3000-150 Coimbra, Portugal

- **Mosteiro de Santa Clara-a-Velha** - Now nothing but stunning ruins, this former monastery on the south bank of the River Mondego was once a retreat for King Dinis' widow, Santa Isabel. She oversaw the church's construction, and she was interred there after her death.

- R. Baixo 57, 3040-266 Santa Clara, Portugal

- **Biblioteca Joanina** - Home to over 300,000 books from medieval times, the Biblioteca Joanina is a sight to behold. It's incredible. Located on the same grounds as Coimbra University, it's an easy place to visit and one you should definitely make the time to see.

- Paco das Escolas, Coimbra 3000-370 Portugal

- **Mondego River Cruise** - For a relaxing sightseeing experience, the Mondego River Cruise is a definite must. See the city in all its glory from the water and travel along Coimbra's ancient waterways.

- **Jardim Botánico (Botanical Garden)** - Portugal's most expansive botanical gardens, Jardim Botánico is a beautiful landscape home to over 1,200 species of trees and plants from around the world.

  - CC Martim de Freitas, 3000-456 Coimbra, Portugal

- **Igreja de Santa Cruz** - Featuring some of the most detailed sculptures and carvings, this church is one of Coimbra's best examples of its history. Dating back to 1131, the Romanesque church features a level of extravagance some churches dream of having.

  - Praça 8 de Maio, 3001-300 Coimbra, Portugal

- **Santa Clara-a-Velha Convent** - Who doesn't love a good convent? This gothic convent was only excavated in 2009. The ancient building is partially in ruins, but it offers a glimpse into the past with detailed histories in the museum.

  - R. Baixo 57, 3040-266 Santa Clara, Portugal

## HIDDEN GEMS IN COIMBRA

While the university is always a focal point for travelers, there are some places which get forgotten that we think you should go and visit:

- **Portugal dos Pequenitos** - Considered the oldest "theme park" in Portugal, Portugal dos Pequenitos is a playground with mini-models of the city's streets and buildings. Despite it being essentially a playground, it's still a great place to take in some of the city's history.

- Largo Rossio de Santa Clara, 3040-256 Coimbra, Portugal

- **Quinta das Lágrimas Gardens** - Surrounding the former royal palace, which is now the only 5-star hotel in Coimbra, the Quinta das Lágrimas Gardens are appealing and tragic. It's a stunning garden paying tribute to two star-crossed lovers with intense romance.

- R. José Vilarinho Raposo 1, 3040-382 Coimbra, Portugal

- **Patio da Inquisição** - Step into history to see the former headquarters for the Inquisition Court from the sixteenth century. Here you can see what's believed to be the beheading block, a grim reminder of this dark moment in Coimbra's history.

- Rua Pedro Rocha, Coimbra 3000-330 Portugal

- **Pet & Tea Cat Café** - While definitely not a must-see, the Pet & Tea Cat Café is a wonderful place to visit. You get to enjoy all the makings of a café, but cats are everywhere, and they love to cuddle. It's lovely, really.

- R. João Cabreira 4, 3000-142 Coimbra, Portugal

## HOW LONG SHOULD YOU STAY IN COIMBRA?

Coimbra is a city where you'll do a lot of walking. Thanks to its tricky terrain, it's going to be a rather strenuous walk at times. The city does have public transportation in the form of streetcars, buses, and electric taxis. So, if walking isn't your style, there are options.

Getting to Coimbra isn't complicated either; it's accessible by shuttle, train, car, and bus. When it comes to how long you should stay in Coimbra, I'd argue two days are enough to get everything you need out of the city.

Here's what a two-day trip to Coimbra would look like:

**Day 1**

- Visit the historic center of Coimbra.
- See the Quinta das Lágrimas Gardens.
- Take a Mondego River Cruise.

**Day 2**

- See one of Portugal's oldest universities.
- While at the university, be sure to visit the Biblioteca Joanina, Capela de São Miguel, and the chapel's bell tower.

**Ideas For A Potential Day 3**

If you want to extend your time in Coimbra to three days, here are some ideas of what you could do:

- Travel to the Gois Region and see the Schist Villages.
- Travel to see the ruins of the Conombriga settlement from Roman times.

## TAKEAWAY

Coimbra is perhaps one of the most fascinating cities in Portugal. It's a treasure trove of historical value with interesting sites and people. Thanks to its reputation as a student city, it fluctuates in terms of its business depending on the school year. Overall, it's a great place to explore and experience and one you should make every effort to see, even if it's just for a day.

Now it's time to take this trip across the water to the autonomous island of Madeira. We're going to explore everything this stunning island has to offer adventurers. There's only really has one option for getting to Maderia, the plane. So pack your bags and prepare to fly; we're going to the beautiful Madeira region.

# CHAPTER 14
# MADEIRA

"Madeira is a wine like no other. It is fine wine in extremis. Heat and air, both the sworn enemies of most wines and wine makers, conspire to turn Madeira into one of the most enthralling of the world's wines as well as the most resilient."
—Richard Mayson

Within the Atlantic Ocean, a ninety-minute flight from mainland Portugal, lies an oasis in the form of lush islands, a year-round spring-like climate, and a fascinating place to visit known as Madeira. You'd likely easily miss Madeira on a map due to its tiny size, but don't let that make you believe that this island chain has little to offer. This autonomous region is home to over 250,000 people, as well as dramatic natural scenery, tropical forests, towering mountains, incredible food, amazing people, and more. They also have Carnival, which is almost identical to the Carnival that takes place in Rio de Janeiro.

In this chapter, we will explore Madeira, and we will help you discover everything you need to know about traveling to this beautiful location. We're not focusing on one particular place but the entire island chain of Madeira, Ponto Santo, and Desertas, which make up the Madeira region.

We've got a lot to cover, so let's dive into the crystal-clear waters of Madeira.

## HISTORY AND CULTURE OF MADEIRA

Madeira has a long and rich history that even predates Portuguese times. Let's take a look at Madeira through the ages:

**Pre-Portuguese Times**

Before Madeira became a Portuguese territory, it wasn't well known in mainland Europe. Plutarch, the philosopher, once mentioned that upon his return to the city of Cádiz in Spain, he'd met several sailors who'd recounted a journey to two islands in the Atlantic 10,000 furlongs from the coast of Africa, which indicates these were likely Madeira and Porto Santo.

Its earliest history is primarily speculation, with there being beliefs that Vikings once came to the islands before Portuguese colonization. But with a lack of evidence, it's unclear what the truth really is about pre-Portuguese times in Madeira.

**Portuguese Discover**

In 1419, Madeira was discovered by the Portuguese through pure chance. It was a storm that forced two of Prince Henry the Navigator's captains to the island of Madeira, which they initially called Porto Santo. Following this initial discovery, less than a year later, an expedition was sent to populate the island, therefore claiming it under Portuguese rule.

In 1425, Madeira was officially made a Portuguese province as the population continued to grow. The majority of the settlers on Madeira were farmers, fishermen, and peasants from northern Portugal. Their reasons for leaving often stemmed from a lack of opportunities in farming due to the nobility owning the bulk of the farmlands, overpopulation, and the reality that Portugal had been ravaged by the Black Death.

During the fifteenth and sixteenth centuries, Madeira would become a mandatory port of call for all European trade routes, the home of Christopher Columbus for several years, and a prominent player in sugar cane production in Europe for some time.

**Seventeenth to Nineteenth Century**

When sugar cane production dramatically declined in Madeira, the region pivoted to producing wine. During the seventeenth and eighteenth centuries, Madeira's wine was considered the most popular luxury in the colonial western hemisphere. Commercial treaties with England increased in Madeira, meaning numerous English merchants settled on the island, taking complete control of the wine trade among England, the West Indies, and North America.

Fun fact: Madeira wine was enjoyed by the Founding Fathers in the United States and used to toast the Declaration of Independence.

The eighteenth century saw Madeira allowing the British Empire to occupy the island due to the Napoleonic Wars. They were allies during this war against the French, who attempted to conquer large swaths of the Iberian Coast.

At the end of the eighteenth century, when John VI of Portugal died, his son Miguel seized power from the rightful heir and proclaimed himself Portugal's "Absolute King."

Madeira didn't accept him as their king and held out hope for the rightful ruler, Maria II. As a result of this defiance, Miguel sent troops to Madeira and overwhelmed their defenses, forcing them to accept him as their king.

**Twentieth Century**

During the twentieth century, the Germans came to Madeira. Initially, they were building a hospital and were welcomed to the island. However, it was discovered soon after that they had nefarious intentions of colonizing Madeira when locals discovered guns and ammunition in barrels being taken to the hospital site. This caused a confiscation of all German property in Madeira and the halting of construction on the hospital (which was restarted in 1930).

Germany declared war on Portugal in 1916 during WWI. During the war, Germany attacked boats in Funchal harbor, destroying numerous ships and even some buildings located near the harbor.

Madeira during WWII was far different. There was always the threat of invasion, and Adolf Hitler even flirted with the idea on numerous occasions. In 1940, he issued a directive to discover the pros and cons of occupying Madeira and the Azores Islands. In the end, they managed to escape the war unscathed.

In 1976, following the 1974 Democratic Revolution, Portugal granted Madeira political autonomy. While it remained a Portuguese territory, it was free to have its own government and legislature.

## CRIME AND SAFETY

As it stands with most places in Portugal frequented by tourists, the crime in Madeira is extremely low. In fact, it's lower than most places in Portugal, with already few crime issues. Even crimes that might be on the minds of tourists, like pickpocketing, are rare. Of course, this doesn't mean you should act like crime doesn't exist. Remain guarded with your valuables, and be cautious walking at night, especially if you're alone.

### Scams

One thing to watch out for, especially in the Funchal area, is scams with taxi drivers overcharging you. Make sure the meter is operational during taxi rides to avoid taxi drivers making up their own figures at the end of the ride.

### Drugs

Madeira doesn't have a drug or drinking spiking problem. While drugs aren't openly sold, they are available in various circles. Drug possession in Madeira is illegal. Another thing to take note of is that there have been several reports throughout the years of cocaine in Madeira being cut with dangerous ingredients like crystal meth, speed, etc.

### Transportation

If you're driving in Madeira, get ready for a different world of drivers. Local drivers can seem rather aggressive in how they drive, but it's more because of their vast experience with the roads and how to navigate them. Be cautious of the roads in Madeira because they are winding and can get extremely steep.

**Hiking**

There is an insane number of hiking opportunities in Madeira. You want to ensure you're being careful on hikes due to water irrigation channels that are linked to hiking trails. There are numerous examples of these channels being dilapidated and hazardous. Also, make sure you're bringing enough water, a rain jacket, extra layers, etc., just in case the weather suddenly turns.

**Weather**

Overall, the weather in Madeira stays in a consistent spring-like state. The sun can sometimes be more intense than you're used to, so sunscreen is a must. Additionally, the odd tropical storm can sneak up on you, and they're intense. Finally, when swimming, be careful of rip currents, which aren't common but are possible.

## HEALTH

Remember that you can use the Portuguese medical emergency number 112 in a health emergency, which works even in Madeira. Other options include seeking assistance from the local authorities or your accommodation.

There are three major public hospitals in Madeira:

- Hospital Dr. Nélio Mendonça (24/7 emergency services)

  - Av. Luís de Camões 6180, 9000-177 Funchal, Portugal

- Hospital dos Marmeleiros (generally reserved for severe cases)

  - 9050 Funchal, Portugal

- Hospital Dr. João de Almada (generally reserved for palliative and elder care)

  - Sítio da, Tv. da Quinta de Santana, 9050-535 Funchal, Portugal

**Pharmacies**

While Madeira is stocked with pharmacies, it doesn't have any pharmacies that operate 24/7. So make sure you get what you need during standard operating hours of 8:30 a.m. - 8:00 p.m.

## FOOD TO TRY WHILE IN MADEIRA

Madeira may be far from mainland Portugal, but they share numerous similarities, and one such similarity is their love of fantastic food. Here are some of the best of the best food offerings in Madeira that you need to try while visiting:

**Espetada Madeirense**

This dish is made using beef cubes that have been placed on a laurel skewers. It's grilled over charcoal or wood. It's not necessarily anything special, but it's absolutely delicious. Cooked for just the right amount of time with the right heat level, it makes for tender beef served best with fried maize.

**Lapas (Limpets)**

Limpets are aquatic snails, and this dish is a Madeiran specialty. It's cooked in a frying pan and covered in butter and fresh lemon juice. Snails aren't everyone's cup of tea, but when in Madeira, right?

**Picadinho**

Served in almost every restaurant in Maderia, picadinho is one of the island's most popular traditional dishes. It starts with small cubes of beef, which are fried before being seasoned with pepper and garlic. It's served in a delicious sauce and surrounded by french fries. Some picadinho dishes use squid and octopus, but you're more likely to find the beef variation.

**Sopa de Trigo**

This is a wheat soup, and it's a dish that makes sense, considering Madeira's strong roots in wheat production. The soup has a gummy texture and is dense, featuring numerous vegetables and usually a type of meat. Every restaurant will have variations of how they serve this dish, but Sopa de Trigo is almost always on the menu.

**Bife de Atum (Tuna Steak)**

Tuna ranks as one of Madeira's most popular food items, and it's often enjoyed in steak form. All tuna served in Madeira is caught locally, and this dish prepares the steak in a marinade of garlic, salt, olive oil, and oregano. Most restaurants either serve it with boiled potatoes or fried maize.

**Cozido Madeirense**

This is Madeira's famous stew. It features salted pork, sausages, and lots of vegetables. The stew is then cooked over a wood fire in a large pot. Thanks to both the ingredients and cooking method, you're in for a hearty and delicious stew that's perfect for dinner.

**Carne Vinha D'Alhos**

While more traditional to a Madeiran Christmas, you can enjoy this dish year-round. Carne Vinha D'Alhos is a pork dish made using garlic, bay leaves, white wine, salt, and pepper, which is then left to marinate for roughly two days. When it's time to be consumed, it's fried, along with some lard and the marinade.

### Castanhetas

Yet another seafood option, castanhetas is a fish found in abundance along the Madeira coastline. This is one of the best seafood dishes around and is cooked simply with olive oil and salt. You can add some lemon juice to give it extra flavor, but this is a dish that won't disappoint.

### Cracas

These calcareous formations come from the rocks along the Madeira coast and are considered a snack packed with flavors of the ocean. This delicacy is definitely not going to be to everyone's liking, but it's worth a try, especially if you love seafood.

## RESTAURANTS TO TRY WHILE IN MADEIRA

Madeira is home to some of Europe's best restaurants, including several Michelin Star restaurants. Here's where you should be dining while visiting Madeira:

Please note addresses, operation hours, and prices are subject to change.

### Casal de Penha

*Beco da Ataíde 1, 9000-604 Funchal, Portugal*

$$

Casal de Penha is a lovely restaurant with sensational views and delicious food. It's the trifecta making for a great experience. It's family-owned and operated and boasts an authentic menu of Portuguese and local cuisines. The seafood at Casal de Penha is a highlight, as it's fresh and cooked with tons of flavor. If the clams "à Bulhão Pato" are available, you should definitely try them as they're delicious.

**Operating Hours:**

Monday - Saturday: 12:30 - 2:30 p.m. (Lunch)

5:30 - 10:00 p.m. (Dinner)

Sunday:Closed

**William**

*Estrada Monumental 139, 9000-098 Funchal, Portugal*

$$$$

If you're looking for something upper-class and elegant, then William is the restaurant for you. This Michelin Star establishment is two stories and offers an authentic gastronomy experience with historical dishes made using the freshest local ingredients possible. William is one of Madeira's most sought-after culinary experiences, and it's easy to understand why.

**Operating Hours:**

Sunday - Tuesday:Closed

Wednesday - Saturday: 7:30 p.m. - 10:00 p.m.

**Villa Cipriani**

*Estrada Monumental 143, 9000-098 Funchal, Portugal*

$$$

One of Madeira's finest restaurants is Villa Cipriani. It's got some of the best views of the ocean, cliffs, and downtown Funchal. This elegant restaurant boasts stunning Italian cuisine, which is only complemented by the striking setting. It's an old-school restaurant with professional staff ready to make the experience as amazing as it possibly can be.

**Operating Hours:**

Monday - Sunday: 6:30 p.m. - 10:30 p.m.

**The Dining Room**

*R. da Casa Branca 7, 9000-088 Funchal, Portugal*

$$$

Located in a historic house surrounded by a lush, stunning garden, the Dining Room is an elegant dining experience worthy of your attention. It features a timely design in a stunning dining room with art, chandeliers, and beautiful decor reminiscent of the English. This all complements the menu, which has gorgeous, colorful dishes made with fresh ingredients. The menu's dishes are international, with a contemporary take on some classics. I'd recommend attempting to get a table on the terrace, as it's great for a warm night in Madeira.

**Operating Hours:**

Monday - Sunday:7:00 p.m. - 10:30 p.m.

**Vila do Peixa**

*R. Dr. João Abel de Freitas 30A, 9300-048 Câmara de Lobos, Portugal*

$$

Located in upper Old Town, Vila do Peixa is a great seafood restaurant to enjoy for lunch or dinner. It features large windows providing a gorgeous view of the city and ocean, and the food is fresh and authentic to maritime cooking in Madeira and Portugal. Overall, it's a great place to enjoy a meal.

**Operating Hours:**

Monday - Sunday:12:00 p.m. - 10:30 p.m.

**Il Gallo d'Ora**

*Estrada Monumental 147, 9004-532 Funchal, Portugal*

$$$$

Ill Gallo d'Ora is often called a culinary Eden, and considering its two Michelin Stars, it's most likely an apt description. Run by renowned French chef Benoît Sinthon, you experience a menu packed with flavors, fresh ingredients, and creative cuisines that look to capture the flavors of Madeira and the surrounding Atlantic. The menu features old dishes reimagined and new dishes invented by Chef Sinthon.

If you're traveling to Madeira, book in advance to ensure you get the chance to dine at one of the most incredible establishments in Portugal.

**Operating Hours:**

Sunday - Monday:Closed

Tuesday - Saturday: 7:00 p.m. - 10:00 p.m.

## NIGHTLIFE IN MADEIRA

Madeira has plenty of nighttime opportunities. Across the island chain, there's a thriving nightlife in just about every central area.

Please note addresses, operation hours, and prices are subject to change.

**Bars**

Here are some of the bars you might want to visit in Madeira if you're looking for a place to relax and have some drinks:

**Café de Teatro**

*Av. Arriaga, 9000-060 Funchal, Portugal*

$$

Join Madeira's artsy crowd in appreciating this beautiful venue. It's a stylish café that serves some fantastic cocktails. Sometimes, there are massive parties in the area, which Café de Teatro plays a part in hosting. This is why Café de Teatro often attracts such a young crowd. Well, that and their cocktails, of course.

**Operating Hours:**

Monday - Friday:8:00 a.m. - 12:00 a.m.

Saturday:9:00 a.m. - 12:00 a.m.

Sunday: 9:00 a.m. - 11:00 p.m.

**Museu Café & Petisco**

*Praca do Município 85, 9000-043 Funchal, Portugal*

$$

The venue with perhaps the most bizarre operating hours, Museu Café & Petisco is a great place to go for a relaxed evening out. They've got a great cocktails and drinks list and wonderful food. You can enjoy a nice meal before letting the night and drinks whisk you away into a state of pure bliss.

**Operating Hours:**

Monday:Closed

Tuesday:12:00 p.m. - 12:00 a.m.

Wednesday - Thursday:12:00 p.m. - 11:00 p.m.

Friday:12:00 p.m. - 12:00 a.m.

Saturday - Sunday: Closed

**23 Vintage Bar**

*Rua de Santa Maria 23, 9060-291 Funchal, Portugal*

$$

While 23 Vintage Bar is a great venue, its business hours aren't the best, seeing as they're only open two days a week. If you're planning a night of clubbing, this might be the perfect place to start your evening, thanks to a laid-back vibe, great cocktails, and decent prices. The outdoor terrace is highly recommended, and they usually have live music playing to enhance the atmosphere.

**Operating Hours:**

Sunday - Thursday:Closed

Friday - Saturday: 8:00 p.m. - 4:00 a.m.

**Trap Bar**

*R. do Favilla 7, 9000-920 Funchal, Portugal*

$$$

At Trap Bar, you can get great drinks in a great atmosphere that is often made even better with live music. This is one of the more interesting places in Madeira as it's open twenty-four hours a day on Fridays and Saturdays, which is highly unusual but perfect if you aren't looking to go back to the hotel. Keep the party going as long as you want, and let loose.

**Operating Hours:**

Monday - Thursday:9:45 a.m. - 11:00 p.m.

Friday - Saturday:24 Hours

Sunday: Closed

**Nightclubs**

Looking for a nightclub to really let loose? You'll find the best and majority of Madeira nightclubs in the capital, Funchal.

**Vespas, Marginal, and Jam**

*Av. Sá Carneiro 7, Funchal, Portugal*

$$

Home to three different venues in one, this venue holds Vespas, Marginal, and Jam nightclubs. Each has its own distinct style and music selection, meaning they cater to different crowds with ease. Vespas remains the most popular option of the three and in all of Madeira.

Vespas is where the younger crowd goes, Marginal is for techno freaks, and Jam is the classic pop music club where people of all generations come and party.

**Operating Hours:**

Sunday - ThursdayClosed

Friday - Saturday: 11:00 p.m. - 8:00 a.m.

**Dubai Club**

*Estrada Monumental 147, 9004-532 Funchal, Portugal*

$$$

Dubai Club is rather pricey. But, if you're looking for a great place to dance and enjoy an interesting vibe from all walks of life, this might be the place for you. During the day, the venue is far more relaxed, but as the sun sets and the hours drag on, the party gets started with local and international DJs providing a diverse range of music.

**Operating Hours:**

Monday - Tuesday: Closed

Wednesday - Sunday:12:00 a.m. - 6:00 a.m.

**Casinos**

Looking to win—or lose—some money? Here's where you can go in Madeira, where they will welcome you and your money with open arms:

**Casino da Madeira**

*Av. do Infante, 9004-513 Funchal, Portugal*

$$ - $$$

Part casino, part club, Casino de Madeira is a great place to get a taste of two very different nights in one. You can enjoy gambling for the majority of the evening before heading over to the club section to dance and celebrate your winnings or forget the losses.

**Casino Operating Hours:**

Sunday - Thursday:3:00 p.m. - 3:00 a.m.

Friday - Saturday: 4:00 p.m. - 4:00 a.m.

**Clubs Operating Hours:**

Sunday - Thursday: Closed

Friday - Saturday: 11:00 p.m. - 4:00 a.m.

## FESTIVALS AND EVENTS IN MADEIRA

Here's a look at some of the festivals and events that take place across Madeira throughout the year:

**February**

- **Carnival** - One of Madeira's best and finest events is Carnival. Styled after the celebration in Rio de Janeiro, this colorful festival brings beautiful music, dancing, floats, imaginative costumes, and a great vibe to the streets of the island.

**April**

- **The Madeira Flower Festival** - Every year in Funchal, the streets are decorated in dazzling colors and fragrances as a parade of flowers brightens an already colorful city.

**May**

- **Our Lady of Fatima** - Held on May 13 every year, this is a celebration and procession in honor of Our Lady of Fatima.
- **The Sé Festival -** Held in Funchal surrounding the City Hall and Cathedral, the Sé Festival is a bright and colorful celebration with music and great food just about everywhere you look.

**June**

- **The Atlantic Festival and Jazz Festival** - Jazz and classical music come together for this wonderful festival across Madeira in numerous venues every Saturday. Local and international acts serenade the people of the island and the tourists that visit.

**August**

- **The Monte Festival** - Another religious celebration. This procession honors Our Lady of Mount Virgin with a parade through the streets near the Funchal parish Nossa Senhora de Monte.

**September**

- **The Wine Festival** - Celebrating the Grape Harvest Season. This festival is a celebration of wine and, therefore, means a lot of drinking, music, ethnic food, and folklore.

**December**

- **Christmas** - A beautiful celebration of Christmas takes over December with stunning decorations and lights to bring the island to life. Madeira takes Christmas very seriously, like most places in Portugal, and as a result, it's a pure celebration and spectacle.
- **New Year's Eve** - Funchal is the place to celebrate New Year's Eve. It's a festival of lights and an insane fireworks display with parties in every corner of the historic city.

## TOURIST SPOTS AND ACTIVITIES IN MADEIRA

Here are some of the amazing tourist spots and activities you can find and do in Madeira:

- **Funchal** - No trip to Madeira is complete without touring the stunning capital of the island. It's Madeira's largest town and has so many wonderful things to see and do because of its long and colorful history.

- Funchal, Madeira, Portugal

- **Funchal Cable Car** - See the city above by taking the famous Funchal Cable Car. It takes you from the city below to the Monte suburb.

- Av. do Mar e das Comunidades Madeirenses, 9060-190 Funchal, Portugal

- **Paragliding and Snorkeling** - Whether you're up in the clouds or under the sea, some amazing water-based activities are waiting for you all along the coast of Madeira. Visit the Calheta municipality for the best options!

- Calheta, Madeira, Portugal

- **Museu de Arte Contemporânea** - Perched up high on a cliff overlooking the city, Museu de Arte Contemporânea provides a wonderful experience of seeing contemporary art and one of the best views on the island.

- Estrada Simão Gonçalves Câmara 37 Ilha da Madeira, 9370-139 Calheta, Portugal

- **Porto Moniz Natural Swimming Pools** - An absolutely incredible place to visit is the Porto Moniz Natural Swimming Pools, which are in the north-west tip of Madeira. It's a series of natural pools along the rugged coastline that make for a relaxing time looking at the ocean, crashing against the rocks. It's a fully functional location with great facilities to make this a purely amazing experience.

- Praça Do Lyra Vila De Porto Moniz, 9270-053 Porto Moniz, Portugal

- **Paul Do Mar** - This traditional fishing village is a great place to go surfing and experience a town almost stuck in time. It's laid-back and a great place to relax and enjoy some time in a quiet part of Madeira.

- Paul Do Mar, Madeira, Portugal

- **Miradouro da Ponta do Rosto** - A truly unique place that has the vibes of the Scottish highlands and Caribbean sea. It's spectacular and offers incredible views. From here, you can even see the planes approaching Funchal airport. Be warned, it's a bit of a walk at two hours one way.
- **Parque Natural da Madeira** - If you're looking for something breathtaking, then Madeira's most popular attraction is the place to go for an

unbelievable experience. Almost in the center of Madeira, this massive park is home to endangered species, stunning natural sights, coastal views, and more.

- **Pico Ruivo** - At over 6,000 feet, this is Madeira's highest peak and perfect for adventurers looking for a thrill. There's a trail that's about 3.5 miles and takes roughly an hour and a half to trek. At the top, you get views that will render you speechless. There are guided tours available, and there's no harm in packing a picnic for the top.
- **Monte Palace Tropical Garden** - This stunning venue is so fun to explore. It's high in the hills above the capital city and is home to thousands of exotic plants, various wildlife, and more. You can take the Funchal Cable car to the general area where the gardens are located, making it perfect for a combined experience. Even better is you can toboggan down, making for a three-in-one experience!

- 9050-288 Funchal, Portugal

- **Risco Waterfall** - While this natural attraction can get busy and is a far walk on a narrow path, it's worth it. The narrow cascading Risco waterfall is beautiful, complemented by misty spray, a crown of clouds, and a dense forest. Go early to try to avoid the larger crowds that go later in the day!

- **Cabo Girão** - This skywalk was installed in 2012 on a 580-meter-high cliff overlooking the coast of Madeira, Funchal, and the small pockets of farmland below. It's free and is an amazing experience for those not afraid of heights.

- Câmara de Lobos, Madeira, Portugal

- **São Vicente** - This stunning coastal village is straight out of a travel guide. It's a great place to visit and a place where you could stay for a while. The area has numerous activities, like climbing the tallest peak on Madeira for some insane views of the island, checking out caves, visiting the Caves and Volcanism Center, and more.

- São Vicente, Madeira, Portugal

- **Machico** - This city holds historical significance as the place where the first settlement was built in Maderia. It's also home to one of Portugal's most magnificent beaches: Praia de Machico. Visit the Museu da Balelia for an in-depth and unique look at the history of the island and city. But don't miss the beach because it's truly something special.

- Machico, Madeira, Portugal

- **Parque Florestal das Queimadas** - The island of Madeira is known for its lush greenery and intertwined relationship with nature. You can experience this on full display at Parque Florestal das Queimadas. This park is filled with stunning waterfalls, lush vegetation, mist-filled gullies, and numerous species of birds.

- Levada do Caldeirão Verde, Portugal

## HIDDEN GEMS IN MADEIRA

Madeira is a popular tourist destination, but even this island has some amazing places that seemingly get overlooked by travelers. Here are some places to visit that are perfect for a true Madeira holiday:

- **Prazeres** - The village of Prazeres is tiny, with a population just shy of 1,000 people. Still, it's such a wonderful place to experience. It's got perfect viewpoints to see a striking sunset, wonderful forests to walk through and explore, and some guided bike tours, which are really fun. It's often overlooked by tourists, but that makes it even better.

- Prazeres, Madeira, Portugal

- **Porto Santo** - This less-developed island is the perfect place to visit in the Portuguese archipelago. It's basically a massive stretch of golden sands, calm waters, and a handful of villas, hotels, and restaurants. It's a great place to spend the day to fully relax in the sun. The island is also home to some windmills and boat tours.

- **Palheiro Gardens** - In the hills of Funchal, the gardens of the Palheiro Estate are proof that nature, of any kind, thrives in Madeira. Previously owned by the Blandy family, who were major players in Madeira's wine history in the nineteenth and early twentieth centuries, it's now a place to see incredible variations of flowers in full bloom.

- Caminho da Quinta do Palheiro, 32 São Gonçalo, 9060-255 Funchal, Portugal

- **Miradouros do Paredão** - You can find this incredible spot between Pico do Areeiro and Curral das Freiras. This viewpoint offers incredible views of the natural beauty in Madeira and is often extremely quiet, making it an even more fulfilling experience.
- **Calheta Sugar Cane Factory** - In the village of Calheta is an old sugarcane factory still in operation, which takes you back in time to Madeira's history as a large sugarcane producer. The best time to visit is between April and May when the sugarcane is being harvested.

- Av. D. Manuel I 29, Calheta, Portugal

## HOW LONG SHOULD YOU STAY IN MADEIRA?

Madeira may be small on a map, but in reality, it's a big place to visit. You're not going to be able to experience everything this island has to offer in a couple of days. So, if you're traveling to Madeira, we recommend staying for at least a week.

Getting to Madeira is relatively easy. You can either travel via plane or cruise ship, both international and local flights. Getting around Madeira is best in a rented car, but there are other options like buses and taxis.

Here's a sample itinerary for you to use when traveling to Madeira for seven days:

**Day 1–2 - Funchal**

Explore the stunning capital city of Madeira: Funchal. There's so much to see and do in this incredible city, so it's perfect for a couple of days.

Day one in Funchal is going to look like this:

- Take the Funchal Cable Car up to the Monte suburbs.
- Visit the Monte Palace Tropical Gardens.
- Toboggan down to Funchal.
- Visit Funchal's old town.

On day two, you're going to want to do the following:

- Visit Santa Catarina Park.
- Enjoy wine tasting at Blandy Wine Lodges.

- Visit the Funchal Cathedral.

**Day 3**

On day three, you're going to explore the northwest parts of Madeira:

- Visit Boca da Encumeada
- See the Paul da Serra plateau.
- Explore the Fanal Wildlife Refuge.
- Visit Ribeira da Janela.
- Visit the natural swimming pools in Porto Moniz.

**Day 4**

On day four, you're going to explore Madeira's east coast:

- See the Cristo Rei viewpoint.
- Walk along the Santa Cruz promenade.
- Explore Santo da Serra.
- Head to the ocean and Pico do Facho viewpoint.
- Watch the sunset at the Ponta do Rosto viewpoint.

**Day 5**

Day five is for central and northeast Madeira:

- Check out the sunrise from Pico do Ariero.
- See the Balcões viewpoint.
- Visit Faial and explore the area.
- Visit the village of Porto da Cruz.

### Day 6

On day six, you want to spend a great day at Porto Santo Island. Here, you can do the following:

- Relax on the beach.
- Take boat tours.
- Go on an off-road 4x4 tour.
- Snorkeling.

### Day 7

On day six, it's time for a day of beachside enjoyment. Pick any beach and attempt the following activities:

- Dolphin and whale watching.
- Paragliding.
- Snorkeling.
- Visit the Cabo Girão for incredible views.
- Dine at the Fajã dos Padres, where the food and wine are traditional.

### Things to Do If You Extend This Itinerary to 10 Days

There are so many things you can do if you're looking to extend your trip to Madeira. Here are some ideas not mentioned in the above seven-day itinerary:

- Spend a day in São Vicente exploring caves and the coast.

- Visit the Machico village.
- Climb Pico Ruive.
- Go and see Risco Waterfall.
- See the village of Prazeres.
- Tour the Miradouros do Paredão.

## TAKEAWAY

Madeira is paradise. That's essentially its brand as an island filled with natural beauty at just about every turn. Even the cities are incredibly beautiful and in touch with the natural beauty, living in perfect harmony. Beyond the island's undeniable aesthetic appeal, it's home to tons of great sights, activities, restaurants, and nightlife opportunities. There's a lot of life to experience from coast to coast on the Madeira island.

Speaking of islands, it's time we head to a collection of islands known as the Azores Islands. This is another autonomous island in Portugal and it's another stunning and impressive experience waiting to be had.

# CHAPTER 15
# THE AZORES ISLANDS

> "My affection hath an unknown bottom, like the Bay of Portugal."
>
> WILLIAM SHAKESPEARE

Following Madeira, we're looking at the Azores Islands, another autonomous region in Portugal. The Azores Islands is made up of nine volcanic islands, which are divided into three main groups:

- Flores and Corvo (West)
- Graciosa, Pico, Terceira, São Jorge, and Faial (Center)
- São Miguel, Formigas Islets, and Santa Maria (East)

Across all nine islands, the Azores' population is over 250,000. What makes the Azores such a great tourist destination can't be pinpointed to just one thing. Some reasons may be the numerous fifteenth-century churches, majestic manor houses, vibrant blue-green lakes, volcanic craters, welcoming year-round climate (57°F - 71°F), and fertile prairies.

In this chapter, we'll dive deep into everything the Azores Islands offer, from the local food to the hidden gems. With nine islands in its collection, there's a lot to say!

## HISTORY AND CULTURE OF THE AZORES ISLANDS

Portuguese explorer Diogo de Silves rediscovered the Azores Islands in 1427. While it had been inhabited 700 years prior, It would take over a decade for the Portuguese to begin settling on the islands, starting with Santa Maria. In 1444, they began settling on São Miguel. At this point, they'd only discovered two of the nine islands.

Thanks to the positioning of the Azores Islands out in the middle of the Atlantic Ocean, the islands began to rapidly expand. São Miguel benefited heavily from wheat and sugar cane production, which was exported to North African garrisons. Later on, the production and exporting of oranges to the English market led to more wealth.

In 1450, Terceira was discovered. Terceira was one of the more pivotal islands in the Azores for numerous reasons. For starters, in 1580, Spanish King Filipe II sought to succeed the Portuguese King Henry, who had no children and no heir. However, D. António, a Lisbon native, was said to be the

Portuguese king's son. Terceira took D. António's side in this fight, leading to numerous attacks from the Spaniards who eventually occupied the island.

Around this time, it's said that the island of Graciosa was first seen. However, the exact year of its discovery and settlement remains unknown. From the beginning, the island was dedicated to agricultural needs like wheat, wine, barley, and aguardiente. Another island where the settlement date is unknown is São Jorge. We know that by 1442, the island was occupied, and its economy was focused on wheat and wine.

Come 1460, the Pico Islands would be settled, with their primary focus being wheat and woad, a type of plant used in the dying of clothes. At the time, the islanders were also prolific sperm whale hunters, but as times have drastically changed, this has not been practiced since 1987.

During the first half of the fifteenth century, Faial Island was spotted and, in 1460, was inhabited by northern Portuguese citizens. Various forms of agriculture and woad production were Faial's claim to fame.

Finally, in 1452, the final islands, Flores and Corvo, were discovered. Flores gained its name from the countless flowers found all across the island. Originally, it was settled by the Flemish Wilhelm Van der Haegen, but he later returned to São Jorge due to the distance between the islands. It was again settled in the sixteenth century. The island became a great place for agriculture, with barley, wheat, corn, and vegetables being their main production points.

## CRIME AND SAFETY

Overall, the Azores is extremely safe with a low crime rate. It's important to note that petty crimes like purse snatching and pickpocketing are uncommon but can occur. You must guard your valuables, avoid walking around with unnecessary and expensive items, don't have too much cash on hand, and remain vigilant, especially at night.

**Beaches and Swimming**

There are some things you should know about swimming in the Azores. Here are some tips to keep you safe:

- Don't dive in unknown waters, as you don't know if there are shallow depths or hidden rocks present that can cause serious injuries or death.
- Don't swim at beaches connecting to rivers because the current can be extremely strong.
- Don't visit any beaches or swim in the water when severe weather warnings are in place.

When it comes to the beaches, you want to know what the warning flags are:

Green = Calm waters

Yellow = Agitated Waters (No swimming permitted)

Red = Dangerous Waters (Not permitted to enter or swim in the ocean)

Checkered Black and White = Lifeguard currently not on duty

**Roads**

The roads across the Azores Islands are narrow and feature numerous blind corners and curves and even hidden driveways. It's important to be cautious while driving and don't go faster than necessary. At night, it's more difficult due to the lack of lighting and livestock wandering about the roads, so be extremely careful.

**Public Transportation**

Public transportation in the Azores is somewhat limited. You're likely going to be making use of taxis, Uber, etc. So, if you are traveling by taxi, be sure to have them run the meter and show you the recorded fare so they don't overcharge you. This is a common scam by taxi drivers when interacting with tourists.

## HEALTH

Remember that you can use the Portuguese medical emergency number 112 in a health emergency, which works even across the Azores Islands. Other options include seeking assistance from the local authorities or your accommodation.

There are three major public hospitals across the Azores Islands:

- Hospital of Horta (Faial)

- Estrada Princ Alberto Do Mónaco Angústias, Horta, Portugal

- Hospital do Divino Espírito Santo (São Miguel)

  - Av. D. Manuel I, 9500-370 Ponta Delgada, Portugal

- Hospital de Santo Espírito da Ilha Terceira (Terceira)

  - Canada do briado 9700-049, 9700-049 Angra do Heroísmo, Portugal

Please note that you need to contact your travel insurance provider immediately should you find yourself in a medical emergency. Any hospital across the Azore Islands will require an upfront payment.

**Pharmacies**

The Azores have numerous pharmacies across all islands in its collection. However, it doesn't have any pharmacies that operate 24/7, so make sure you get what you need during standard operating hours.

## FOOD TO TRY WHILE IN THE AZORES ISLANDS

When you're in the Azores Islands, you'll be treated to so many new and exciting culinary experiences, it's best you prepare yourself. Here are some of the dishes you need to try while visiting the Azores Islands:

**Bolos Lêvedos**

With such a rich history in wheat production, it's no surprise that one of the Azores Islands delicacies is a type of bread known as Bolos Lêvedos. This bread is best enjoyed after being cooked on a griddle and tastes sweet with a soft texture. It's divine and can even be enjoyed on its own, but add some cheese and meat to truly blow your mind.

**Cozido**

While available across the Azores, this is a São Miguel specialty. This is more because they cook it traditionally using geysers, also known as natural caldeiras. The dish itself is a stew of meat and vegetables that are stewed for a long time throughout the day using caldeiras. If you want to try it, we recommend phoning in to order it well in advance (24 hours) because it's so popular it sells out quickly.

**Alcatra**

This stunning braised beef is one of the most delicious things you'll ever taste. It's cooked for several hours and just falls apart, in the best possible way, when you look at it. It can be served in a variety of ways, but more often than not, it's served with potatoes, rice, and sweet bread.

**Red Bean Cake**

While this may not sound appetizing, red bean cake is shockingly delicious. Made using—you guessed it—red beans, this cake is not only delicious, but it's also moist. If you end up trying it, just know anything you think you know going in will turn out to be wrong. This shatters all expectations.

**Malasadas**

This Azores São Miguel original has become so popular that it's spread throughout the world. It's simply fried dough that's light, fluffy, and perfect for stuffing in ingredients like pineapple, chocolate, caramel, passionfruit, etc.

## RESTAURANTS TO TRY WHILE IN THE AZORES ISLANDS

Because there are so many individual islands in the Azores Islands, this is going to be a long list of restaurants. Of course, it depends on which island you're on. I've included at least one or two from every island in the collection:

Please note addresses, operation hours, and prices are subject to change.

**Michel Restaurant**

*Rua Eng° José Cordeiro Antiga da Calheta 55, 9500-311 Ponta Delgada, Portugal*

$$

This quaint restaurant provides dinners with a gourmet food experience at a reasonable price. You can enjoy some of the finest modern Portuguese cuisines with a fusion twist. The staff at Michel Restaurant are friendly and know what they're doing, making the experience much more eloquent. The biggest thing to know about this restaurant is that booking days in advance is recommended, considering it's a smaller venue that's very popular.

**Operating Hours:**

Monday - Wednesday: 12:30 p.m. - 2:30 p.m. (Lunch)

7:00 p.m. - 9:30 p.m. (Dinner)

Thursday:12:30 p.m. - 2:30 p.m. (Lunch)

7:00 p.m. - 10:30 p.m. (Dinner)

Friday:12:30 p.m. - 2:30 p.m. (Lunch)

7:00 p.m. - 9:30 p.m. (Dinner)

Saturday:7:00 p.m. - 9:00 p.m. (Dinner Only)

Sunday: Closed

**Lan's Pizzeria**

*Rua Manuel da Ponte 41 São Sebastião, Ponta Delgada, São Miguel 9500-085 Portugal*

$

Sometimes a simple pizza will do, and then there's Lan's Pizzeria that offers not only pizzas but dishes of Portuguese, Thai, and Italian origin. Even some of their pizzas have interesting twists to honor these cultures. Here, the aim of the game is something for everyone at low prices. They deliver tenfold. This establishment truly goes above and beyond to create a phenomenal experience.

**Operating Hours:**

Monday - Saturday: 12:00 p.m. - 3:00 p.m. (Lunch)

6:00 p.m. - 10:00 p.m. (Dinner)

Sunday: Closed

**Balcony Restaurant**

*Avenida Infante Dom Henrique, 113, Ponta Delgada, São Miguel 9500-770 Portugal*

$$$$

One of the finest dining experiences to be had in the Azores is easily the Balcony Restaurant. Located in the Grand Hotel, this restaurant offers stunning food, ocean views, and world-class service. Their menu is filled with contemporary interpretations of some of Portugal's most famous dishes. This restaurant is a perfect place to get some of the best food you can across the Azores.

**Operating Hours:**

Monday - Sunday: 7:00 p.m. - 10:00 p.m.

**Caffe 5 "Cinq"**

*Rua Carlos Dabney, Madalena, Pico 9950-327 Portugal*

$$

Caffe 5 "Cinq" is a cozy café/restaurant that serves a variety of traditional Portuguese dishes and a few standard international dishes. This level of options means if you're not a fan of Portuguese food, there are alternatives. Desserts are particularly popular at Caffe 5 "Cinq," especially the crepes. There's definitely something for everyone on the menu, so you'll be hard-pressed to not find something you like.

**Operating Hours:**

Monday - Saturday: 9:00 a.m. - 11:00 p.m.

Sunday: Closed

**Restaurante O Pescador**

*R. Conselheiro José Cardoso 11, 9760-411 Praia da Vitória, Portugal*

$$$

This is one of the Azores Islands' oldest restaurants and it's among the most popular across the islands, especially in Terceira. Serving high-quality authentic Portuguese dishes, this is a venue that knows what it's doing. The wine list is expansive, the staff is incredibly knowledgeable, the food portions are large, and the atmosphere is impeccable. Overall, Resaurante O Pescador is one of the Azores' finest restaurants.

**Operating Hours:**

Monday - Friday: 12:00 p.m. - 10:00 p.m.

Saturday: 12:00 p.m. - 5:00 p.m.

Sunday: Closed

**Gastro Bar Principe**

*Estrada Principe Alberto do Monaco Apartamentos Príncipe, Ground floor, Horta, Faial Island 9900-038 Portugal*

$$$

This modern upmarket restaurant boasts a great menu of modern Portuguese and European cuisines. Gastro Bar Principe is run by a host of international chefs, all bringing something unique to this wonderful establishment. They have a seasonal menu to take advantage of the best ingredients of the time but also to keep things new and exciting. Overall, this is a great restaurant to experience in Horto.

**Operating Hours:**

Monday - Saturday: 7:00 p.m. - 10:00 p.m.

Sunday: Closed

**O Branquinho**

*Ribeira do Belo 48, 9800-210 Rosais, Portugal*

$$ - $$$

O Branquinho is a great restaurant on São Jorge that serves up some of the best modern Portuguese food on the island. There's a focus on seafood, but that doesn't mean there aren't a hefty number of meat options, too. There's even something for vegetarians. The restaurant itself is comfortable and cozy, with a view into the kitchen. It's a great spot to enjoy a meal, be it lunch or dinner.

**Operating Hours:**

Monday: 12:00 - 2:00 p.m. (Lunch)

6:30 - 10:00 p.m. (Dinner)

Tuesday - Sunday: 12:00 - 2:00 p.m. (Lunch)

7:00 - 10:00 p.m. (Dinner)

**Ponta Negra Restaurante & Bar de Praia**

*Ponta Negra São Lourenço, S/N, 9580-114 VPT, Portugal*

$$

Located in the prime location on the bay and surrounded by vineyards, this venue is a stunning seafood restaurant that also serves a host of traditional Portuguese dishes. From beautiful views to delicious food, Ponta Negra is the perfect place to eat and relax in Santa Maria.

**Operating Hours:**

Monday: Closed

Tuesday - Saturday: 11:30 a.m. - 10:30 p.m.

Sunday: 11:30 a.m. - 9:30 p.m.

## NIGHTLIFE IN THE AZORES ISLANDS

Nightlife is going to vary across the different islands in the Azores. The good news is there are some specks of nightlife here and there, and these are the places you will want to check out!

Please note addresses, operation hours, and prices are subject to change.

**Bars**

Here are some of the bars you may want to visit in the Azores Islands if you're looking for a place to relax and have some drinks:

**A Quinta**

*Avenida Dr Manuel Arriaga, 9675-022 Furnas, Portugal*

$$

A Quinta is a chic bar with a heavy focus on connecting with nature. By that, we mean it's open-air with a roof and curtains separating you from the outside. It's a stunning venue perfect for a chilled evening of drinking and hanging out with friends or your partner. The kitchen is open most of the day, closing at 10:00 p.m.

**Operating Hours:**

Monday: Closed

Tuesday - Thursday: 12:00 p.m. - 12:00 a.m.

Friday - Saturday: 12:00 p.m. - 2:00 a.m.

Sunday: 12:00 p.m. - 12:00 a.m.

**Bar Do Pi**

*Av. Infante Dom Henrique, Ponta Delgada, Portugal*

$

Located on Ponta Delgada on São Miguel, Bar Do Pi is a simple, no-frills waterhole. It's a great place to get a drink because the drinks are ridiculously cheap, and it's open extremely late for a bar. Of course, the trade-off is that the venue isn't amazing overall. But after a few drinks, you won't even notice, so there's a bright side!

**Operating Hours:**

Sunday - Thursday: 2:00 p.m. - 2:00 a.m.

Friday - Saturday: 2:00 p.m. - 4:00 a.m.

**Blues Bar**

*Av. Álvaro Martins Homem, 9760-412 Praia da Vitória, Portugal*

$$

If you love music and drinking and wish there was a place to do both on the Azores Islands, welcome to the Blues Bar. Featuring musicians from around Portugal, the Blues Bar is a great place for a relaxing night out with great drinks and company. It's a stylish bar with great seating inside and out. Also, the Blues Bar's cocktails are pretty great.

**Operating Hours:**

Monday: Closed

Tuesday - Thursday: 12:00 p.m. - 2:00 a.m.

Friday - Saturday: 12:00 p.m. - 4:00 a.m.

**Lava Jazz**

*Av. Roberto Ivens, 9500-239 Ponta Delgada, Portugal*

$$

On São Miguel, there's a great jazz club, and even if you're not a fan of jazz, you will love this venue. The sultry music provides an incredible atmosphere, and combined with the amazing drinks on offer, it's sure to be a great night out at Lava Jazz. They've also got tapas, which are absolutely delicious.

**Operating Hours:**

Sunday - Monday: Closed

Tuesday - Thursday: 7:00 p.m. - 11:00 p.m.

Friday - Saturday: 8:30 p.m. - 12:00 a.m.

**Nightclubs**

It's a limited selection, but there are several options when it comes to nightclubs in the Azores Islands:

**Raiz**

*9500-094 Ponta Delgada, Portugal*

$$

One of the Azores' premier nightclubs is Raiz. The crowd is young, the music is loud, the drinks are flowing, and the dance floor is filled with people living their best lives. That's the kind of stuff you want from a club, and Raiz is happy to give it to people. This is a great place to come and party while traveling across the Azores Islands.

**Operating Hours:**

Sunday - Thursday: Closed

Friday - Saturday: 12:00 a.m. - 5:00 a.m.

## FESTIVALS AND EVENTS ACROSS THE AZORES ISLANDS

Here are all the festivals and events you need to know about across the Azores Islands throughout the year:

**February**

- **Mardi Gras** - Mardi Gras is a four-day celebration across the islands known as Carnaval by the locals. This festival is filled with music, dancing, partying, and drinking, all while people wear colorful costumes and masks with floats touring the streets.

**May**

- **The Festival of Senhor Santo Cristo dos Milagres (Lord Holy Christ of Miracles)** - Taking place in May, around Easter, this festival is the Azores Islands' largest religious event. Pilgrims from around the world gather to parade the streets of the city, decorated with flowers.
- **Holy Ghost Festivals** - This is an important festival amongst the people of the Azores and dates back to medieval times. It takes place at any time between May and September and involves parades, feasts, and celebrations.

**June**

- **The Sanjoaninas Festivities in Angra do Heroísmo** - This festival is a Terceira exclusive and is a large religious celebration.

**August**

- **Nossa Senhora de Lourdes** - This festival takes place in Pico, starts on the last Sunday of August, and lasts a week. It celebrates the patron saint of the whalers. It features numerous cultural and social events connected to the whale hunting traditions of the past.
- **Nossa Senhora dos Milagres** - Taking place every August 15 in Corvo, this is a celebration of Our Lady of Miracles.

**September**

- **Festa das Vindimas** - The wine harvesting festival takes place every year during the first week of September. It's a great excuse to drink some delicious wines from the Azores.

**December**

- **Christmas** - Most towns across the Azores Islands go all out to celebrate Christmas with decorations, celebrations, great food, and drinks. It's a very jovial time to be in the Azores.
- **New Year's Eve** - Considering there are nine islands in the Azores, the type of party you're going to get is going to be vastly different depending on where you are. Try to stick with the larger islands in the more populated areas if you're looking for a party.

## TOURIST SPOTS AND ACTIVITIES ACROSS THE AZORES ISLANDS

With nine islands in the Azores, best believe there's a lot to see and do. Here are some of the best tourist spots across the Azores:

- **Capelinhos** - Between 1957 and 1958, the Capelinhos volcano erupted and created a new island while damaging large swaths of surrounding land. Visit the new island and see the ruins of the old city that once stood in Capelinhos' shadow. They've also converted an old lighthouse into a museum that helps express the area's history.

- Faial Island, Azores Islands, Portugal

- **Montanha do Pico** - This volcano isn't just the highest point in the Azores but also in Portugal overall at 2,351 meters. It's one of the best places to hike because, despite its daunting appearance, it's easy to scale without advanced equipment. On a good day, you can see the islands of São Jorge, Terceira, Faial, and Graciosa from the top.

- Pico Island, Azores Islands, Portugal

- **Monte Brasil** - Yes, another volcano; that's what the Azores have in abundance. This one is different, though. You can find trails to the summit of Monte Brasil from Angra do Heroísmo. At the top, you can see monuments to Portuguese occupation, an incredible view of the city below, and gun emplacements dating back to the twentieth century World Wars.

- Angra do Heroismo, Terceira, Azores Islands, Portugal

- **Sete Cidades Massif** - The most incredible place to see across the Azores is the Sete Cidades Massif. It features twin blue and green lakes and lush vegetation. All of this is shielded thanks to the massive volcanic crater. While volcanos can cause immense destruction, this proves they're also the creators of undeniable beauty, as this massif is the result of 38,000 years of successive volcanic events.

- Ponta Delgada, São Miguel, Azores Islands, Portugal

- **Angra do Heroísmo** - This stunning city on the island of Terceira features buildings still showcasing their flawless 1700s architecture. It's a small city, but one with immense character. The Rua da Sé features mosaic pavements, which is something special. But just about everything in this town is impressive, from the colors used for the homes to the stunning cathedral.

- Angra do Heroísmo, Terceira, Azores Islands, Portugal

- **Lagoa das Furnas** - In São Miguel, there's a lake where signs of volcanic activity are present. You can view small calderas belching steam from a raised boardwalk and, if you're lucky, see some locals using them to cook local dishes.

- Adjacent to the town of Furnas, São Miguel, Azores Islands, Portugal

- **Caldeira** - This is a fun place to visit. Once similar to Sete Cidades Massif on São Miguel, the eruption of Capelinhos to the east resulted in this once vibrant lake becoming an essentially dry crater. There's stunning plant life, and the crater's rim is 400 meters up, presenting a challenging yet doable trail.

- Faial, Azores Islands, Portugal

- **Diving, Whale and Dolphin Watching, and Wave Sports** - Across the Azores, you'll find numerous opportunities for whale and dolphin sightings, diving, snorkeling, boat rides, and various other watersports. Considering the biggest draw of the Azores is nature and beaches, these are the kinds of activities you should be seeking out along the coast.

- **Poça da Dona Beija** - Want to have an interesting experience? The hot spring complex on the island of São Miguel is the best place to experience something different. Take a soak in hot spring water with a temperature of 104°F.

- Lomba Das Barracas 1, Furnas, Portugal

- **Marina da Horta** - On Faial Island, you'll find the main recreational harbor: Marina da Horto. It's located in one of the most breathtaking cities in Portugal that's small but gorgeous. There's a lot of fun to be had with loads of water-based activities available, as well as great restaurants, bars, and cafés along the streets overlooking the marina. Beyond the marina, exploring the city is something you should do while in the Horto municipality.

- Marina da Horta, Praça Infante Dom Henrique, 9900-017 Horta, Portugal

## HIDDEN GEMS ACROSS THE AZORES ISLANDS

With so many islands in its collection, it's not a surprise that some sites have become hidden gems for tourists. Here are some of the best-hidden gems across the Azores:

- **Pico Vineyards** - Explore the historic and beautiful vineyards in Pico and experience the wine culture of the area, maybe even try some of the local offerings. This UNESCO site is great for a visit, thanks to guided tours, museums, sights, and most importantly, wine.

- Pico, Azores Islands, Portugal

- **Islet of Vila Franca do Campo -** This tiny islet located off the coast of São Miguel is accessible via a boat service. It's a stunning islet that's rich in vegetation and perfect for a beach day in what is a unique and beautiful spot.

- Located off the South Central coast of São Miguel, Azores Islands, Portugal

- **Algar do Carvão** - Located in the heart of Terceira, this ancient lava tube is just waiting to be explored. You can descend 100 meters down the tube, entering the magma chamber of this extinct volcano. It's an incredible experience and one definitely worth doing if you've got the time.

- Angra do Heroismo. Terceira. Azores Islands, Portugal

- **Lagoa do Fogo** - Yet another stunning crater lake and the location of the Azores' largest body of water, Lagoa do Fago is a great place for a beautiful adventure. Before you go, make sure to check the weather because the crater is frequently covered in mist.

- Água de Pau Massif, São Miguel, Azores Islands, Portugal

## HOW LONG SHOULD YOU STAY IN THE AZORES ISLANDS?

The Azores Islands are a collection of islands, and one, two, or even three days simply aren't going to cut it. So, our recommendation is to stay for at least ten days. At a minimum, we'd stay a week.

Getting to the Azores Islands requires flying into their central airport, Ponta Delgada Airport (PDL). From there, you can take another flight to any of the nine islands in the Azores. You can also travel between the islands and towns by boat.

Traversing the individual islands provides multiple opportunities for getting around. For starters, most of the islands have car and scooter rentals available. Fair warning, though, the roads in the Azores aren't like the roads you might be used to as they're steep, narrow, twisting, and cloudy, thanks to the elevation. Another mode of transportation is taxis. Unfortunately, they're notoriously unreliable. Finally, the least recommended option is cycling around the islands. This isn't something I'd recommend if you're not up for the challenge and endless hill climbing.

Here's a sample itinerary for you to use when traveling to the Azores Islands for ten days:

**Day 1–3 - Terceira**

You're going to start your Azores journey in Terceira. This is considered the party island in the Azores. June is one of the best times to visit because of the Sanjoaninas street parties. Beyond the partying aspect of Terceira, it's home to stunning hiking trails and volcanic landscapes. So get ready for a lot of adventures on foot, taking in the natural beauty of Terceira and the Azores Islands overall.

Here's what day one in Terceira will look like:

- Visit the colorful churches in Angra do Heroismo.
- Hike Monte Brazil.
- Take in the sunset at the beach.

Here's what day two in Terceira will look like:

- Hike in Serreta.
- Take a dip in the Biscoitos Natural Pools.
- Visit Algar do Carvão and explore the dormant volcanoes.
- Explore the Gruto do Natal Cave.

Here's what day three in Terceira will look like:

- Enjoy a snorkeling boat tour through the Deep Blue Azores Diving Center.

  - Alternatively, take a jeep tour around the island.
  - Alternatively, go whale watching.

- Check out the insane views at the Miradouro Serra do Cume Viewpoint and enjoy a bite to eat and something to drink.

**Day 4–6 - São Jorge**

After a wonderful time in Terceira, you're going to either take a ferry or fly to the island of São Jorge.

On day one in São Jorge (day four overall), you're going to want to do the following:

- Dive into the beautiful Simao Dias Natural Pools.

- Explore the island.

On day two (day five overall), you're going to become one with nature by enjoying a stunning hike.

- Caldeira de Santo Cristo Hike.

On day three in São Jorge (day six overall), here's what you'll be getting up to:

- Visit Cafe Nuns, Europe's only coffee plantation.
- Hike in Fajã dos Vimes.

**Day 7–8 - Pico**

On day seven of your Azores Island tour, you'll ferry to the island of Pico. This is the most volcanic island in the Azores and also the second largest. On Pico, there are vineyards, volcanic caves, hiking trails, tidal pools, and more.

Here's what day one in Pico (day seven overall) is going to look like:

- Tour the Lajes do Pico harbor.
- Go on a whale and dolphin watching tour.

Your second day in Pico (day eight overall) is going to be another hike:

- Hike the famous Mount Pico.
- Relax the rest of the day.

**Day 9 - Faial Island**

On day nine, you will take a day trip to Faial Island. What you choose to do on your day trip is up to you. You may not be able to complete the majority of the available activities, but here are some options:

- Hike Cabeco do Canto.
- Enjoy some mountain biking.
- Go sailing.
- Enjoy a whale-watching tour.

If you're looking for something to cut, maybe skip whale watching as it's available on other islands where you're spending far more time.

**Day 10 - São Miguel**

Depending on your travel plans, your last day in the Azores might not look anything like this itinerary. If you're going back to mainland Portugal, then your flight may be later in the day. But if you're returning home, then you might be pressed for time.

Here are some activities you can try to do on the island of São Miguel:

- Bath in the hot springs.
- See Sete Cidades Lake.
- Hike the Praia-Lagoa do Fogo.

## TAKEAWAY

The Azores Islands is one of Portugal's most magnificent offerings. It's impossible to come and stay for a few days; this will either be the entire trip or the bulk of a trip to Portugal. It's the perfect place to enjoy a truly relaxing vacation.

We've explored so many amazing places, and we barely scratched the surface. In the next chapter we're going to look at some smaller locations across Portugal that you should consider visiting while touring the country.

# CHAPTER 16
# OTHER PLACES TO CONSIDER

Not every place in Portugal is worth an entire chapter, but that doesn't mean they're not worth a visit. In this chapter, we will discuss the numerous places in Portugal that you should consider traveling to. Most of these are small villages tucked into parts of the country that are on the way to more prominent destinations, but they all have something to offer.

## ÉVORA

In the heart of Alentejo lies the city of Évora. This beautiful city is complemented by a rich and important history. Dating back to the days of the Romans, in the fifteenth century the Portuguese kings chose Évora as their residence, which is why this place became so significant. Thanks to its historical value, it was made a UNESCO World Heritage Site in 1986.

Visit the city square, Praça do Giraldo, located in the heart of Évora. It has eight roads connecting to this prominent square. Filled with sidewalk cafés, shops, the Church of Santa Antão, and a marble drinking fountain, it's worth a visit.

Here are some other points of interest when visiting Évora:

- Roman baths
- Graça Church
- São Francisco Church
- Museum of Évora
- Eugénio de Almeida Foundation
- Palace of D. Manuel
- Ermida de São Brás chapel
- Cromeleque dos Almendres

With so many places to see, great food to eat, and adventures to be had, a stay in Évora won't disappoint.

## AVEIRO

This stunning city lies next to the ocean and has numerous channels that local boats meander through. It's like a version of Venice in Portugal. Enjoy a sightseeing tour around the city through the channels or tour the city by foot or bike. It's completely flat, making it an easy city to walk around.

The predominant architectural style in Aveiro is Art Nouveau, and it's stunning. Most of the Art Nouveau buildings lie on the main channel, making the city look incredible from the water. But even inland, it's beautiful. Many of these features make Aveiro one of the most romantic cities, not just in Portugal, but all of Europe. This city is vibrant and full of life, creating a unique experience.

Here are some other points of interest when visiting Évora:

- Aveiro Museum
- Convent of Jesus
- Chapel of Senhor das Barrocas
- Misericordia Church
- São Jacinto Dunes Natural Reserve
- Alegre Porcelain Factory
- Costa Nova
- Aveiro University Campus
- Barra Light (The highest lighthouse in Portugal)

This is one of those cities that can easily fall under the radar, but it's also one you alter your itinerary to visit. It's simply too beautiful to pass up.

## ÓBIDOS

Close to the capital, Lisbon, Óbidos is a small medieval town that's been incredibly preserved over the centuries. It's a picturesque town on the Atlantic coast, on higher ground that once had immense strategic value. Dating back to before the Roman invasion, Óbidos was eventually chosen by the king and gifted to the queen, becoming part of the Queen's estate known as the Casa das Rainhas. The castle that was built still stands today. Here, you'll find a rich religious history and architecture.

Here are some other points of interest when visiting Évora:

- Santa Maria Main Church
- Misericórdia Church
- Church of São Pedro
- Senhor Jesus da Pedra Sanctuary
- Óbidos City Museum
- Medieval Market
- El Rey Beach
- Foz do Arelho Beach
- Muralhas da Cidade
- Porta da Vila
- Castelo de Óbidos
- Rua da Talhada

Throughout the year, there are several festivals and events that are amazing to attend, like the International Chocolate Festival, the Harpsichord and Baroque Classical Music Seasons, and the Opera Festival.

This town is great to visit during Christmas because it goes all out decorating just about every inch of available space.

## THE MINHO REGION

Roughly sixty-three miles outside Porto, the Minho is home to the Rio Minho, a broad river with major cultural and historical significance for Portugal, as it acts as a border between them and Spain. The Minho region is home to a plethora of postcard-like locations. Here, you'll find high mountains, historic towns, Atlantic beaches, dreamy rivers, rolling vineyards, mysterious archeological sites, and ancient religious foundations. Basically, this area has a lot to offer to tourists looking for somewhere to spend their day.

Here are some other points of interest when visiting the Minho:

- The weekly market at Barcelos
- Summer carnival Romaria hosted at the Viana do Castelo
- Guimarães (Medieval Town)
- Braga (ecclesiastical center)
- Costa Verde
- Viana do Castelo (Coastal Town)
- Lima Valley
- Parque Nacional da Peneda-Gerês (National park)
- Rio Minho

In the Minho, one of Portugal's oldest regions, you'll find a simpler life where nature remains almost untouched in most parts of the landscape. It's beautiful, tranquil, and something worth experiencing. Get out of the city and explore Portugal's natural beauty. While you can find that all over the country, it's nowhere near as concentrated as it is in the Minho region.

## SETÚBAL PENINSULA

Welcome to a secluded paradise. Setúbal Peninsula is an intriguing location in Portugal. Suppose you're looking to travel somewhere less populated by tourists. In that case, you can't go wrong with the Setúbal Peninsula, which is considered a hidden gem in Portugal. For starters, here you'll likely find the best seafood in the country. All their seafood is caught fresh from Setúbal Bay. Restaurants serve just about all the seafood classics like squid, cod, sole, gilt-head sea bream, sea bass, sardines, oysters, barnacles, and black scabbard fish. Now, how is that for options?

Getting to the Setúbal Peninsula is easy if you travel by the Vasco da Gama Bridge. The city itself is rich with historical architecture, old city palaces, beautiful town squares with stonework, narrow streets, and monuments.

Here are some other points of interest when visiting The Setúbal Peninsula:

- The Franciscan Convento de Jesus
- Sixteenth-century Sao Felipe Fortress
- Wine tastings at various vineyards
- Costa da Caparica Beach
- Setubal Port
- Palmela (A link to ancient Portugal)

- Reserva Natural do Estuario de Sado
- Fossil Rock Formation
- Parque Natural da Arrabida

This slice of paradise is worth visiting if you can spare a day or two. The natural elements of the Setúbal Peninsula are what make it worth visiting.

## THE DOURO VALLEY

A place you will want to visit if you're a wine lover is the wine country known as the Douro Valley. Just east of Porto, vineyards populate the hills of the Douro Valley. Here, you can get a firsthand experience of Portuguese viniculture. Learn about their wine production methods, taste the wine, and enjoy the beautiful, calm atmosphere of the valley.

Here are some other points of interest when visiting The Douro Valley:

- Hiking trails
- Wine tastings
- Vineyard tours
- Boat rides along the Douro River
- Kayaking, canoeing, or water-skiing on the Douro River

- Douro Museum
- Côa Valley Archaeological Park
- Lamego Museum
- Bird-watching locations
- Lamego City
- Castle of Numão

In 1756, boundaries were established for the Doura Valley vineyards. This makes the Douro Valley the oldest demarcated wine region. As a result, it became a UNESCO World Heritage Site. The Douro Valley is accessible by road, cruise ship, or train, making it easy to get to and from the wine region.

## TAKEAWAY

We focus so much on the major areas in Portugal that these smaller, yet still incredible, locations can get lost in the process. If you've got a day to spare or are looking for something off the typical path that tourists take, these are some of the places you'll want to visit.

In the next chapter, we will present you with some sample itineraries to help with the planning of your trip. They are guidelines for what certain vacation timelines can look like. You'll even see some of these locations popping up in the itineraries.

# PART THREE
# SAMPLE ITINERARIES

## TEN DAYS IN PORTUGAL

In this ten-day itinerary, we're going to be focusing on the following areas:

- Porto (+ Douro Valley Day Trip)
- Lisbon (+ Sintra Day Trip)
- The Algarve

**Day 1–3 - Porto (+ Douro Valley Day Trip)**

Hopefully, you'll be arriving in Porto in the early hours of the morning so you can explore the city on day one.

Here's what you should do on your first day in Porto:

- Take a walking tour of Porto and experience the nation's second-largest city while learning more about its history.
- Find one of Porto's many Miradouros (viewpoints) to see the city in all its glory.
- If you can get in, visit the Livraria Lello, a beautiful bookstore most famous for hosting J. K. Rowling while she was writing the Harry Potter series—a portion of which she wrote in Livraria Lello!
- Enjoy some of the many amazing and delicious food offerings in Porto.

You can take your day trip to Douro Valley anywhere within these three days. We suggest day 2. While we recommend doing only two things in the Douro Valley, they will take up the bulk of your day. Trust me.

- Explore the various historic wineries in the Douro Valley and enjoy some wine tastings.
- Enjoy a boat cruise along the Douro River.

When traveling to Douro Valley, you can either take the train, travel by car, or go with a tour company.

**Day 4–6 - Lisbon (+ Sintra Day Trip)**

Lisbon is Portugal's capital and biggest city. There are a ton of things to do and see while visiting the city. You're only here for a few days, so you won't get to do everything, but let's look at what you should be doing.

Day one in Lisbon (day four overall) is going to look like this:

- Throughout your first day, try to visit as many miradouros as you can to see the city in all its glory from various vantage points.
- Enjoy a walking tour to take in as much of the city's history as you can.
- Ride the famous Tram 25 and visit the historic neighborhood of Belem.

Day two in Lisbon (day five overall) is going to be another busy day exploring. Here's what you should get up to:

- Visit the Igreja de São Roque.
- See the Padrão dos Descobrimentos monument.
- Go to the Oceanário de Lisboa.

For your day trip to Sintra (day six overall), you're going to want to see the following:

- Pena Palace is a must-see attraction in Sintra and is a true focal point of the entire city.
- See the Moorish Castle and look over the city from high above.
- Visit Sintra's old city center.
- If you have time, see the Quinta da Regaleira, which is an incredible site.

**Day 7–10 - The Algarve**

For the final leg of your Portuguese tour, you're heading to the Algarve region, where you'll split your time exploring various parts of the area.

Day one in the Algarve (day seven overall) will be spent in Lagos and surrounding areas. For your day in Lagos, why not ditch the historical sightseeing and instead take a load off with a beach day? Visit either

- Ponta da Piedade
- Praia de Dona Ana
- Praia do Camilo

Day two (eight overall) in the Algarve will be spent exploring the Seven Hanging Valleys Trail. It's a seven-mile hike along the coastline with alternative routes available. This is a great way to explore the Algarve's stunning natural landscape further.

Day three (day nine overall) should be spent exploring Sagres and the western areas of the region. Here's what your day should look like:

- Explore the town of Sagres.
- Visit the fishing town of Salema.

- Enjoy more beach time at Praia da Arrifana, Praia da Mareta, or Praia do Beliche.

On day four in the Algarve (day ten overall), you will be flying home, so take what little time you have left and enjoy what you can in the Algarve, ensuring it's part of your journey to the airport.

## ONE WEEK IN PORTUGAL (LISBON AND PORTO)

One week in Portugal isn't going to feel like enough when you're through the week. But let's make this week count. Here's a one-week itinerary taking you to Lisbon, Sintra, Porto, the Douro Valley, and several other towns along the way.

**Day 1–2 - Lisbon**

Here's what you should do on your first day in Lisbon:

- Visit the city Cathedral.
- Explore the ruins of Carom Convent.
- Check out the impressive Arco da Rua Augusta.
- Go on the Santa Justa Lift and get a great view of the city.
- Ride Tram 28 to Castelo de São Jorge.

Day 2 in Lisbon should contain the following activities:

- Visit the historic neighborhood of Belem.
- See the Jerónimos Monastery.
- Check out the famous LxFactory.

**Day 3 - Sintra**

Here's what you will do on your day trip to the town of Sintra:

- Visit Pena Palace and Pena Park.
- See the Moorish Castle.
- Tour the insane Quinta da Regaleira.

**Day 4 - Óbidos, Batalha, Fatima & Nazaré**

Day four is going to be a busy day. I'd recommend renting a car to make this easier. Along the way to your next main destination, Porto, you will make several stops to explore historic places in Portugal.

- Visit the medieval town of Óbidos.
- Visit the town of Batalha.
- Visit the town of Fatima.
- Visit the town of Nazaré.

You might not have time to visit all of these locations; just cut the one you think is the least interesting to you and your journey. The alternative is a day trip to one or two of these options. If it was a choice, I'd say go on a day trip to the beaches of Nazaré. Just make sure you're spending the night in Porto so you can start exploring first thing in the morning.

**Day 5–6 - Porto**

Here is what you should do on your first day in Porto:

- Join a walking tour to experience the ins and outs of the city.
- Visit the Igreja do Carmo and Igreja de Santo Ildefonso churches.
- See the famous Livraria Lello bookshop.
- Visit Porto Cathedral and climb the Clergies Towers.
- Take an afternoon river cruise along the Douro River.

Day 2 in Porto should contain the following activities:

- Enjoy a day on the coast of Porto by exploring the city's many beaches.
- Spend the afternoon in Gaia on the opposite side of the Douro River where you can enjoy wine tastings.

**Day 7 - Douro Valley**

Your final day is going to be spent exploring the Douro Valley, which is Portugal's most famous wine-growing region. You'll be able to enjoy wine tastings, great food, and stunning views of the valley.

## TWO WEEKS IN PORTUGAL (LISBON, PORTO, AND ALGARVE)

For the two-week itinerary, we're going to take the one-week itinerary that explores Lisbon and Porto and add a week in the Algarve.

While in the Algarve, you will want to take a less structured approach and instead just explore. Consider skipping the main cities of Faro and Lagos, and just move around exploring the region and its natural beauty. I'd recommend basing yourself in Albufeira, where the beaches are immaculate, and there are so many great bars and restaurants. While in the region, you'll find that you can enjoy hikes, sea caves, kayaking, and numerous other outdoor activities in most old towns.

While in the Algarve, don't miss the towns Sagres and Tavira.

If you want something more structured, adapt the itineraries available in Chapters 10 and 11.

## THREE WEEKS IN PORTUGAL (LISBON, PORTO, ALGARVE, AND MADEIRA)

If you're extending your stay in Portugal to three weeks, then it's time to take this party off the mainland in the third week by traveling to the autonomous island of Madeira. You'll stick with the week one and two plan already laid out, but now you're adding Madeira to the mix.

Madeira is full of dramatic landscapes, lush green foliage, soaring mountains, great beaches, and so much more. This island offers some of the best hiking opportunities in Europe. There's also just so much to see on the island.

If you want something more structured, adapt the itinerary from Chapter 15 to fit your time in Madeira.

## TWO-WEEK TRIP IN PORTUGAL

Here's an alternative itinerary for traveling to many possible locations across Portugal:

**Week 1**

In your first week, you will spend time in Lisbon, Cascais, Sintra, Óbidos, and Porto.

**Day 1–2 - Lisbon**

While visiting Lisbon, you will want to pack as much into your stay as possible. Here are some of the things you should try to do while in the city:

- Ride Tram 28.
- Walk through the Alfama neighborhood.
- Visit the Castelo de São Jorge.
- Tour the Sé de Lisboa Cathedral.

- Visit the Praça do Comércio.
- Check out the 148 ft high Elevador de Santa Justa in Rua da Prata.
- Have a meal at the Time Out Market.
- Visit some of the many clubs, bars, and restaurants around Lisbon.
- Check out some of the museums.
- Explore the historic Torre de Belém.
- Go to the LxFactory for a cultural experience with great food, art, and more.

**Day 3 - Cascais**

Time to visit Cascais for a beach day. Close to Lisbon, you'll find picturesque beaches and a colorful town filled with great restaurants, shops, and cafés. Here are some of the things you can see and do in Cascais besides the beautiful beaches and charming town:

- Boat tours.
- Check out the Cidadela de Cascais, a fortified structure with museums, shops, and more.
- Visit the Santa Marta Lighthouse Museum for a panoramic view of Cascais.
- See the Boca do Inferno (Hell's Mouth), where the waves crash against rock walls.
- Catch an incredible sunset at Cabo da Roca on your way to Sintra. You can either stay in Lisbon, Cascais, or Sintra for the night.

### Day 4 - Sintra

Time to explore the mountainous town of Sintra, where castles are just about everywhere, ready to be explored by tourists and locals alike. Sintra has retained much of the original architecture from its illustrious history, making it an incredible place to visit.

Thanks to a wide array of castles, there's a lot to see in Sintra. Some are beyond incredible and will leave you breathless, thanks to stunning views and architecture maintained throughout the centuries. While in the area, enjoy some of the local cuisine, including the desserts. Try to stay the night in Sintra to fully enjoy everything this village has to offer.

### Day 5 - Óbidos

This will be one of the most exciting places you will visit while exploring Portugal. Óbidos is a medieval town, and it makes an impression almost immediately. As you arrive, you see the entrance adorned with eighteenth-century tiles. Here are some things to check out in Óbidos:

- Santa Maria Church
- Óbidos Castle
- Rua Direita Main Street
- Hotel Castelo de Óbidos

### Day 6–7 - Porto

While on your way to Porto, you should consider a stop in the village of Nazaré. It's halfway between Óbidos and Porto and has beautiful sights, like the Nazaré Canyon. Once you're done there, it's straight on to the wine region of Porto. As a city, Porto is charming. Not as busy as Lisbon, but with just as much to do and twice the charm.

Here are some of the things you should do in Porto:

- Check out the 250-foot Torre dos Clérigos.
- Visit one of the world's most beautiful bookstores called Lello Bookstore.
- Head to the Praça da Liberdade and enjoy food and coffee at one of the many cafés or restaurants.
- Visit the São Bento Railway Station and view the tile panels which depict the nation's history.
- See the Porto Cathedral from the twelfth century.
- View the sunset at the Cais do Ribeira, which overlooks the Douro River in the valley.
- Visit the Monastery of Serra do Pilar, which has some incredible views.
- Go to wine tastings and wine cellars to experience the taste of Porto wines.

**Week 2**

In your second week, you will spend time in Braga e Guimarães, Coimbra e Fátima, Lagos, Sagres, and Lisbon.

**Day 8 – Braga e Guimarães**

On day 8, you will visit two places: Braga and Guimarães. The distance between the two cities is twelve miles, and they are only thirty-five miles outside Porto. Here, you can enjoy tours of these historic cities and visit historic centers. A highlight in Braga is the steps of the Bom Jesus do Monte Sanctuary.

**Day 9 – Coimbra e Fátima**

Take a trip to the city of students, Coimbra. Home to one of the world's oldest universities, Coimbra is an incredible place to visit thanks to its unique city design, medieval streets, stairways, slopes, and the stunning waterfront.

You'll also visit Fátima to explore various religious attractions like the Shrine of Fátima. This complex features both a shrine and a chapel. Neither location is significant in size, so you won't have to rush your visit to both. Take your time and take it all in.

**Day 10–11 – Lagos**

Once in Lagos, you'll likely want to stay longer than two days. It's a beautiful region with a rich and diverse landscape, many beaches, great restaurants, and markets. Of course, there are historical sites to add to that list, making it a tight two days in paradise.

Here is how you should spend your two days in Lagos:

- Visit the best beaches in Lagos: Praia do Camilo and Praia Dona Ana.
- See the sunset at Ponta da Piedade.

- If you have time, visit Marinha Beach, which has been consistently voted one of Europe's most beautiful beaches.
- Get to Benagil Beach for a boat trip to Benagil Cave.
- Try the 7 Hanging Valleys Trail, a 3.5-mile (one-way) hike.
- Visit the Carvoeiro Village for beautiful colored homes perched on cliffs.

**Day 12–13 – Sagres**

The final true stop on this itinerary is Sagres, a beautiful small coastal town. It's time to relax and enjoy the last few days of your vacation. You'll find stunning beaches, dramatic cliffs, great food, and more here.

You can check out the following places in Sagres for the best experience:

- Sagres Fortress
- Amado Beach
- Cordoama Lookout
- Beliche Beach
- Cabo São Vicente

**Day 14 - Lisbon**

As with all good things, your Portugal trip has come to an end where it all began. It's time to travel back to Lisbon, where you'll return to your home country. Depending on when your flight leaves the airport, you can get back to the city early and enjoy a short day in the city before leaving.

## THREE-WEEK PORTUGAL ROAD TRIP

If you're lucky enough to travel to Portugal for three weeks, you're in for the best trip ever. You can experience more of Portugal than most, especially if you plan on making it a road trip. Let's take a look at what a 3-week trip to Portugal looks like:

**Week 1**

In your first week, you will spend time in Lisbon, Cascais, and Sintra.

**Day 1–2 - Lisbon**

Four days in Lisbon is more than enough time to get to all the major sites while having a relaxing time in this major Portuguese city.

On day one, you're going to want to do the following:

- Get the annoying stuff like checking into your hotel out of the way as soon as you can.
- Immediately start exploring, starting with the Alfama neighborhood, which is Lisbon's oldest neighborhood. Here, you can explore the labyrinth-like alleyways and enjoy the street's history.
- Visit the Carmo Convent and take in the breathtaking views that the Santa Justa Lift has to offer.

- Enjoy a famous Lisbon treat, Pastél de Nata, at Manteigaria.
- Take in the sunset at the São Jorge Castle.
- Get dinner at one of the many amazing restaurants in Lisbon.
- If you have the energy, maybe hit a bar for a nightcap or a club for some dancing. But this can be done any night, so there is no pressure on day one!

Day two takes you to the Belém district by the Tagus River. It's twenty minutes from the main city by car, but there are other means of transportation to get to the area. Here you will:

- Tour the famous Belém Tower.
- See the striking Monument of the Discoveries.
- Visit the beautiful architectural marvel that is the Jerónimos Monastery.
- Tour the Palácio Nacional da Ajuda, which is an incredibly beautiful place
- Finally, finish off the day by exploring LxFactory, a great place to see art, shop, enjoy a bite to eat, and more.

**Day 3–4 - Lisbon**

Day three in Lisbon is all about seeing the city from as many angles as you can while visiting a few monuments.

- Explore the Lisbon Cathedrals, and if you're able,

climb the towers!

- Visit the Bairro Alto neighborhood, and while you're there, consider having lunch at Miradoura de Santa Luzia, which is a great restaurant with a killer view of the city.
- Ride Tram 28 for one of the best tours of the city.

Day four, your last day, is for all the things you couldn't get to on days one, two, and three. Here's what I'd do if we were you:

- Visit the famous Pink Street.
- Have a wonderful lunch at Mercato da Ribeira.
- Go and see the Statue of Cristo Rei.
- Ride the cable cars by the water. Maybe even take a HippoTour.
- Enjoy a final, peaceful night in Lisbon, preferably somewhere with live music.

**Day 5 - Cascais**

While you're going to remain in Lisbon for accommodation, you'll be taking a day trip to Cascais, the seaside city. About twenty miles outside of Lisbon, this city is great for a beach day with a bit of sightseeing.

While in Cascais, be sure to do the following:

- You're going to spend either the morning or the afternoon at the beach. Whatever you decide is up to you. Afternoon makes more sense to us to avoid being tired from the sun for the rest of the day.

- Visit the Palacete Seixas, which is a twentieth-century seaside palace.
- Tour the Museu Condes de Castro Guimarães with its stunning art collection, prehistoric archeological remains, and more.
- Have a relaxing afternoon before making your way back to Lisbon.

**Day 6–7 - Sintra**

Most people make Sintra a day trip. In this itinerary, it's recommended you stay or visit for two days and take in all that Sintra has to offer.

Here's what day one will look like:

- Visiting Sintra and not going to the Pena Palace is a sin. This is one of the best sites in Sintra, with its unrivaled views. It's not to be missed. It's not the easiest place to get to and can take a while, so if you're there, you should also tour Pena Park, which is below the palace.
- Depending on your appetite for adventure, head next to the Moorish Castle. The good news is that it's not far from Pena Palace!

Day two in Sintra is going to be far less strenuous than day one, but still eventful:

- Start your morning in the old center of Sintra.
- Visit the park and Palace of Monserrate deep in the mountains.
- Take in the magical Quinta da Regaleira.
- If you have the time and energy, visit Cabo da Roca to say you went to Europe's westernmost point.

**Week 2**

In your second week, you will spend time in Óbidos, Coimbra, Piódão & Foz d'Égua, Costa Nova and Aveiro, and Porto.

**Day 8 - Óbidos**

After enjoying Sintra, you will want to hit the road for Coimbra. On the way, you will make a day stop in the medieval town of Óbidos, which is less than halfway to your final destination. This is a great day trip opportunity. Here's what you'll do while visiting Óbidos:

- Explore the well-preserved medieval walls, which offer stunning views of Óbidos.
- Walk the streets of this town that's almost stuck in time.
- Try to find the fourteen hidden bookstores of Óbidos.
- Visit the colorful and beautiful Porta da Vila, made up entirely of Azulejo tiles.

### Day 9 - Coimbra

Today is the day you explore the student city of Coimbra. This historical place has so much to offer visitors who are willing to traverse the tricky hilly terrain. Here's what you're going to want to do in Coimbra:

- Visit the oldest university in Portugal, Coimbra University.
- See the stunning and historical Palace of Schools and Joanina Library.
- Visit the iconic historical landmark Igreja de Santa Cruz, a gorgeous church.
- Finally, check out the Manga Cloister, a peculiar monument by the Igreja de Santa Cruz church.

### Day 10 - Piódão & Foz d'Égua

Want to see authentic Portugal? You'll want to drive to the mountainous Arganil region, where you will find several villages like Piódão and Foz d'Égua. This area has major day-trip appeal. Here, you'll find historical towns on steep hills accompanied by picturesque streams. You'll want to explore the town, eat the food, and experience the historical value these places hold. Be prepared for a long day, as getting to these places can take up to three hours.

*Alternative: If you're not interested in traveling this far to explore Piódão and Foz d'Égua, you can cut this day out and either spend another day in Coimbra, or move up the itinerary and spend an extra day in Porto.*

**Day 11 - Costa Nova and Aveiro**

Coimbra remains home base, and Day 11's day trip takes you to Costa Nova and Aveiro. While it's two hours away, it's worth the journey. Our favorite is Aveiro, a stunning little waterfront city with small canals and gondolas. Costa Nova is a more coastal town with striped beach houses, holiday homes, and lots of restaurants.

**Day 12–14 - Porto**

From Coimbra, you'll make a short one-and-a-half-hour drive to Porto, Portugal's second-largest city.

On day one of your trip to Porto, here's what you should be doing:

- You'll start on the other side of the Douro River overlooking Porto, in the small town of Vila Nova de Gaia, where the wine is stored.
- Enjoy a wine tasting.
- Visit some great vantage points on the Teleferico de Gaia cable cars.

Day two in Porto is going to be far busier! We suggest getting a good pair of walking shoes. Here's what you'll be up to:

- The first stop is the stunning Cais de Ribeira, which is vibrant and colorful, perfect for starting off the day.
- Tour the Sé do Porto, a beautiful Porto cathedral.

- Visit the Sao Bento Station, one of Portugal's most incredible train stations.
- Nearby, you'll find a cluster of sites to see, including the Igreja dos Congregados, the colorful Largo da Pena Ventosa alley, and the Clerigos Tower.
- Finally, you'll visit the Livraria Lello bookshop.

After a grueling day two, you're going to have a far more relaxed and less structured day three. Here's what you'll get up to on day three:

- Explore hidden alleys.
- See the Rua de Santa Catarina.
- Visit a couple more chapels, namely the Church of Santo Ildefonso and Chapel of Souls.
- To cap it all off, watch the sunset from the Dom Luis I Bridge by taking the Funicular dos Guindais.

**Week 3**

In your final week, you will spend time in Marvão, Elves, Évora, Faro, Albufeira, Ferragudo, and Lisbon.

**Day 15 - Marvão**

The unfortunate reality of traveling to Marvão from Porto is the distance. It's a long drive, three and a half hours, to be exact. Marvão is a medieval city on the border with Spain, and it's beautiful. Week three is all about exploring smaller places and not staying more than a day, which makes it an exciting leg of the journey.

Here, you're going to simply explore the city. Take it all in. From the entrance gate to the high medieval walls. This small city exists on a rocky slope at the highest point. You'll stay the night before, making a much shorter journey in the morning to Elvas.

**Day 16 - Elvas**

Traveling only an hour and seventeen minutes from Marvão, you'll arrive at the beautiful little city of Elvas. It's a day trip on your way to Évora.

Here's what you'll be enjoying in Elvas:

- Republic Square and the Cathedral. This also features some incredible architecture thanks to the Santa Clara archway.
- See the Pelourinho de Elvas, which is a symbolic pillar dating all the way back to the sixteenth century.
- The must-see landmark in Elvas is the Castelo de Elvas. It's incredible and such a sight to behold.
- The final two destinations aren't technically in Elvas but on the outskirts, so if you have the time, you should visit the Amoreira Aqueduct and the Forte de Nossa Senhora da Graça.

Once you're done here, it's straight on to Évora for two nights.

**Day 17–18 - Évora**

The historic capital of the Alentejo region, Évora, dates back to Roman and Celtic times, and the history in the area showcases this beautifully. Due to its geography, Évora is considered the hottest place in Portugal. Be sure to check the weather before going to ensure it's still a place you want to visit.

Here's what day one in Évora is going to look like:

- Visit the famous Chapel of Bones and immediately afterward make your way to the St. Francis Monastery.
- Tour the Évora Public Gardens and locate the Évora Royal Palace within the grounds.
- Visit the Fingidas ruins, which are fake ruins built of architectural materials from all over Évora.

Day two is going to be somewhat busier. Here's what you'll be up to:

- Start by exploring Giraldo Square.
- Visit the Évora Cathedral and get tickets to the Gothic Tower.
- Explore the Roman ruins of the UNESCO site, the Temple of Diana.

- View the Roman Arch of Dona Isabel.
- Finally, visit the second-oldest university in Portugal, Évora University.

**Day 19 - Faro**

Get ready for yet another long day of driving. Faro is roughly three hours away from Évora. We recommend traveling in the morning after some well-needed rest from exploring Évora. We also recommend visiting the city as a day trip and spending the afternoon traveling to your next destination.

While in Faro, here's what you're going to be visiting:

- Old Town.
- Arco da Vila Cathedral.
- Palacio Pousada.

I wouldn't recommend staying longer than necessary. Faro is a great city, but unless you're staying for more than a day, it's best to move on to your next destination.

**Day 20 - Albufeira**

While this is a vacation, it's clear you've worked for it, and now it's time to wind down a bit in the final days. Albufeira is known for being Portugal's party city, but it's also a great place to relax. Honestly, we wouldn't over-plan your time in Albufeira. Get to the beach, explore the city, and enjoy a beautiful sunset. Just relax.

### Day 21 - Ferragudo

Your final day trip is to a beautiful village an hour from Albufeira. This fishing village has a stunning beach, great restaurants, and lovely viewpoints. After Albufeira, it's a great place to relax even more.

Here are some things to do and see while in Ferragudo:

- Walk along the Marina.
- Rua Infante Dom Enriqeu and Rua Infante Santo for some killer photos.
- Visit the Igreja de Nossa Senhora da Conceição. You don't even have to go in because the outside alone is something to behold.
- Relax on the Praia da Angrinha, which is the most beautiful beach in the area.
- On the Praia da Angrinha is an incredible castle, the Castelo de São João do Arade.

### Day 22 - Lisbon

Your final day is more about tying up loose ends. Depending on your time management, you may be able to spend some more time in Lisbon (after traveling two hours from Albufeira) for some last-minute exploring before departing home. Maybe grab another bite of authentic Portuguese food and enjoy a nice walk around before heading to the airport. This day really bends to the will of your travel to Lisbon and the time of your flight, so take it as it comes.

# CONCLUSION

Parabéns!

That means congratulations, because you've just completed a comprehensive look at what traveling in Portugal can look like, and look at you now! You're more knowledgeable than ever when it comes to this magical place you plan to explore on your vacation.

Thanks to your research, you know why Portugal is the place to vacation, how to book tickets, how to budget, navigating their transportation network, all while having insight into all the main places in Portugal worth a visit. So once again, parabéns!

It's time to take this knowledge and plan your ultimate trip! You know where to go, what to do, and how to do it. Now it's time to make it a reality. Each chapter in this book is there to refer to when planning your adventure. So, don't get stressed out. This information isn't going anywhere.

Portugal is probably one of the best places to visit in the world. Once you're there, you'll feel so at home in this gorgeous country. You'll find experiences you can't find anywhere else. While the planning may be daunting, it will all be worth it when you arrive in paradise. At least, that's how it felt when we finally made it to Portugal after months of planning.

All we can say now is, good luck! But at this point, do you really need it?

# REFERENCES


Introduction

Statistics Portugal - web portal (no date). Available at: https://www.ine.pt/xportal/xmain?xpgid=ine_tema&xpid=INE&tema_cod=1713

Travels, S. (2021) Pros and cons of spontaneous travel - spellbound travels. Available at: https://spellboundtravels.com/2019/04/02/pros-and-cons-of-spontaneous-travel/

Keene, E. (2021) 8 Advantages To Having A Travel Itinerary, Travel Information. Available at: https://pinkpangea.com/2015/05/travel-itinerary/

Chapter 1

Wheeler, D.L. et al. (2023) Portugal | History, flag, Population, Cities, Map, & Facts. Available at: https://www.britannica.com/place/Portugal

*The history of Portugal* (2022). Available at: https://www.portugal.com/history-and-culture/the-history-of-portugal/

D, P. (2023) "16 Totally Unbiased Reasons You'll Want to Visit Portugal," The Planet D: Adventure Travel Blog [Preprint]. Available at: https://theplanetd.com/visit-portugal/

Sousa, I. (2021) "10 Reasons to Visit Portugal," Ecotours Portugal, 16 April. Available at: https://www.ecotoursportugal.com/en/travel-blog/portugal-4/10-reasons-to-visit-portugal-306

Rosa, N. (2023) "17 fun facts about Portugal you probably never knew," Real Word [Preprint]. Available at: https://www.trafalgar.com/real-word/fun-facts-about-portugal/

Chapter 2

Hintoft, V. (2020) "Flights to Portugal: Tips and tricks to finding the best deals," bePortugal [Preprint]. Available at: https://beportugal.com/flights-to-portugal/

Ramaswamy, M. (2021) "Getting to Portugal | How to travel to Portugal," Rough Guides, 26 April. Available at: https://www.roughguides.com/portugal/getting-there/

Chapter 3

Budget travel abroad: The Ultimate Checklist (no date). Available at: https://www.transitionsabroad.com/publications/magazine/0707/budget_travel_tips_for_checklist.shtml

Shannon (2022b) "25 top tips for travelling on a budget," We Are Global Travellers [Preprint]. Available at: https://weareglobaltravellers.com/2020/05/tips-travelling-on-a-budget/

Trip, B.Y. (no date) Portugal travel cost - Average price of a vacation to Portugal: food & meal budget, daily & weekly expenses | BudgetYourTrip.com. Available at: https://www.budgetyourtrip.com/portugal

Chapter 4

Expatica (2023) Public transportation in Portugal: a guide for expats | Expatica. Available at: https://www.expatica.com/pt/living/transportation/public-transportation-in-portugal-419519/

Chapter 5

Sylvester, P. (2021) "Handy Portuguese phrases for travelers in Portugal," Copyright (C) 2004-2023 World Nomads [Preprint]. Available at: https://www.worldnomads.com/explore/europe/portugal/its-portugal-they-speak-portugese

Katie (2017) 10 Must-Know Words and Phrases for your trip to Portugal. Available at: https://www.languagetrainers.com/blog/10-must-know-words-and-phrases-for-your-trip-to-portugal/

Tips on accommodations in Portugal | Frommer's (no date). Available at: https://www.frommers.com/destinations/portugal/planning-a-trip/tips-on-accommodations

Gajjar, S.H. (2023) Tipping in Portugal: Should you or should you not? Available at: https://devourtours.com/blog/tipping-in-portugal/?cnt=PH

Portuguese culture - do's and don'ts (2018b). Available at: https://culturalatlas.sbs.com.au/portuguese-culture/portuguese-culture-do-s-and-don-ts

Team, T. (2023) "Dos and dont's in Portugal - etiquette for travelers," Tatonka Blog, 4 May. Available at: https://blog.tatonka.com/en/dos-and-donts-portugal/

Cultural do's & don'ts in Portugal - through the eyes of an expat (2017). Available at: https://meetngreetme.com/blog/dos-donts-culture-in-portugal-expat-shares-advice/

anothertravel (2023) Portuguese culture customs and etiquette | anothertravel. Available at: https://www.anothertravel.com/europe/portugal/culture-etiquette/

Fox, J.D. (2023) "25 Essential Tips For Your First Trip To Portugal," Julie Dawn Fox in Portugal [Preprint]. Available at: https://juliedawnfox.com/tips-first-trip-portugal/

The Atlas Heart (2023) The Atlas Heart. Available at: https://theatlasheart.com/portugal-travel-guide/

## Chapter 6

Pt, C. (2021) 10 facts you didn't know about Lisbon. Available at: https://www.collegiate-ac.pt/en/student-news/curiosities-about-lisbon/

De Sousa Rebelo, L., Gaspar, J.B. and Ehrlich, B. (2023) Lisbon | History, culture, Economy, & Facts. Available at: https://www.britannica.com/place/Lisbon

History of Lisbon - From its foundation to the twentieth century (no date). Available at: https://www.lisbon.net/history

Ilimtour (2017) "Islamic heritage of Al Andalus: Lisbon," Ilimtour [Preprint]. Available at: https://ilimtour.com/islamic-heritage-al-andalus-lisbon/

Renaissance Lisbon: how was Lisbon back in its the golden age? (2022). Available at: https://lisbonwalker.com/packages/renaissance-lisbon/

Giddings, P. (2023) "Is Lisbon safe? Course it is if you use common sense..." lisbonlisboaportugal.com [Preprint]. Available at: https://lisbonlisboaportugal.com/lisbon-tour/is-lisbon-safe-tourist-female-sole-travellers-dangerous.html

Australian Government (N/A). Available at: https://www.smartraveller.gov.au/destinations/europe/portugal

Hopkins, E. (2022) "Top 10 Best Hospitals In Portugal: Public & Private," Viv

Europe [Preprint]. Available at: https://viveurope.com/hospitals-in-portugal/

Hirsch, D. and M. (2023) "10 Lisbon Food Favorites – What To Eat In Lisbon," 2foodtrippers [Preprint]. Available at: https://www.2foodtrippers.com/what-to-eat-in-lisbon/

Scatena, J. (2021) "13 best restaurants in Lisbon," Condé Nast Traveler, 2 February. Available at: https://www.cntraveler.com/gallery/best-restaurants-in-lisbon

Calles, A.R. (2022) "Visiting Lisbon? check out these 10 awesome restaurants," TheTravel [Preprint]. Available at: https://www.thetravel.com/best-restaurants-in-lisbon/

Taborda, J. (2023) Lisbon Street Food: bifana, prego, salgado, & more. Available at: https://devourtours.com/blog/lisbon-street-food/?cnt=PH

Santos, N. (2020) "Best street food markets in Lisbon," Culture Trip, 19 May. Available at: https://theculturetrip.com/europe/portugal/lisbon/articles/best-street-food-markets-in-lisbon/

Bergin, J. (2022) "Lisbon Nightlife 2023: Secret gems you can't miss on a night out!," Pilot Plans, 25 April. Available at: https://www.pilotplans.com/blog/lisbon-nightlife

Guru, L. and Guru, L. (2022) "12 months of festivals and events in Lisbon," Lisbon Guru [Preprint]. Available at: https://www.lisbonguru.com/festivals-events-all-year-round/

Giddings, P. (2023b) "Top 10 of Lisbon," LisbonLisboaPortugal.com [Preprint]. Available at: https://lisbonlisboaportugal.com/lisbon-tour/lisbon-sightseeing-activities-things-to-do-see.html

Santos, N. (2022) "Secret spots in Lisbon the locals wish you didn't know about," Culture Trip, 12 May. Available at: https://theculturetrip.com/europe/portugal/articles/11-secret-spots-in-lisbon-the-locals-wish-you-didnt-know-about/

Livingston, L. (2023) "20 hidden gems and secret spots in Lisbon Portugal," The Geographical Cure [Preprint]. Available at: https://www.thegeographicalcure.com/post/lisbon-s-best-kept-secrets

The 7 Best Beaches In Lisbon To Suit Every Taste (2019). Available at: https://www.oliverstravels.com/blog/best-beaches-lisbon/

Akkam, A. (2018) "10 best museums in Lisbon," Condé Nast Traveler, 13 November. Available at: https://www.cntraveler.com/gallery/best-museums-in-lisbon

9 best live music spots in Lisbon (2022). Available at: https://www.portugal.com/activities-experiences/9-best-live-music-spots-in-lisbon/

Lisbon Street Art Tours - Home (no date). Available at: http://www.lisbonstreetarttours.com/

Bounce (2022) "Lisbon On a Rainy Day: 12 Things To Do," Bounce [Preprint]. Available at: https://usebounce.com/guides/lisbon/lisbon-on-a-rainy-day

Kaz (2023) "17+ Fun Things To Do In Lisbon With Kids 2023 | Lisbon For Kids," Travel Mad Mum, 28 June. Available at: https://travelmadmum.com/lisbon-with-kids/

Mikkelsen, S. (2019) How Long To Spend In Lisbon. Available at: https://www.webjet.com.au/travel/destinations/how-long-to-spend-in-lisbon/

Prowse, A. (2023) "LISBON, PORTUGAL: COMPLETE 3-DAY ITINERARY," We Are Travel Girls [Preprint]. Available at: https://wearetravelgirls.com/lisbon-3-day-itinerary/

## Chapter 7

The Editors of Encyclopaedia Britannica (1998) Sintra | Portugal's historic town & palaces. Available at: https://www.britannica.com/place/Sintra

UNESCO World Heritage Centre (no date) Cultural landscape of Sintra. Available at: https://whc.unesco.org/en/list/723/

Sintra: Health & Safety - Tripadvisor (no date). Available at: https://www.tripadvisor.com/Travel-g189164-s206/Sintra:Portugal:Health.And.Safety.html

Christoffer, S. (2019) "Living in Sintra: What You Need to Live in Portugal's Fairytale City," bePortugal [Preprint]. Available at: https://www.beportugal.com/sintra/

Delahay&Co (no date) The Cuisine of Sintra | Mad About Sintra. Available at: https://www.madaboutsintra.com/regional_cuisine.html

Gajjar, S.H. (2023a) 4 essential restaurants in Sintra you can't skip. Available at: https://devourtours.com/blog/restaurants-sintra/?cnt=PH

Claire (2023) "How to Eat Your Way in Sintra in One Day - The Perfect Guide," Authentic Food Quest, 22 March. Available at: https://www.authenticfoodquest.com/eat-your-way-in-sintra/

Best Nightlife in Sintra | Frommer's (no date). Available at: https://www.frommers.com/destinations/sintra/nightlife/overview

Events & festivals (2015). Available at: http://www.ezportugal.com/sintra-portugal/things-to-do-sintra/events-festivals-sintra

Top eventos (no date). Available at: https://visitsintra.travel/pt/programe-a-sua-visita/top-eventos

Meeuwesen, J. (2020) "15 best things to do in Sintra (Portugal)," The Crazy Tourist [Preprint]. Available at: https://www.thecrazytourist.com/15-best-things-sintra-portugal/

Top 10 Must-See Attractions in Sintra (no date). Available at: https://www.sintraportugaltourism.com/guide/top-10-attractions-and-things-to-do-in-sintra.html

www.thingstodopost.org (no date) 9 Hidden Gems Things to do in Sintra That You Shouldn't Miss. Available at: https://www.thingstodopost.org/9-hidden-gems-things-to-do-in-sintra-that-you-shouldn-t-miss-687596

Tiffany, A. (2023) "Best Beaches In Sintra (Portugal) - An Ultimate Guide (2023) - Just Go Exploring," Just Go Exploring, 17 August. Available at: https://justgoexploring.com/destinations/best-beaches-in-sintra-portugal-an-ultimate-guide/

Johnson, J. (2023) "Visiting Sintra with Kids: Is it Really that Magical?," Those Johnson Boys, 19 April. Available at: https://thosejohnsonboys.com/sintra-with-kids/#Getting_from_Lisbon_to_Sintra

From Lisbon to Sintra: 4 best ways to get there (no date). Available at: https://www.planetware.com/portugal/from-lisbon-to-sintra-best-ways-to-get-there-p-1-67.htm

Jurga (2023) "Visiting Sintra, Portugal: What to see & Itinerary for 1, 2, or 3 days," Full Suitcase Family Travel Blog [Preprint]. Available at: https://fullsuitcase.com/sintra-itinerary/

## Chapter 8

Editor At Surfertoday.com and Editor at SurferToday.com (2023) "41 things you didn't know about Nazaré," Surfertoday [Preprint]. Available at: https://www.surfertoday.com/surfing/things-you-didnt-know-about-nazare

Tobey, A. (2021) Nazare Traditions and Historic Culture - BOOMER Magazine. Available at: https://www.boomermagazine.com/nazare-traditions-and-historic-culture/

Portugal, T.I. (no date) "Nazare," Portugal Travel Guide [Preprint]. Available at: https://www.travel-in-portugal.com/nazare

TasteAtlas (2023) "3 local foods you have to try in nazaré," Taste Atlas, 22 August. Available at: https://www.tasteatlas.com/local-food-in-nazare

Where to eat: the 21 best restaurants in Nazare (no date b). Available at: https://wanderlog.com/list/geoCategory/74840/where-to-eat-the-best-restaurants-in-nazare

MARIA DO MAR, Nazare - Restaurant reviews, photos & phone number - Tripadvisor (no date). Available at: https://www.tripadvisor.com/Restaurant_Review-g315902-d1576933-Reviews-Maria_do_Mar-Nazare_Leiria_District_Central_Portugal.html

Planet, L. (no date) Drinking and nightlife Nazaré, Estremadura - Lonely Planet. Available at: https://www.lonelyplanet.com/portugal/central-portugal/nazare/nightlife

Cultural events – Festivals - Nazaré - Portugal - Petit Futé (no date). Available at: https://www.petitfute.co.uk/v45378-nazare/c1170-manifestation-evenement/c1050-manifestations-culturelles-festivals/

Nazaré, Portugal Events, Calendar & Tickets | Eventbrite (no date). Available at: https://www.eventbrite.com/d/portugal--nazar%C3%A9/events/

NazareWaves (no date) Nazaré Big Waves News - Nazaré Big Waves Surf - Portugal. Available at: https://nazarewaves.com/

Top 10 Must-See Attractions in Nazaré (no date). Available at: https://www.nazareportugaltourism.com/guide/top-10-things-to-see-and-do-in-nazare.html

Tripadvisor (no date) Igreja de Nossa Senhora da Nazare. Available at: https://www.tripadvisor.com/Attraction_Review-g315902-d1568672-Reviews-Igreja_de_Nossa_Senhora_da_Nazare-Nazare_Leiria_District_Central_Portugal.html

Tripadvisor (no date a) Ermida da Memória (Nazaré) - Tripadvisor. Available at: https://www.tripadvisor.com.br/Attraction_Review-g315902-d8477644-Reviews-Ermida_da_Memoria-Nazare_Leiria_District_Central_Portugal.html

Tripadvisor (no date c) Thalasso (Nazare) - All you need to know BEFORE you go. Available at: https://www.tripadvisor.com/Attraction_Review-g315902-d4764636-Reviews-Thalasso-Nazare_Leiria_District_Central_Portugal.html

Nazaré Funicular - Tourist Guide (no date). Available at: https://www.nazareportugaltourism.com/guide/elevador-da-nazare.html

Nazare Surf School (no date). Available at: https://nazaresurfschool.pt/

Barra Surf Club Nazaré (no date). Available at: https://www.barrasurfclub.com/

De Portugal, T.C. (2023) Municipal Market of Nazaré. Available at: https://togetherness.centerofportugal.com/article/municipal-market-of-nazare

Rent A Bike Nazaré | E-motion Nazaré - E-bike Rental Nazaré (no date). Available at: https://www.e-motionnazare.com/

Nazaré skatepark - Skateparks Detail - Trucks and Fins (no date). Available at: https://trucksandfins.com/en/spots/skateparks/Nazare-skatepark/143

NazareWaves (no date b) Tourism Nazare - Nazaré Big Waves Surf - Portugal. Available at: https://nazarewaves.com/en/Home/InfoForTourists

a world of destinations (2021) Best Things to do in Nazaré, Portugal - a world of destinations. Available at: https://aworldofdestinations.com/things-to-do-nazare-portugal/

Ourcrossings (2022) Portugal travel guide: Discovering The Best of Nazaré In A Day. Available at: https://ourcrossings.com/2019/08/26/discovering-the-best-of-nazare-in-a-day/

## Chapter 9

The Editors of Encyclopaedia Britannica (2023) Porto | History, population, Map, climate, & facts. Available at: https://www.britannica.com/place/Porto-Portugal

Porto Lounge Hostel & Guesthouse (no date). Available at: https://portoloungehostel.com/porto-history

Culture & Traditions of Porto (no date). Available at: https://www.visitar-porto.com/en/what-to-do/culture.html

Is it safe to visit Porto? (no date). Available at: https://porto-north-portugal.com/porto-guide/is-it-safe-to-visit-porto.html

Travelsafe-Abroad (2020) How safe is Porto for travel? (2023 Updated) • Travel safe - abroad. Available at: https://www.travelsafe-abroad.com/portugal/porto/

Teleport (no date) Safety and crime in Porto, Portugal - Teleport Cities. Available at: https://teleport.org/cities/porto/safety/

Hopkins, E. (2023) "Top 5 best hospitals in Porto," Viv Europe [Preprint]. Available at: https://viveurope.com/best-hospitals-in-porto/

Mak, Q. (2023) "17 Best Porto Food: What to eat in Porto - ms travel solo," ms travel solo, 31 May. Available at: https://www.mstravelsolo.com/best-porto-food/

Renée, J. &Amp; (2023) "Porto Food Guide: 15 Must-Try Restaurants in Porto, Portugal," Will Fly for Food [Preprint]. Available at: https://www.willflyforfood.net/porto-food-guide-15-must-eat-restaurants-in-porto-portugal/

Bounce (2022b) "Where To Find The Best Street Food In Porto," Bounce [Preprint]. Available at: https://usebounce.com/guides/porto/best-street-food-porto

Cardona, J. (2013) "Porto's nightlife," Local Porto [Preprint]. Available at: https://www.localporto.com/porto-nightlife-bars-clubs-discos/

After dark: A guide to nightlife in Porto | Orbzii (2022). Available at: https://www.orbzii.com/see-do/nightlife-porto/

Events & festivals in Porto (no date). Available at: https://www.visitar-porto.com/en/whats-on/porto-events.html

Fiorentino, F. (no date) 23 Top Attractions & Things to do in Porto. Available at: https://www.touropia.com/tourist-attractions-in-porto/

Trails, S.C. (2020) "Porto's 11 Hidden Gems," Secret City Trails [Preprint]. Available at: https://www.secretcitytrails.com/2019/09/04/portos-12-hidden-gems/

Geeks, H. and Matt (2023) "11 Hidden Gems to Porto (and guide to the best FUN things to do in Porto)," Hostelgeeks [Preprint]. Available at: https://hostelgeeks.com/hidden-gems-porto-secrets/

Keighran, M. (2022) "The most beautiful beaches in and around Porto," Culture Trip, 17 October. Available at: https://theculturetrip.com/europe/portugal/articles/the-10-most-beautiful-beaches-in-and-around-porto/

Keighran, M. (2022) "The most beautiful beaches in and around Porto," Culture Trip, 17 October. Available at: https://theculturetrip.com/europe/portugal/articles/the-10-most-beautiful-beaches-in-and-around-porto/

Johnston, D. (2023) "2 days in Porto: The perfect Porto itinerary," Road Affair [Preprint]. Available at: https://www.roadaffair.com/2-days-in-porto-itinerary/

Chapter 10


Ribeiro, S. (2023) "5 Interesting Facts about Faro – Portugal," Simone Ribeiro [Preprint]. Available at: https://midlandstraveller.com/2022/07/22/5-interesting-facts-about-faro-portugal/

AlgarveTips, B. (2020) History of Faro: A brief summary | AlgarveTips. Available at: https://www.algarvetips.com/cities/faro/history-of-faro/

Famous historical places in Faro - Historic places, landmarks, monuments: TripHobo (no date). Available at: https://www.triphobo.com/places/faro-portugal/things-to-do/historical

Famous historical places in Faro - Historic places, landmarks, monuments: TripHobo (no date). Available at: https://www.triphobo.com/places/faro-portugal/things-to-do/historical

Faro evening safety - Faro Forum - Tripadvisor (no date). Available at: https://www.tripadvisor.com.ph/ShowTopic-g189116-i1083-k12330823-Faro_evening_safety-Faro_Faro_District_Algarve.html

Crime in Faro (no date). Available at: https://www.numbeo.com/crime/in/Faro

Faro food Guide: What to try in the Algarve capital (2023). Available at: https://www.portugalist.com/faro-food/

McCann, J. (2022) "Feast on fresh seafood and regional cuisine at Faro's best restaurants," Culture Trip, 12 May. Available at: https://theculturetrip.com/europe/portugal/articles/where-to-eat-in-faro-top-10-local-restaurants/

www.thingstodopost.org (no date b) Algarve, Portugal Food Guide: 6 Pizza food Must-Eat Restaurants & Street Food Stalls in Faro. Available at: https://www.thingstodopost.org/algarve-portugal-food-guide-6-pizza-food-must-eat-restaurants-street-food-stalls-in-faro-216337

Planet, L. (no date a) Drinking and nightlife Faro, The Algarve - Lonely Planet. Available at: https://www.lonelyplanet.com/portugal/the-algarve/faro/nightlife

Tripadvisor (no date d) THE 10 BEST Nightlife activities in Faro (Updated 2023) - Tripadvisor. Available at: https://www.tripadvisor.com/Attractions-g189116-Activities-c20-Faro_Faro_District_Algarve.html

Events and festivals in Faro in 2023: TripHobo (no date). Available at: https://www.triphobo.com/places/faro-portugal/events-festivals

14 Top-Rated Tourist Attractions in Faro (no date). Available at: https://www.

planetware.com/tourist-attractions-/faro-p-faro-faro.htm

www.thingstodopost.org (no date a) 7 Hidden Gems Things to do in Faro That You Shouldn't Miss. Available at: https://www.thingstodopost.org/7-hidden-gems-things-to-do-in-faro-that-you-shouldn-t-miss-782500

10 of the Best Beaches in Faro (no date). Available at: https://www.travel-in-portugal.com/beaches/faro

kimkim (2023) "How to get to the Algarve," Kimkim [Preprint]. Available at: https://www.kimkim.com/ab/getting-to-algarve

Faro, Portugal: a tourism guide for 2023 (no date). Available at: https://www.algarve-tourist.com/Faro-portugal-guide.html

Abroad, U. (2022) 3 days in Faro, Portugal: The perfect Algarve itinerary (2023). Available at: https://www.urbanabroad.com/3-days-in-faro/

## Chapter 11

Traveller, I. (2020) "10 Interesting facts about Lagos, Portugal | Isolated traveller," Isolated Traveller, 22 November. Available at: https://www.isolatedtraveller.com/10-interesting-facts-about-lagos-portugal/

AlgarveTips, B. (2020b) History of Lagos: A brief summary | AlgarveTips. Available at: https://www.algarvetips.com/cities/lagos/history-of-lagos/

City Walk: Lagos Introduction Walking Tour, Lagos, Portugal (no date). Available at: https://www.gpsmycity.com/tours/lagos-introduction-walking-tour-5345.html

Thomas, D. (2020) "Why the Algarve is a safe place to visit," Portugal Resident, 13 August. Available at: https://www.portugalresident.com/why-the-algarve-is-a-safe-place-to-visit/

Crime in Lagos (no date). Available at: https://www.numbeo.com/crime/in/Lagos-Portugal

Nayler, M. (2022) "The best restaurants in Lagos, Portugal," Culture Trip, 4 November. Available at: https://theculturetrip.com/europe/portugal/articles/the-best-restaurants-in-lagos-portugal/

Petit-Hem (2023) "Food guide - where to eat in Lagos, Algarve," PETIT-HEM, 5 May. Available at: https://www.petit-hem.com/post/lagos-food-guide

Informação, S. (2022) "Lagos Food Fest returns with proposals for all tastes," Sul Informação, 11 July. Available at: https://www.sulinformacao.pt/en/2022/07/lagos-food-fest-regressa-com-propostas-para-todos-os-gostos/

Writer, D.G. | C. (no date) 5 best nightlife experiences in Lagos - What to do at night in Lagos - Go Guides. Available at: https://in.hotels.com/go/portugal/best-nightlife-lagos

Algarve Fun (2020) The Best Festivals in the Algarve - Culture, Music, Food & more. Available at: https://www.algarvefun.com/algarve-tips/festivals-in-the-algarve/

Raes, V. (2020) "15 best things to do in Lagos (Portugal)," The Crazy Tourist [Preprint]. Available at: https://www.thecrazytourist.com/15-best-things-lagos-portugal/

Lagos Portugal; the best sights, attractions and things to see and do in 2023 (no date). Available at: https://www.lagosportugalguide.com/lagos-algarve/lagos-portugal-sights-activities-things-to-do-see.html

Bba (2020) "Hidden Gems To Seek Out In Lagos," Big Blue Adventures [Preprint]. Available at: https://www.bigblueadventures.com/adventure-travel/portugal-west-algarve-lagos/

Lagos in 3 days; a suggested tour and itinerary for 2023 (no date). Available at: https://www.lagosportugalguide.com/lagos-algarve/lagos-3-days.html

Mollie (2022) "A guide to Lagos, Portugal," We Are Global Travellers [Preprint]. Available at: https://weareglobaltravellers.com/2020/10/lagos-travel-guide/

## Chapter 12

Bloom Consulting (2020) "5 curiosities about Braga," Bloom Consulting - Journal [Preprint]. Available at: https://www.bloom-consulting.com/journal/5-curiosities-about-braga/

Visit | History and Heritage | Presentation (no date). Available at: https://www.cm-braga.pt/en/0101/conhecer/historia-e-patrimonio/apresentacao

Visit | History and Heritage | Museums (no date). Available at: https://www.cm-braga.pt/en/1201/conhecer/historia-e-patrimonio/museus

Visit | History and Heritage | Religious Heritage (no date). Available at: https://www.cm-braga.pt/en/0101/conhecer/historia-e-patrimonio/patrimonio-religioso/apresentacao

Crime in Braga (no date). Available at: https://www.numbeo.com/crime/in/Braga

Braga Food: Six regional dishes to try in Braga (2023). Available at: https://www.portugalist.com/braga-food/

Hengstenberg, K. (2021) "What and where to eat in Braga?," Travel Tomorrow

[Preprint]. Available at: https://traveltomorrow.com/what-and-where-to-eat-in-braga/

www.thingstodopost.org (no date d) Northern Portugal, Portugal Food Guide: 10 Mediterranean food Must-Eat Restaurants & Street Food Stalls in Braga. Available at: https://www.thingstodopost.org/northern-portugal-portugal-food-guide-10-mediterranean-food-must-eat-restaurants-street-food-stalls-in-braga-216977

Nightlife in Braga (2015). Available at: http://www.ezportugal.com/braga-portugal/things-to-do-braga/nightlife-braga-portugal

Planet, L. (no date a) Drinking and nightlife Braga, The Minho - Lonely Planet. Available at: https://www.lonelyplanet.com/portugal/the-north/braga/nightlife

Braga events and Festivals (2015). Available at: http://www.ezportugal.com/braga-portugal/things-to-do-braga/events-festivals-braga

18 top tourist attractions in Braga & easy day trips (no date). Available at: https://www.planetware.com/tourist-attractions-/braga-p-bra-brag.htm

Braga day trip and suggested tour and itinerary (no date). Available at: https://porto-north-portugal.com/braga-portugal/braga-day-trip-tour.html

Tripadvisor (no date d) THE 10 BEST Hidden gem attractions in Braga District (Updated 2023). Available at: https://www.tripadvisor.com/Attractions-g2618580-Activities-zft12156-Braga_District_Northern_Portugal.html

Braga City Council (no date). Available at: https://www.cm-braga.pt/en/0101/conhecer/natureza-espacos-verdes-e-praias-fluviais/apresentacao

Trotter, G. (no date) Braga, Portugal | A 2-day itinerary. Available at: https://www.theglobetrotter.co.uk/2020/10/braga-portugal-itinerary.html

## Chapter 13

Traveller, I. (2020b) "20 Interesting Facts about Coimbra | Isolated Traveller," Isolated Traveller, 4 March. Available at: https://www.isolatedtraveller.com/20-interesting-facts-about-coimbra/

Salty (2021) "Coimbra – Portugal's original capital," Go Discover Portugal Travel [Preprint]. Available at: http://godiscoverportugal.com/coimbra/

Coimbra's historical highlights | Trip.com (no date). Available at: https://www.trip.com/things-to-do/detail/37025813/

Coimbra: Health & Safety - Tripadvisor (no date). Available at: https://www.

tripadvisor.com/Travel-g189143-s206/Coimbra:Portugal:Health.And.Safety.html

Crime in Coimbra (no date). Available at: https://www.numbeo.com/crime/in/Coimbra

Coimbra Food: The Best Typical Foods To Try in Coimbra (2023). Available at: https://www.portugalist.com/coimbra-food/

Admin (2021) Eating in Coimbra - restaurants and hamburgers | InLife Portugal. Available at: https://inlifehousing.com/blog/where-to-eat-in-coimbra-restaurants-for-all-kind-of-tastes/

Nightlife in Coimbra (2015). Available at: http://www.ezportugal.com/coimbra-portugal/things-to-do-coimbra/nightlife-coimbra-portugal

Events and festivals (2015). Available at: http://www.ezportugal.com/coimbra-portugal/things-to-do-coimbra/events-festivals-coimbra

19 top tourist attractions in Coimbra & easy day trips (no date). Available at: https://www.planetware.com/tourist-attractions-/coimbra-p-coim-coim.htm

Fox, J.D. (2023b) "28 Things To Do In Coimbra: Why You Definitely Need More Than 1 Day," Julie Dawn Fox in Portugal [Preprint]. Available at: https://juliedawnfox.com/things-to-do-coimbra/

Tripadvisor (no date f) THE BEST hidden gem attractions in Coimbra (Updated 2023). Available at: https://www.tripadvisor.com/Attractions-g189143-Activities-zft12156-Coimbra_Coimbra_District_Central_Portugal.html

Coimbra itineraries and tours for 1, 2 and 3 days (no date). Available at: https://myportugalholiday.com/coimbra-portugal/coimbra-1-2-3-day-tour-itinerary.html

## Chapter 14

Garcia, I. (2021) "Nine things you need to know about Madeira," Time Out Madeira [Preprint]. Available at: https://www.timeout.com/madeira/things-to-do/fun-facts-nine-things-you-need-to-know-about-madeira

Systems, W. (no date) Madeira Island History. Available at: https://madeira.best/guide/facts-about/madeira-island-history

Hatton, W. (2021) "Is madeira safe to visit?," Copyright (C) 2004-2023 World Nomads [Preprint]. Available at: https://www.worldnomads.com/travel-safety/portugal/how-safe-is-madeira

Systems, W. (no date a) 18 dishes you absolutely must try during your vacation in Madeira Island. Available at: https://blog.madeira.best/18-dishes-you-absolutely-must-try-during-your-vacation-in-madeira-island

Pré check-in online (no date). Available at: https://www.madeirarent.pt/new/Gastronomic-Tour-in-Madeira

Funchal MICHELIN Restaurants - The MICHELIN Guide Portugal (no date). Available at: https://guide.michelin.com/en/pt/ilha-da-madeira/funchal/restaurants

Systems, W. (no date c) Nightlife in Madeira Island. Available at: https://blog.madeira.best/nightlife-in-madeira-island

Guide To Madeira Nightlife | Thomas Cook (no date). Available at: https://www.thomascook.com/holidays/portugal/madeira/things-to-do/nightlife

Madeira Nightlife (no date). Available at: https://www.madeira-web.com/en/things-to-do/nightlife.html

Madeira Island - Festivals and events (no date). Available at: https://www.madeira-a-z.com/what-to-do/madeira-festivals.html

Pinches, B. (2023) "Top 24 Most Beautiful Places To Visit In Madeira - Global-Grasshopper," Global Grasshopper – travel inspiration for the road less travelled, 22 July. Available at: https://globalgrasshopper.com/destinations/europe/10-beautiful-places-visit-madeira/

Raes, V. (2022) "15 best things to do in Madeira (Portugal)," The Crazy Tourist [Preprint]. Available at: https://www.thecrazytourist.com/15-best-things-madeira-portugal/

Jurga (2023a) "8 hidden gems of madeira that most tourists never see," Full Suitcase Family Travel Blog [Preprint]. Available at: https://fullsuitcase.com/madeira-hidden-gems/

Systems, W. (no date b) How many days do you need in Madeira? Available at: https://blog.madeira.best/how-many-days-do-you-need-in-madeira

Ronan, L. (2023) "7 Days in Madeira Itinerary: The Best Way to See Madeira [2023]," Faraway Lucy [Preprint]. Available at: https://www.farawaylucy.com/madeira-itinerary-7-days/

## Chapter15

Jones, J. (2015) 25 Fun Facts About The Azores Islands. Available at: https://travelingwiththejones.com/2015/10/05/25-fun-facts-about-the-azores/

Azores GreenMark - The Azores (no date). Available at: https://www.azoresgreenmark.com/acores/history/

Canada, G.A. (2023) Travel advice and advisories for Azores. Available at: https://travel.gc.ca/destinations/azores

Azores Travel Vaccinations | Health Information | Travel Doctor Network (no date). Available at: https://www.traveldoctor.network/country/azores/#:~:text=Hospitals%20are%20located%20on%20Faial,you%20have%20travel%20health%20insurance

Crew, W. (2023) "The Azores Food Guide – What to eat in the Azores, Portugal," Wanderlust Crew [Preprint]. Available at: https://wanderlustcrew.com/the-azores-food-guide/

Kris (2022) "Best restaurants in the Azores you need to try," Wapiti Travel [Preprint]. Available at: https://www.wapititravel.com/blog/en/restaurants-in-azores/

Choice Hotels International (2019) Nightlife in Azores. Available at: https://traveltop6.com/portugal/azores/nightlife

Azores: Festivals - Tripadvisor (no date). Available at: https://www.tripadvisor.com/Travel-g189123-c91599/Azores:Portugal:Festivals.html

About The Azores | Escape to the Authentic with unbeatable travel deals to the Azores and beyond (no date). Available at: https://azoresgetaways.com/en-us/azores/azores-festivals-and-events

Raes, V. (2020b) "15 best things to do in the Azores (Portugal)," The Crazy Tourist [Preprint]. Available at: https://www.thecrazytourist.com/15-best-things-azores-portugal/

"Best things to do in the Azores" (2023) Times Travel [Preprint]. Available at: https://www.thetimes.co.uk/travel/destinations/portugal/europe/azores/best-things-to-do-azores

GmbH, H. (no date) Hidden Gems the Azores » Blogger tips for your next trip to the Azores. Available at: https://www.holidu.com/magazine/hidden-gems-azores

Greta (2023) Azores Itinerary: 10 EPIC Days In The Azores Islands, Portugal. Available at: https://gretastravels.com/azores-itinerary/

Kris (2023) "The perfect Azores itinerary for first-time visitors ( 2023 edition)," Wapiti Travel [Preprint]. Available at: https://www.wapititravel.com/blog/en/azores-itinerary/

Chapter 16

Évora, World Heritage site | www.visitportugal.com (no date). Available at: https://www.visitportugal.com/en/destinos/alentejo/73787

Luisseco (2023) "Visit Evora – Top 10 reasons to come to Alentejo, Portugal," Visit Évora [Preprint]. Available at: https://www.visitevora.net/en/visit-evora/

Visita a Aveiro | www.visitportugal.com (no date). Available at: https://www.visitportugal.com/en/content/visit-aveiro

Aveiro Center of Portugal (2023). Available at: https://www.centerofportugal.com/destination/aveiro

Óbidos | www.visitportugal.com (no date). Available at: https://www.visitportugal.com/en/node/73768

Obidos, Portugal; a day-trip and holiday guide for 2023 (2023). Available at: https://myportugalholiday.com/portugal-guides/obidos-portugal.html

Ramaswamy, M. (2021b) "The Minho Travel Guide | What to do in The Minho," Rough Guides, 26 April. Available at: https://www.roughguides.com/portugal/minho/

Mwh (2023) "Meandering through the Minho," Portugal Travel Guide [Preprint]. Available at: https://portugaltravelguide.com/north-portugal/

German Press Agency - DPA (2021) Magical, secluded paradise of Portugal's Setubal peninsula. Available at: https://www.dailysabah.com/life/travel/magical-secluded-paradise-of-portugals-setubal-peninsula

WineTourism.com (2023) Your 2023 guide to Setubal Peninsula wine region. Available at: https://www.winetourism.com/wine-region/setubal/

The Douro Valley | www.visitportugal.com (no date). Available at: https://www.visitportugal.com/en/content/douro-valley

Rabinowitz, J. (2022) "Reasons why Portugal's Douro Valley should be on your bucket list," Culture Trip, 20 December. Available at: https://theculturetrip.com/europe/portugal/articles/11-reasons-why-portugals-douro-valley-should-be-on-your-bucketlist/

Part 3

Hansen, M. (2023) "How to plan an amazing Portugal itinerary (10 days)," Wheatless Wanderlust [Preprint]. Available at: https://wheatlesswanderlust.com/10-days-in-portugal-itinerary/

Steph (2023) "Ultimate Portugal itinerary: 1, 2 & 3 week plans," Big World Small Pockets [Preprint]. Available at: https://www.bigworldsmallpockets.com/portugal-itinerary/

Cotrim, C. (2022) "The perfect Portugal Itinerary from 7 to 14 days + practical tips," Boundless Roads [Preprint]. Available at: https://www.boundlessroads.com/portugal-itinerary/

Laura (2023) "The Ultimate guide to road trip in Portugal," The Historian Traveller [Preprint]. Available at: https://thehistoriantraveller.com/road-trip-portugal/#Portugal_itinerary_3_weeks

Printed in Great Britain
by Amazon

34165506R00255